Handbook of Theory
for Practice Teachers
in Social Work

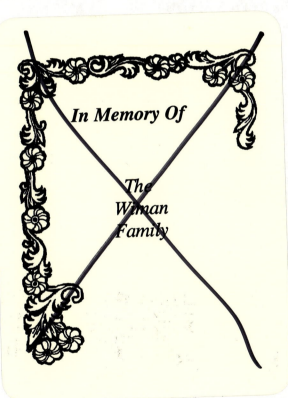

of related interest

Introducing Network Analysis in Social Work
Philip Seed
ISBN 1 85302 034 6

Grief in Children:
A Handbook for Adults
Atle Dyregrov
ISBN 1 85302 113 X

The Abuse of Elderly People:
A Handbook for Professionals
Jacki Pritchard
ISBN 1 85302 122 9

Social Work in the Wake of Disaster
David Tumelty
ISBN 1 85302 060 5

Dramatherapy with Families, Groups and Individuals:
Waiting in the Wings
Sue Jennings
ISBN 1 85302 014 1

Play Therapy with Abused Children
Ann Cattanach
ISBN 1 85302 120 2

Storymaking in Bereavement:
Dragons Fight in the Meadow
Alida Gersie
ISBN 1 85302 065 6

Handbook of Theory for Practice Teachers in Social Work

Edited by Joyce Lishman

Jessica Kingsley Publishers
London

First published in the United Kingdom in 1991 by
Jessica Kingsley Publishers Ltd
118 Pentonville Road
London N1 9JN

The right of the contributors to be identified as authors of these articles has been asserted by them in accordance with the Copyright, Designs and Patents Act 1988.

Copyright © 1991 the contributors and the publisher

British Library Cataloguing in Publication Data
Handbook of theory for practice teachers in
  social work.
  1. Great Britain. Welfare workers. Professional education
  I. Lishman, Joyce
  361.0071141

  ISBN 1-85302-098-2

Printed in Great Britain by
Billing & Sons Ltd, Worcester

Contents

Introduction

Joyce Lishman

This volume was commissioned by the North of Scotland Consortium for Education and Training in Social Work in order to provide a comprehensive handbook of relevant theory for practice teachers teaching and supervising students on Diploma in Social Work programmes. CCETSW Paper 30 (1989) makes clear that in relation to the Diploma in Social Work 'knowledge will only be assessed in relation to practice.' One implication of this requirement is that assessment of relevant theory is likely to be carried out, relatively more than in the past, in practice by practice teachers. It therefore becomes even more necessary that practice teachers and university/college lecturers share an empirical and theoretical base. Educational institutions need to select and teach knowledge and theory relevant to the practice of social work in a range of contexts and settings. Practice teachers need to reinforce the understanding and application of knowledge and theory in practice.

The purpose of this volume is to provide a range both of models of understanding human experience and behaviour and of models of social work intervention. Authors were asked to describe a model (of understanding or intervention) and analyse it critically, with reference to its relevance to social work, and in such a way as to enable practice teachers and students to develop a greater understanding of that particular model of behaviour or intervention.

The first part of the volume describes theories of human behaviour and includes papers on the development of the individual throughout the life cycle, and on a psychodynamic approach to understanding human experience and behaviour, in particular the relation of past to present experience and of inner and outer reality. Aldgate's paper examines attachment theory, in particular in relation to children, and Rochford's paper examines loss and bereavement both in relation to social work clients and to students.

Selections such as this inevitably have omissions: further chapters on cognitive development through the life cycle and on understanding family structures and systems would have been relevant. So far the focus appears to be entirely on the individual but Davis's paper identifies the powerful structural influences on individual lives whereby poverty, gender and race, for example, critically and overpoweringly affect adversely the life chances of people who become social work clients.

Hardiker and Barker's chapter addresses the general theme of discipline knowledge for social work and analyses the use of social theory (often implicit and ill defined) by social workers. They remind us of the need for a critical understanding of the function of knowledge in social work. While this volume is predominantly welfare oriented, social work has to address the 'structural realities of our changing society, such as punishment in the community, the move to private and voluntary-based welfare and homelessness and poverty.'

These 'structural realities' have to be borne firmly in mind in reading the second section of this volume on models of intervention. While the paper on community social work acknowledges and addresses structural issues the majority of papers present models of intervention with individuals, families or groups. These models - counselling, behaviour modification, task-centred work, crisis intervention and a life-space approach - are relevant and necessary to the practice of social work where intervention with individuals, families or groups is an important component of local authority and voluntary agency social work. Students need to have access to a range of techniques and approaches in order effectively to help individuals and families to change and problem solve.

However, there remains in social work a dilemma and tension between this individualistic problem-solving base and the reality for many clients that problem solution lies at a political and structural, rather than individual, level.

Part I

**MODELS OF UNDERSTANDING
HUMAN DEVELOPMENT
AND BEHAVIOUR**

Chapter 1

Attachment Theory and Its Application to Child Care Social Work - An Introduction

Jane Aldgate

Over 30 years ago John Bowlby wrote his seminal papers on attachment (see, for example, Bowlby 1958). Since then, his name has been synonymous with the construct of attachment in British child development theory.

Bowlby would be the first person to acknowledge that times have changed since the 1950s. Divorce has had its impact on the lives of many children; although there have always been reconstituted families, today the pattern of those families is more flexible, with many children living in one household and maintaining links with non-custodial parents in another. In addition, there is a rich diversity of family types, responding to the transitions being made towards a multi-cultural society and to the emancipation of women in the work-force (see Rapoport et al 1982).

In spite of the changes in family life, attachment theory still holds a central place in the social worker's repertoire of basic theory although it has been refined from the early days as a result of research, developments in psychological theory and changes in social work practice. It is, however, still important, and forms the theoretical base for several important areas of social work intervention, including child abuse (Corby 1989) and direct work with children (Aldgate and Simmonds 1988).

Although attachment is a construct which can be applied universally to adults and children alike, this paper will be selective and primarily consider the relevance and application of attachment theory for work with children who have experienced faulty or unresolved severed attachments. Its main aim is to unpick some of the mythology that surrounds the construct of attachment and evaluate its usefulness for child care social work.

What is attachment?

If asked, many of us would probably be able to come up with a definition of attachment; but do we really know the facts? What exactly is attachment? Harris believes that it is not a static theory but a developing theoretical construct with particular relevance for work with children and caregivers. We need to develop a 'working knowledge' of this construct, 'recognising that systematic, research-based testing of attachment theory is a slow and painstaking process' (Harris 1984 pp. 24-25).

Attachment theory has its roots in many different psychological theories. Harris, for example, includes 'ethology, psychoanalysis, anthropology, cognitive psychology, developmental biology, neurophysiology and systems theory' (Harris 1984, p.24). Space precludes a detailed review of these here but readers might like to consult Bowlby's original work (Bowlby 1961, 1973, 1980 and 1979), and also look at the recent reviews by Harris (1984 and 1986) and Corby (1989).

For a definition of attachment, the first place to turn to is the original source - Bowlby himself. He has modified his views considerably since 1958. This is his revised definition:

> What, for convenience, I am terming attachment theory is a way of conceptualizing the propensity of human beings to make strong affectional bonds to particular others and of explaining the many forms of emotional distress and personality disturbance, including anxiety, anger, depression, and emotional detachment, to which unwilling separation and loss give rise (Bowlby 1984, p.27).

Bowlby amplifies his theory thus:

> Briefly put, attachment behaviour is conceived of as any form of behaviour that results in a person attaining or retaining proximity to some other differentiated and preferred individual, who is usually conceived as stronger and/or wiser. While especially evident during early childhood, attachment behaviour is held to characterize human beings from the cradle to the grave. It includes crying and calling, which elicit care, following and clinging, and also strong protest should a child be left alone or with strangers. With age, the frequency and the intensity with which such behaviour is exhibited diminish steadily. Nevertheless, all these forms of behaviour persist as an important part of man's behavioural equipment. In adults, they are especially evident when a person is distressed, ill, or afraid. The particular patterns of attachment beha-

viour shown by an individual turn partly on his present age, sex, and circumstances and partly on the experiences he or she has had with attachment figures earlier in his or her life (Bowlby 1984, p.28).

Jean Harris and Vera Fahlberg have also recently written about attachment. Harris says:

> Everyone knows what attachment means. It is one word for children, lovers, brothers and sisters and friends. We know that some attachments are stronger and more persistent than others, that human life is poor in their absence and that their loss or disruption leads to grief. Much of the world's literature springs from our need to describe, share and celebrate human attachment (Harris 1984, p.24).

Fahlberg describes attachment as 'an affectionate bond between two individuals which endures through time and space and serves to join them emotionally' (Fahlberg 1981a, p.7). She catalogues the reasons why attachment is especially important for children.

Attachment helps the child:

— attain his or her full potential
— sort out what he or she perceives
— think logically
— develop a conscience
— become self-reliant
— cope with stress and frustration
— handle fear and worry
— develop future relationships
— reduce jealousy (Fahlberg 1981a, p.7).

Attachment is a protective mechanism which enables young children to explore their environment knowing that they can return to the safety of significant adults. Seeing attachment like this makes it legitimate for adults and children to feel frightened when they are separated unwillingly from their familiar attachment figures. Probation officers in prisons are all too aware that one of the tasks they are frequently asked to undertake is to contact family or significant friends to reassure them and the prisoner that their relationship still continues. The most frightening thing for children is to be afraid and be separated from their attachment figures simultaneously. This, Fahlberg (1981a) suggests, is what makes moves in care so frightening. Bowlby makes a useful comparison between children's anxiety over unwanted separation from an attachment figure to 'the anxiety that the General of an expeditionary force feels when communications with his base are cut or threatened' (Bowlby 1986, p.62).

The conditions under which attachments will develop are diverse. Understanding these diversities and what may lead to normal and abnormal attachment are an essential part of assessing children and families. What is particularly relevant to social workers dealing with children is to recognize that, given the right conditions, children are resilient to change and have the potential to adapt to different patterns of attachment.

It used to be thought that there was 'a critical period' for the development of attachment between babies and mothers. Fathers seemed very peripheral in these early writings, perhaps a reflection of a much more rigid division of labour by gender rather than any reflection on the parenting capacity of each gender. If attachment did not take place, it was argued, children's development would be seriously affected. Where separation took place in early childhood, it was likely that the effects of this would be long lasting. While it is obviously advantageous that early secure attachments can be established between children and their carers, it does not necessarily follow that if children are subsequently separated from their primary attachment figures they will be irreversibly damaged. Recent research work by Herbert et al (1982) refutes the notion of 'a sensitive period' in the formation of mother-to-infant attachment. If this were so, they argue, the adoption of small babies, let alone older children, would be a non-starter. Attachment is not a mechanical, all or nothing phenomena, but far more complicated and subject to later modification.

In addition, current thinking suggests that there is room, in our multi-cultural society, for a variety of acceptable patterns of attachment between young children and their families (Clarke and Clarke 1976). Although it is common, even with small children, for hierarchies of attachments to be present with certain adults taking on more importance than others - research indicates that infants are capable of making deep attachments to several significant people (Schaffer and Emerson 1964, Schaffer 1977). Sylva and Lunt summarize the current thinking:

> There is no scientific foundation for the myth of the blood bond or the belief that the biological mother alone is uniquely capable of caring for her child. This loving relationship may be carried out or shared by one or several other adults provided that they show certain qualities. What are these qualities? Sensitivity, consistency, stimulation and responsiveness are some of the qualities important to the early relationship in a young child's life (Sylva and Lunt 1982, pp.50-51).

Knowing the qualities adults should provide to foster good attachments in their children is only one side of the process. The other is to match these with children's requirements for healthy emotional development. Kellmer-Pringle provides us with a now classic definition of children's needs. This definition can be universally applied in different cultures and social circumstances:

1. basic physical care

2. affection

3. security

4. stimulation of innate potential

5. guidance and control

6. responsibility

7. independence (see Kellmer-Pringle 1975).

All these needs are as relevant to the development of good attachments as they are to children's general physical and emotional development. As Sheridan (see, for example, Department of Health 1989) has pointed out, the two are very much interlinked. Faulty attachments often result when affection and security have been inconsistent in the early years. A major consequence can be an imbalance between dependency and the development of independence (see Fahlberg 1981a for an elaboration of this point).

Good-enough parenting and attachments

Clearly, what is significant to children's development is the quality of care offered by parenting figures. The building of attachments is an interactive process. Children will respond to the parenting they are offered. In turn, that parenting behaviour will have been influenced by many factors, including, as Quinton and Rutter (1984) suggest, the parent's own childhood experiences. However, no-one has perfect parents, a fact which led Winnicott (1965) to develop his concept of 'good-enough' parenting. The essential features of this concept is that there is a baseline for reasonable parenting behaviour which can be identified. This includes consistency, adequate stimulation, appropriate affection, pride in children's development and achievements and expecting from children behaviour appropriate to their age and development. Parents who fall below this baseline will be in danger of placing their children's emotional health at risk. One consequence may be the development of faulty patterns of attachment.

Bowlby believes that the worst patterns of parenting likely to contribute to the development of faulty attachments in children include:

    a. One or both parents being persistently unresponsive to the child's care-eliciting behaviour and/or actively disparaging and rejecting him or her

b. Discontinuities of parenting, occurring more or less frequently, including periods in hospital or institution

c. Persistent threats by parents not to love a child, used as a way of controlling him or her

d. Threats by parents to abandon the family, used either as a method of disciplining the child or as a way of coercing a spouse

e. Threats by one parent either to desert or even to kill the other or else to commit suicide (each of these is more common than might be supposed)

f. Inducing a child to feel guilty by claiming that his behaviour is or will be responsible for the parent's death or illness (Bowlby 1984, p.30)

These are extremes of behaviour, but some elements can often be seen in the parents of children whose attachments are inadequate.

Consequences of faulty attachments

The consequences of faulty attachments will vary according to the severity of the problem. There are two main concepts which are useful for social workers in relation to the emotional damage which can result. The first is privation, where children have lacked any opportunity to form affectional bonds (Rutter 1972). Many early studies of children brought up in institutions provided searing evidence of the consequences of privation (see Dinnage and Pringle 1967). The second concept, more often faced by social workers, is deprivation - where children have experienced some early affectional bonds but where these have been disrupted and not replaced by others. The worst outcome seems to be where children in care have experienced many changes of placements and there are no adults in their lives who represent stability. In these circumstances, children may become confused about who they are and who they belong to. Sometimes they may wrongly blame themselves wholly for yet another move, and try to protect themselves from further hurt and rejection by shutting off from the possibility of new attachments.

Loss and attachment theory

It can therefore be seen that loss has special relevance to attachment theory. Some children whose early attachment problems have not been replaced with compensating attachment figures have gaps in their development and seem to be 'stuck' or 'frozen' at an earlier age. Much direct work with children has concentrated on addressing this issue. Fahlberg divides the way children can become 'stuck' into four areas:

- developmental delays in any or all of the three major areas - physical, cognitive and psychological.
- the child may have developed abnormal patterns of behaviour - maladaptive patterns.
- unresolved separation issues may cause the child to become stuck.
- misperceptions can hinder the usual progression of growth and change (Fahlberg 1984, p.17).

The social worker's task is to help children close the gaps, to put together the missing bits of the past and make sense of them sufficiently so that enough integration may occur for them to relate to others in a realistic and positive way. Some examples of how this has been done in practice may be found in Aldgate and Simmonds (1988).

For further details and useful checklists for assessing attachment, readers might like to refer to Fahlberg's volume, *Attachment and Separation*, BAAF (1981a). Additional material is to be found in Bowlby (1984 and 1986), BAAF (1984) and Batty (1986).

In child care social work, separations are often concerned with the movement of children in and out of care. In child abuse cases, sometimes the only way to protect children is to remove them from danger, although such action should only be taken when there really is no alternative, because of the significance for a child of the breaking of attachments both in the long and the short term. Stevenson summarizes the impact of admission to care on children. During this event, 'We are breaking prematurely the lifeline of the developing child' (Stevenson 1968, p.9). The same could be said of moves in care where attachments have been made or returning to birth families. But what is the significance of this break? What are the consequences of separation for children in the short and the long term? Is it important that a child's lifeline is repaired and if so, what part can social workers play in this? This chapter now attempts to address these questions. It makes no attempt to be comprehensive but selects literature and research which social workers may find to be useful in embarking on intervention with children and their families who have experienced severed attachments.

Children's immediate reactions to separation and loss

Because attachment is a protective mechanism, anxiety and fear are the major emotions which many children will experience when separated from adults to whom they are attached, but are only the first part of the process of reaction, which has been well documented (see, for example, Fahlberg 1981b, Jewett 1984, and Kubler-Ross 1972). It may also include some or all of the following emotions:

shock, alarm, denial and disbelief, yearning and pining, searching, anger or guilt, disorganisation, despair and finally, reorganisation and integration.

Children may go through some or all of these stages, not necessarily in the order given. Their experiences of attachment will have a primary influence on their likely reactions to separation but there are other factors which may determine the way they respond, including cultural expectations, age, gender, temperament, cognitive appraisal and 'set' and social circumstances before and after separation.

Cultural expectations

Cultural reactions to separation and loss may be significant in determining children's ability to resolve their feelings (Kaffman and Elizir 1983). Jewett (1984) and Black (1984) argue that one major problem for children in Western cultures is the denial of mourning rituals. It is also well known that the loss of cultural reference points may bring very special problems for immigrants (Cheetham 1972, Lim 1983), while Small (1986) has drawn attention to the problems of identity confusion some black children may have when living in transracial placements or being placed in children's homes where all the staff are white.

Age of children at separation

Age is a major factor affecting children's responses to the breaking of attachments. Children's perceptions and understanding of death, for example, may vary with age and related cognitive ability (Orbach et al 1985). Reactions will also vary with age. Black (1984), for example, found that one year after bereavement, younger children tended to show aggressive symptoms while the older ones showed sadness and depression.

Secondly, age may act as a protective factor against stress in young children (Rutter 1981). Even though very young babies may sense changes around them (Fahlberg 1982), it is likely that 'children below the age of six or seven months are relatively immune because they have not yet developed selective attachments and therefore are not able to experience separation and anxiety' (Rutter 1981, p.337).

Children of above school age may also be protected to some extent because advantage may be taken of 'an older child's ability to understand situations and develop strategies for dealing with them' (Rutter 1985, p.606). Research on children admitted to hospital (Stacey et al 1970) has shown that these children have the cognitive skills to appreciate that separation 'does not necessarily mean abandonment or loss of a relationship and to understand better what is involved in hospitalization and why unpleasant medical or surgical procedures may be necessary' (Rutter 1981, p.337).

Children who are least likely to be protected by their age are those between six and thirty-three months (Benians 1982). In this age group, children do not have the cognitive ability to make total sense of what is happening to them and the younger child may find it difficult to hold attachment figures in mind for the duration of a separation or to understand the nature of death (Rutter 1981 and 1985). These young children need special attention when coming into care to ensure they are placed with families who can offer a consistent experience. Any parental visits should occur daily to avoid detachment (Cooper 1986).

Gender

One area which sometimes receives little attention is that of gender differences. Overall, boys appear to be more vulnerable to the effects of severed attachments than girls (Rutter 1981, Wallerstein and Kelly 1980 and Hetherington 1980). The reasons for these differences are so far unclear but the outcomes, as social work research has suggested, is that the negative experiences of the care system are likely to cause more deterioration in the behaviour of boys than in girls (Rowe and Lambert 1973). Social workers may find it useful to alert themselves to these differences when they are working with children in care and adapt their plan and style of intervention accordingly.

Temperamental characteristics

Children are individuals with different temperaments and personalities. Research on child abuse has suggested that a child's temperament may affect the way adults respond to him or her (Lynch 1975). So, in separation, children's temperamental responses may well influence the way they are perceived and responded to by adults. Research in this area is still in its infancy (Rutter 1972, 1981) but, given that temperament is a variable often accounted for in the linking of children and foster or adoptive families (Aldgate and Hawley 1986 and Tizard 1977), it should not be discounted.

Cognitive appraisal and set

Alongside temperament, there are two important individual attributes which may influence the outcome of a separation experience: cognitive appraisal and 'cognitive set' (Rutter 1981 and 1985).

There are two main points. Firstly, reactions will depend on perceptions of the event or 'cognitive appraisal'. This has much in common with

Fahlberg's fourth reason (Fahlberg 1984) why children become 'stuck' in their development (see above p.15). Separation or loss may be seen as positive or threatening. A change of school may be anticipated by one child with pleasure and by another with terror. Stacey et al (1970) found that children who were accustomed to brief happy separations from parents, time spent with grandparents for example, tended to react better to hospital admissions than children who had never experienced separation from their primary parent figures. Cognitive appraisal may be influenced by the intervention of adults - parents, carers or social workers, in preparing children for impending changes.

Secondly, allied to cognitive appraisal of an event is a child's 'cognitive set'. This is best defined as 'a sense of self-esteem and self-efficacy which makes successful coping more likely'. The corollary of this is 'a sense of helplessness which increases the likelihood that one adversity will lead to another' (Rutter 1985, p.603). Rutter's views have much in common with the work done on the relationship between identity and well-being of children in care (Weinstein 1960, Colon 1973, Thorpe 1980). It is a concept which warrants urgent attention when applied to black children in care, who may, through exposure to institutionalized racism, be encouraged to deny their positive racial identity (Maxime 1986, Small 1986).

Naturally, the children most likely to develop a positive 'cognitive set' are those who, within the context of their own culture and community, have been exposed to 'secure, stable, affectional relationships, and experiences of success and achievement' (Rutter 1985, p.607). But recent work (Quinton et al 1984, Rutter and Quinton 1984) suggests that success and achievement do not need to be general. Even where parents have been unable to provide an environment to facilitate optimal child development, children may find compensation in success at school or in sports or in relationships with other adults. Furthermore, compensatory experiences of success and achievement may be retained to enable an individual to cope in adult life. These new pieces of research have major implications for social work with children experiencing separation and loss. They urge us to move away from a problem-focused intervention to one which identifies strengths and coping mechanisms, drawing evidence from all areas of children's social and developmental activities. Such an approach demands a sophisticated understanding of cultural, ethnic and racial differences.

Furthermore, the potential influence of 'cognitive set' adds weight to the permanency planning movement. Children who move from place to place may well lose a sense of control over their lives and develop 'learned helplessness' (Seligman 1975). It also adds credibility to the emphasis in child care legislation that children's wishes and feelings should be taken into account in making decisions about their future. It is well known that school-aged children are likely to blame themselves for an untimely separation. Appropriate involvement of children in the analysis of why, for example, a foster placement may have failed will help them place their part in the event in perspective. Disruption meetings (see Fitzgerald 1983) are now commonly held in social work agencies. These should offer older children the opportunity to present their views. After all, the process of negotiation between parents and children in many families, irrespective of class, ethnicity or race, is one way by which children gain confidence to assert themselves and at the same time learn to accept appropriate boundaries set by adults. Self-control is as much a part of learning to achieve as is praise for success.

Reasons for separation

A final factor likely to influence children's reactions to separation, linked to 'cognitive set', is the environment in which children have been living before the separation occurred. This links with the idea of the development of faulty attachments described earlier. The exposure over a long period of time to a multiplicity of disadvantage, including persistent tension and disharmonious relationships with and between parents or carers are likely to take their toll on children's coping abilities. It is this association with unsatisfactory family relationships rather than severing of attachment itself which 'may serve to sensitize and increase vulnerability to later losses' (Rutter 1981, p.349). In other words, the reasons for separation rather than the separation itself may have more effect on children in the long-term.

Clearly, it is very important that special attention be paid to such children at the point of entry to care to provide them with maximum stability and protect them from further disadvantage.

What happens after separation

An understanding of the circumstances prior to separation and the various factors which may pre-dispose children's reactions are essential parts of a social work assessment to make the best possible plans for children and their families. Children are least likely to recover when, after a separation, they return to families where multiple long-standing psycho-social problems are still in existence. If children remain in separation from their families in care, they are likely to be most disadvantaged if they experience multiple carers and little stability (Keane 1983, Wolkind and Rutter 1973, Rowe and Lambert 1973, Thorpe 1980). In extreme circumstances, some of these experiences may pre-dispose children who have grown up in care to become poor parents (Quinton and Rutter 1984).

The most devastating effects for any child are likely to occur when separation or loss is part of 'a chain of adversity' (Sylva and Lunt, p.37). Here, no one factor, including the separation itself, is responsible for damaging a child but, circumstances before, during and after separation contribute to children's disadvantage.

Attachment theory and permanency planning

Clearly, a primary social work task with children who have been separated from attachment figures is to prevent a 'chain of adversity' reaction. To this end, it is desirable to consider any social work activity with children in the context of permanency planning. This does not mean a rigid equation in which permanence equals adoption, (an unfortunate interpretation which has been prevalent in much British child care work over the last decade) but rather an ecologically-based approach (see Maluccio et al 1986) which reflects the spirit of the new children's legislation (DHSS 1987).

The primary aim of this approach is to endorse the importance of kinship attachments for children and to prevent long term family breakdown. At the same time, it is flexible enough to recognize that sometimes a hierarchy of attachment figures is the only way to supplement any 'less than good-enough' parenting. It recognizes that there is a place for shared parental responsibility. Local authority care should not be a last resort. Controlled separation, for example, through the use of respite care, give hope for the development of a positive service which sees voluntary care, or 'accommodation' as it will be called under the new legislation, aiming to enhance rather than sever kinship attachments (see Aldgate et al 1989; Swanson 1988; Webb 1989).

It also recognizes that some children will need permanent alternative families who can repair their faulty attachments. Even here, it is necessary to distinguish between protecting a child from further developmental harm and the importance of retaining strong kinship attachments which exist in spite of less than good enough parental behaviour. Readers might like to look at the seminal article by Jenkins (1981) which discusses how the simultaneous existence of old and new attachments may be perfectly compatible.

Increasingly, with a more sophisticated knowledge of attachment theory, researchers and child care writers are realizing that children can grow up in one family and retain links with another. One of the most experienced researchers on adoption and fostering, John Triseliotis, believes that this is perfectly acceptable:

> Children can develop their personality and identity within the concept of two sets of parents, provided there is clarity in their minds about

what is happening and that the stability and continuity of care is maintained and not threatened (Triseliotis 1983, p.31).

He supports his case by citing the growing body of evidence from divorce studies which suggests that the maintenance of contact with non-custodial parents is important to children's emotional development (see Triseliotis 1983). The critical factor for success may lie in the adults concerned not seeing themselves as rivals for children's affections but offering something different and complimentary (Jenkins 1981, Benians 1982, Adcock 1984).

The permanency plan in these cases should take into account the individual requirements of the child and the ways in which they mesh with those of both the old and the new families. As Maluccio et al suggest (1986), there can be many variations of permanence in alternative families provided the basic parameters of stability and continuity of relationships to promote children's growth and functioning are met. To this end, Thoburn catalogues 16 routes for permanence for children who cannot be rehabilitated with their own families. They are:

'1. Secure fostering with the current foster family

2. Secure fostering with a new foster family

3. Custodianship with foster parents or relatives with whom the child is already living

4. Placement before custodianship with known relatives or friends

5. Foster placement with strangers with a view to custodianship if all goes well

6. Foster placement with a new family with a view to adoption if all goes well

7. Foster placement leading quickly to adoption

8. Placement directly for adoption.

The eight routes can each be with or without contact with natural parents or siblings placed elsewhere, making 16 routes in all' (Thoburn 1985, p.30).

Children's potential to recover from severed attachments

How can social workers effect good attachments within the model of permanency planning outlined? Research evidence suggests that deprivation can be reversed but privation is more difficult to counteract in later life (Rutter 1972), although there have been clinical accounts of partial recovery from extreme early privation (Skuse 1984).

But it is also essential to know what are the circumstances most likely to promote children's recovery. First and foremost are stability and quality in relationships with adults, as a comparison of post-separation circumstances drawn from research studies suggests. Firstly, even young children, who seem distressed, may recover from short separations when returned to a family who can continue to meet their developmental needs (Heinike and Westheimer 1965, Rutter 1981). In addition, although many children show behaviour problems following bereavement or divorce, the recovery rate from these problems is also high (Black 1984). A major factor which will affect recovery is family functioning. The psychological and physical health of parents and the relationship between parents and parents and children will affect the outcome for children (Rutter 1981, Richards and Dyson 1982).

Traditionally, it has been thought that the placement of older children in alternative families is a high-risk activity. It is true that many older children in care may have long-standing behaviour and emotional problems (see Berridge and Cleaver 1987) but these are not insurmountable. Rushton and Treseder (1986), for example, assert 'there should be no doubt that where permanent substitute families can be found, these placements have a high probability of positive outcome', (1986, p.54). They draw on research evidence from five major studies to support their view that older children are capable of developmental recovery (see *Adoption and Fostering*, 1986, 10, 3, 55, or Aldgate and Simmons 1988, p.63).

In spite of some methodological problems of making comparisons between different samples of children, Rushton and Treseder are able to conclude from reviewing these studies that 'the best predictors of success are the attitudes, emotional climate and nature of the new parent-child relationships' (Rushton and Treseder 1986, pp.55-56). To this conclusion they have recently added supporting evidence from findings from their own research (see *New Families for Older Children*, BAAF 1989). This new research, alongside that of Thoburn and her colleagues, not only confirms the findings of others but also advances our knowledge about successful attachments in alternative families and is worth consulting in detail (Rushton et al 1988; Thoburn et al 1986).

Finally, Adcock provides us with a helpful summary of the conditions which help children to recover from faulty attachments as:

1. A change in the pattern of early relationships through time

2. Repeated experiences in other relationships that break the pattern of earlier experiences

3. An especially strong emotional experience within a single relationship that breaks the pattern of earlier experiences (Adcock 1988, p.31).

The social work task

Assessment and planning for permanency

Having looked, albeit briefly, at some of the background of attachment theory and its application in research and child care theory, there remains the vital issue of how to begin intervention with families who have attachment problems.

The first task is to assess the specific nature of the problem. This calls for detailed evaluative assessment of the child, the parents or carers and of the interaction between the two. The process is summarized by Adcock:

> To plan a permanent family life for a child therefore, social workers must not only recognise the importance of providing continuity of care but also the importance of assessing children's difficulties in the context of their past history, their home circumstances, school and the effect of past decisions made by professionals about them. As Herbert (1985) says, the term 'problem child' is an over-simplification. It makes it sound as though the problem belongs to the child alone whereas it may be the 'problem situation' which needs attention rather than the child. A treatment plan should be based on assessment of the child, his or her environment and the interaction between the two (Adcock 1988, p.23).

She goes on to describe the sources of information for this assessment:

> To make an assessment it is necessary to acquire factual information from files and records, to observe and to talk with children, parents, carers and professional workers. Assessing children means getting to know them and creating an atmosphere of trust in which they feel free to communicate both verbally and non-verbally. To this end, play is likely to be one important medium of communication (Adcock 1988, p.23).

There are now some excellent 'paper tools', (a term developed by the writer and practitioner John Fitzgerald), available to help the assessment process. I have selected a few that I consider to be helpful. There are many others. Sound foundation guidance is provided by the Department of Health's publication, *Protecting Children* (Department of Health 1989). Here, there are not only comprehensive family assessment schedules, but an introduction to the use of flow charts, which are especially helpful in charting the changes and severed attachments which have occurred in children's lives (see Batty 1984). This information gives an indication of the severity of attachment problems. These tools can be applied to all children, not only those who are at risk of abuse.

Comprehensive guidance which takes into account permanency planning is to be found in Bryer's workbook *Planning in Child Care* (BAAF 1988). Especially useful is the blueprint for planning (pp.40-46) an excellent paper tool which breaks down the complex tasks of assessment, process of intervention and evaluation into manageable sections. This workbook is designed for senior and basic grade workers and can easily be adapted to the context of student supervision. Another substantial text which has much information relevant to attachment problems is Thoburn's volume on child care practice (Thoburn 1988).

Additional guidance on assessing children is to be found in Adcock (1988). Fahlberg's checklists (1981a) have already been mentioned and are useful but care must be taken to ensure that they are not used in a way that is culturally specific. Those with an interest in family therapy may like to dip into Bentovim et al (1982) for a family therapy approach to assessment.

Intervention with adults

Once an assessment of the problem has been made, the appropriate intervention can be selected, planned and undertaken.

Planning is essential for success (see Bryer 1988; Thoburn 1988). It is also essential that parallel work is conducted with children and adults simultaneously.

Take, for example, the necessary work which goes into preparing a child to move from one set of attachment figures to another. Firstly, the worker must consider the readiness of the families to receive children. Families need to be well motivated, flexible (Fitzgerald et al 1982) and above all, realistic about what they may expect from a child. Families need adequate information and details of children's difficulties with concrete examples of the context in which these problems may manifest themselves. Families should not be pressurized into taking children who will not 'fit' into their existing family patterns of attachment. They should be treated as colleagues rather than clients, with priority being given to the families' own views of what they need in order to make a placement work. Request for support and information should be taken at face value and dealt with in a straightforward and businesslike manner (Aldgate and Hawley 1986). Families need a high level of tolerance of stress (Thoburn 1985) and may also require a tolerance of a child's dependent and other difficult behaviour over time (Tizard 1977; Rushton and Treseder 1986).

Equally important is the work to be done with birth parents or former carers. Birth parents may often feel that 'the price of the permanent alternative plan is admission of parental failure' (Jackson and Dunne 1981, p.154). These parents will need help in their own right either to prepare for children's restoration or to free them from their former responsibilities (Boswell 1981) yet enhance their sense of competence by recognizing their continuing role as information givers and their value as attachment figures. The companion volumes by Maluccio and Sinanoglu (1981) and Sinanoglu and Maluccio (1981) give some useful practice examples of how parents of children in care may be helped to improve their parenting skills. Another useful anthology is that edited by Blumenthal and Weinberg (1984). A comprehensive behavioural approach to change is given by Stein, Gambril and Wiltse (1978) who believe that motivation for change is a major factor in assessing potential but also show how to construct a problem profile and measure outcome.

Direct work with children

Alongside the work with old and new adult attachment figures must be the work with children who are about to face or have already experienced unwilling separations from attachment figures. Essential features of the social work role with children facing change are:

— preparing children for separation

— honesty from workers about the need for separation or why loss has occurred

— giving children permission and the opportunity to express their feelings to protect them from later emotional cut-offs

— preserving continuity with the past, preferably by maintaining links with kin.

If children are moving to new carers or are returning home after a substantial absence, they need to be ready for change. This includes having made sense of their past through some re-working of painful experiences and coming to terms with severed and faulty attachments. Older children must have been given 'psychological permission' from their former carers or parents to make new attachments. Finally, children need to be well motivated and be prepared to make the placement work (Fitzgerald et al 1982). The same applies in restoration work.

Children's wishes in this respect are very important and, although it is clearly wrong to place the burden of decision-making on the shoulders of young children (Atherton 1986) the older child and, in particular the adolescent, has a right both legally and morally to a consideration of his or her wishes. Sadly, consumer research on children in care (Page and Clarke 1977 and Stein and Ellis 1983, Stein and Carey 1986) demonstrates that children's views are often not directly taken into account in making decisions about their lives. Not listening to children's opinions about what they feel and what they want is, however, short sighted because, if children are not truly motivated to accept change, they may put in jeopardy even the most meticulous plan.

Readers may like to consult the following texts for detailed guidance on direct work with children facing the severing of attachments through separation or loss: (Jewett 1984; Fahlberg 1981a, 1981b and Fitzgerald 1983; Aldgate and Simmonds 1988; Bryer 1988; Thoburn 1988).

There follows a very brief review of two of the more popular techniques used by social workers but caution should be exercised when embarking on direct work without careful planning of the purpose and duration of intervention. Good supervision must also be built into the process.

A favourite technique to begin the process of repairing the gaps in children's history and attachments is the compilation of a life story book. Fahlberg sees it as 'an opportunity to identify strong feelings about past events, to resolve issues, to correct misperceptions.' She goes on to say:

> The life book can help:
>
> 1. to organise past events in the chronological schema;
>
> 2. to aid in ego development;
>
> 3. to increase self esteem;
>
> 4. a child to re-read at his own pace
>
> 5. a child to share in orderly fashion its past with selected others;
>
> 6. to build a sense of trust for the worker who aids in compiling the book;
>
> 7. to gain acceptance of all facets of the child's life and help the child accept his own past;
>
> and
>
> 8. to facilitate bonding (Fahlberg 1981b, p.52).

Another favourite technique is the eco-map, also developed by Fahlberg. Ryan and Walker summarize its uses:

> This was originally developed as an initial interviewing tool to open communication between the child and social worker. It shows the child and various people, places and concerns which form a part of his or her life. Children can discuss these elements and how they relate to the mans so gain an understanding of their life as a whole and why they are where they are (Ryan and Walker 1985, p.32).

Further guidance on these techniques and others can be sought from Lightbown 1979, Fahlberg 1981b, BAAF 1984, Ryan and Walker 1985. Practice examples of the techniques used with individual children are scattered through Aldgate and Simmonds (1988).

What social workers can do to prepare themselves

Working with children and their families who have experienced severed or faulty attachments places considerable demands on social workers but there are certain things workers can do to prepare themselves for the task in hand. The first guiding principle is that work with children is no different from work with adults and must be set within the context of a professional relationship.

Children in their everyday lives are used to contact with adults who are there for a specific purpose - playgroup leaders, teachers, childminders, doctors. Even very young children have a rudimentary understanding of different roles which adults play in their lives. The qualities which children often admire in these adults are kindness and firmness. Young children appreciate teachers who have a natural sense of authority, provide clear boundaries and yet can demonstrate a partiality towards them as individuals. It will be the same with social workers: children will see them for what they are as individuals, but they are also quite capable of recognizing the role of social worker, provided this is made clear. The fact that the social work task often involves touching deep emotional areas in children makes it difficult to preserve the boundaries of the relationship from the adult's side. But this is essential for if we do not, 'if we side-step the professional nature of our work and mislead children into thinking that we are available indefinitely as their best friend, we are badly letting them down' (Winnicott 1986, p.47).

Being professional does not mean denying empathy (Winnicott 1986). This discipline can only be achieved by developing great self-awareness. Because experiences of loss are universal, seeing children in distress may evoke recollections of workers' own experiences. In addition, some faulty attachments may awaken memories of a less than perfect childhood. Some of these emotions about workers' own attachments may not have been resolved. They may get in the way of work with the child unless they are confronted and examined in supervision. Fitzgerald, talking about separation resulting from disruption of placements urges workers to ask themselves 'Am I having too much pain at the thought of disruption even to listen?' (Fitzgerald 1983, p.40). Pain may not only stem from the worker's own memories of separation or poor parenting; it will also involve a complex mixture of emotions, including anger towards adults who are seen to have put the child in this predicament, guilt about the inadequacy of resources or the breakdown of a family placement in which there has been a high investment of time and energy. Furthermore, there may be an overwhelming desire to protect children from exposure to pain by avoiding the subject of separation or cruelty (Maluccio et al 1986) and not exposing children to further comings and goings of important attachment figures. But the grieving process must be allowed to take place. Tears must be comforted but not stopped (Stevenson 1968). Sometimes, one wonders if the problem lies more with the adult's wish not to witness distress than with the child's inability to cope with more than one set of attachment figures. A more positive approach may be that which recognizes the normality of grieving at the departure or memory of an adult who is an important attachment figure. An hour spent at Heathrow Airport may be quite illuminating in relation to this issue!

Workers have also to confront the problem that they cannot repair years of deprivation in a short period. Sometimes a worker has to settle for partial success (see Aldgate and Simmonds 1988, especially Chapter 4). To this end, it is important to be realistic about the prognosis for recovery and not to make over-optimistic plans. Far better to anticipate the possibility of new attachments failing and prepare contingencies in case they do rather than invest everything in a totally successful outcome, then be paralyzed by despair if it fails. Imagine how the child will feel!

The task of helping children with problems related to attachment is made all the more difficult in Social Service Departments by the fact that this is only part of a wider context of work. At admission to care or at a change of placement, the social worker not only has the role of offering direct help to children but will be working with significant adults. The worker will also be a resource finder, a negotiator and, in some cases, where children are being compulsorily removed from their parents, an authority figure - all these activities to be accomplished in a very short space of time by working at an intensive pace. The work demands a great deal of physical and emotional energy. Workers will often find themselves dealing with deeply felt emotions, both within themselves and within their clients. Sometimes, the complexity of the intervention legitimately demands separate workers for parents and children. Whatever model of service delivery is adopted, it is essential that problems are shared and that workers avail themselves of adequate support. Above all, it is helpful to remember that attachment is a universal phenomenon important for the well-being of every one of us. The child clients of social workers are no different from anyone else in this respect but their status as children places a special responsibility on social workers to offer them intervention which will achieve the best possible outcome.

References

Adcock, M. (1984), 'Alternatives to Adoption', *Adoption and Fostering*, 8, 1, 12-15.

Adcock, M. (1988), 'Assessing Children's Needs' in Aldgate, J. and Simmonds, J. (eds), *Direct Work with Children*, Batsford, 22-35.

Ahmed, S., Cheetham, J. and Small, J., (eds) (1986), *Social Work with Black Children and their Families*, Batsford.

Aldgate, J. and Hawley, D. (1986), *Recollections of Disruption*, National Foster Care Association (NFCA).

Aldgate, J. and Simmonds, J., (eds) (1988), *Direct Work with Children* Batsford.

Aldgate, J., Pratt, R. and Duggan, M. (1989), 'Using Care Away From Home to Prevent Long-term Family Breakdown', *Adoption and Fostering*, 13, 2, 32-37.

Atherton, C. (1986), 'The Family's Experience of Difficulties in Access', in *Promoting Links, Keeping Families and Children in Touch*, Family Rights Group, 40-101.

Batty, D. (1984), 'The Use of Flow Charts', in British Agencies for Adoption and Fostering, (BAAF), *In Touch with Children*, 50.

Batty, D. (ed.) (1986), *Working with Children*, British Agencies for Adoption and Fostering, (BAAF).

Benians, R. (1982), 'Preserving Parental Contact: a Factor in Promoting Healthy Growth and Development in Children', in Family Rights Group (ed.), *Fostering Parental Contact*, Family Rights Group, 7-25.

Bentovim, A., Gorell-Barnes, G., and Cooklin, A. (1982), *Family Therapy: Complimentary Frameworks of Theory and Practice*, Academic Press.

Berridge, D. and Cleaver, H. (1987), *Foster Home Breakdown*, Basil Blackwell.

Black, D. (1984), 'Sundered Families: the Effect of the Loss of a Parent', *Adoption and Fostering*, 8, 2, 38-43.

Blumenthal, K. and Weinberg, A. (eds.) (1984), *Establishing Parent Involvement in Foster Care Agencies*, Child Welfare League of America.

Boswell, A. (1981), 'Relinquishing', *Adoption and Fostering*, 5, 3, 22-24.

Bowlby, J. (1958), 'The Nature of the Child's Tie to His Mother', *International Journal of Psychoanalysis*, 39, 350-373.

Bowlby, J. (1961), *Attachment* (Attachment and Loss 1), Hogarth Press.

Bowlby, J. (1973), *Separation: Anxiety and Anger*, (Attachment and Loss 2), Hogarth Press.

Bowlby, J. (1979), *The Making and Breaking of Affectional Bonds*, Social Science Paperbacks, Tavistock.

Bowlby, J. (1980), *Loss: Sadness and Depression*, (Attachment and Loss 3), Hogarth Press.

Bowlby, J. (1984), 'The Making and Breaking of Affectional Bonds', in BAAF, (ed.), *In Touch With Children*, 27-40.

Bowlby, J. (1986), 'The Making and Breaking of Affectional Bonds', in BAAF (ed.), *Working with Children*.

British Agencies for Adoption and Fostering (ed.) (1984), *In Touch with Children - A Training Pack*, BAAF.

Bryer, M. (1988), *Planning in Child Care*, BAAF.

Cheetham, J. (ed.) (1982), *Social Work and Ethnicity*, George Allen & Unwin.

Clarke, A. M. and Clarke, A. D. B. (1976), *Early Experience: Myth and Evidence*, Open Books.

Colon, F. (1973), 'In Search of One's Past: an identity trip', in *Family Process*, 12, 429-438.

Cooper, C. (1986), 'The Growing Child', in Batty, D. (ed.) op. cit., 5-37.

Corby, B. (1989), 'Alternative Theory Bases in Child Abuse', in Stainton-Rogers, W., Hevey, D. and Ash, E., (eds) *Child Abuse and Neglect - Facing the Challenge*, Batsford in association with The Open University, 30-39.

Department of Health and Social Security (DHSS) (1985), *Social Work Decisions in Child Care*, HMSO.

Department of Health and Social Security (DHSS) (1987), *The Law on Families and Children*, HMSO.

Department of Health (1989), *Protecting Children*, HMSO.

Dinnage, R. and Kellmer Pringle, M. (1967), *Residential Child Care: Facts and Fallacies*, Longmans.

Fahlberg, V. (1981a), *Attachment and Separation*, British Agencies for Adoption and Fostering (BAAF).

Fahlberg, V. (1981b), *Helping Children When They Must Move*, British Agencies for Adoption and Fostering (BAAF).

Fahlberg, V. (1982), *Child Development*, British Agencies for Adoption and Fostering (BAAF).

Fahlberg, V. (1984), 'The Child who is Stuck', in Adcock, M. and White, R. (eds), *In Touch with Parents*, British Agencies for Adoption and Fostering (BAAF), 17-20.

Fitzgerald, J. (1983), *Understanding Disruption*, British Agencies for Adoption and Fostering (BAAF).

Fitzgerald, J., Murcer, B. and Murcer, B. (1982), *Building New Families*, Basil Blackwell.

Harris, J. (1984), 'An Introduction to Attachment Theory and its Place in Child Care Practice', in BAAF op. cit., 24-26.

Harris, J. (1986), 'An Introduction to Attachment Theory and its Place in Child Care Practice', in Batty, D. (ed.) op. cit., 49-55.

Heinike, C.M. and Westheimer, I.J. (1965), *Brief Separations*, Longmans.

Herbert, M. (1985), *Caring for your children*, Blackwell.

Herbert, M., Sluckin, W. and Sluckin, A. (1982), 'Mother - to Infant Bonding' in *Journal of Child Psychology and Psychiatry*, 23, 2.

Hetherington, E.M. (1980), 'Children and Divorce', in Henderson, R. (ed.), *Parent-Child Interaction*, Academic Press.

Jackson, A. D. and Dunne, M. J. (1981), 'Permanency Planning in Foster Care with the Ambivalent Parent', in Maluccio, A. N. and Sinanoglu, P. A. *Partnership with Parents: working with parents of children in foster care*. Columbia University Press, 151-164.

Jenkins, S. , 'The Tie that Bonds', in Maluccio, A. N. and Sinanoglu, P. A., ibid.

Jewett, C. (1984), *Helping Children Cope with Separation and Loss*, Batsford.

Kaffman, M. and Elizir, E. (1983), 'Bereavement Responses of Kibbutz and non-Kibbutz Children Following the Death of the Father', in *Journal of Child Psychology and Psychiatry*, 23, 3, 435-442.

Keane, A. (1983), 'Behaviour Problems among Long-Term Foster Children', in *Adoption and Fostering*, 7, 3, 53-62.

Kellmer-Pringle, M. (1975), *The Needs of Children*, Hutchinson.

Kubler-Ross, E. (1972), *Death and Dying*, Tavistock Publications.

Lightbown, C. (1983), 'Life Story Books', in *Adoption and Fostering*, 7, 3, 9-15.

Lim, S. P. (1983), 'Loss - From the Chinese Point of View', in British Association of Social Workers, (BASW), *Loss, Proceedings of the British Association of Social Workers, Summer School on Loss*, 55-58.

Lynch, M. (1975), 'Ill Health and Child Abuse' in *The Lancet*, 2, 317.

Maluccio, A. N. and Sinanoglu, P. A. (1981), *The Challenge of Partnership: Working with Parents of Children in Foster Care*, Columbia University Press.

Maluccio, A. N., Fein, E. and Olmstead, K. A. (1986), *Permanency Planning for Children - Concepts and Methods*, Tavistock Publications.

Maxime, J. E. (1986), 'Some Psychological Models of Black Self Concept', in Ahmed et al, op. cit., 100-116.

Orbach, I., Gross, Y., Glaubman, H. and Berman, D. (1985), 'Children's Perceptions of Death in Humans and Animals has a Function of Age, Anxiety and Cognitive Ability', in *Journal of Child Psychology and Psychiatry*, 26, 3, 453-463.

Page, R. and Clarke, G. A., (eds) (1977), *Who Cares?*, National Children's Bureau.

Quinton, D. and Rutter, M. (1984), 'Parents with Children in Care - II, Intergenerational continuities', in *Journal of Child Psychology and Child Psychiatry*, 25, 211-229.

Rapoport, R., Fogarty, M. and Rapoport, R. N. (eds) (1982), *Families in Britain*, Routledge and Kegan Paul.

Richards, M. P. M. and Dyson, M. (1982), *Separation, Divorce and the Development of Children: a Review*, Department of Health and Social Security, HMSO.

Rowe, J. and Lambert, L. (1973), *Children Who Wait*, Association of British Adoption and Fostering Agencies (ABAFA).

Rushton, A. and Treseder, J. (1986), 'Research: Developmental Recovery', in *Adoption and Fostering*, 19, 3, 54-56.

Rushton, A., Treseder, J. and Quinton, M. (1989), *New Families for Older Children*, BAAF.

Rutter, M. (1972), *Maternal Deprivation Reassessed*, Harmondsworth: Penguin.

Rutter, M. (1985), 'Resilience in the Face of Adversity', in *British Journal of Psychiatry*, 147, 598-611.

Rutter, M. and Quinton, D. (1984), 'Long Term Follow up of Women Institutionalized in Childhood: Factors Promoting Good Functioning in Adult Life', in *British Journal of Developmental Psychology*, 18, 225-234.

Ryan, T. and Walker, R. (1985), *Making Life Story Books*, British Agencies for Adoption and Fostering (BAAF).

Schaffer, H. R. (1977), *Mothering*, Fontana - Open Books.

Schaffer, H. R. and Emerson, P. E. (1964), *The Development of Social Attachments in Infancy*, Monographs of Social Research in Child Development, 29, 4.

Seligman, M. E. P. (1975), *Helplessness: on Depression, Development and Death*, W. H. Freeman.

Sheridan, M. (1986), 'Chart Illustrating the Developmental Progress of Infants and Young Children', in Batty, D. (ed.), op. cit., 89-101; or Department of Health, op. cit., 88-93.

Sinanoglu, P. and Maluccio, A. N. (eds) (1981), *Parents of Children in Placement - Perspectives and Programmes*, Child Welfare League of America.

Skuse, D. (1984), 'Extreme Deprivation in Early Childhood - II. Theoretical Issues and a Comparative Review', *Journal of Child Psychology and Psychiatry*, 25, 4.

Small, J. (1986), 'Transracial Placements: Conflicts and Contradictions', in Ahmed, S. et al, op. cit., 81-99.

Stacey, M., Dearden, R., Pil, R. and Robinson, D. (1970), *Hospitals, Children, and their Families: the Report of a Pilot Study*, Routledge and Kegan Paul.

Stein, M. and Carey, K. (1986), *Leaving Care*, Basil Blackwell.

Stein, T. J., Gambrill, E. D. and Wiltse, K. T. (1978), *Children in Foster Homes - Achieving Continuity of Care*, Praeger.

Stein, M. and Ellis, S. (1983), *Gizza Say?*, National Association of Young People in Care (NAYPIC).

Stevenson, O. (1968), 'Reception into Care - Its Meaning for all Concerned', in Tod, R. J. N., *Children in Care*, Longmans, 8-19.

Swanson, M. (1988), 'Preventing Reception into Care: Monitoring a Short Stay Refuge for Older Children', in Freeman, I. and Montgomery, S. *Child Care: Monitoring Practice*, Jessica Kingsley Publishers, 46-60.

Sylva, K. and Lunt, I. (1982), *Child Development - a First Course*, Grant McIntyre.

Thoburn, J. (1985), 'What Kind of Permanence?', *Adoption and Fostering*, 9, 4, 29-34.

Thoburn, J. (1988), *Child Placement: Principles and Practice*, Community Care.

Thoburn, J., Murdoch, A. and O'Brien, A. (1986), *Permanence in Child Care*, Basil Blackwell.

Thorpe, R. (1980), 'The Experiences of Children and Parents Living Apart', in Triseliotis, J. (ed.), *New Developments in Foster Care and Adoption*, Routledge and Kegan Paul, 85-100.

Tizard, B. (1977), *Adoption: A Second Chance*, Open Books.

Triseliotis, J. (1983), 'Identity and Security', *Adoption and Fostering*, 7, 1, 22-31.

Wallerstein, J. S. and Kelly, J. B. (1980), *Surviving the Break-Up: How Children and Parents Cope with Divorce*, Grant McIntyre.

Webb, S. (1989), *The Feasibility of Using Respite Care in a Social Services Department*, Thesis for the MSc in Applied Social Studies, University of Oxford.

Winnicott, C. (1986), 'Face to Face with Children', in Batty, (ed.) op. cit. 38-48.

Winnicott, D. W. (1965), *The Maturational Process and the Facilitating Environment*, Hogarth.

Wolkind, S. N. and Rutter, M. (1973), 'Children Who Have Been in Care - an Epidemiological Study', in *Journal of Child Psychology and Psychiatry*, 14, 97-109.

Chapter 2

Erikson's Life Cycle Approach to Development

Alastair Gibson

At certain ages, according to Erikson's (1965) life cycle approach to development, we encounter expectable life crises which create a conflict within ourselves as individuals and between ourselves and significant other people in our lives. How we cope with these conflicts affects the development of our personality and patterns of behaviour.

This is very much a psychosocial theory; although it may owe its roots to certain aspects of Freudian theory, it is firmly committed to the importance of relationships as a central factor in the development of personality. There are important features from psychodynamic theory which are inherent in an understanding of the life cycle approach and it would be useful to mention these briefly before considering the life crises.

First, the concept of the ego assumes importance. The ego is the central functioning part of the personality which is conscious, aware and determines our day to day activities and relationships in a rational, reality-based way. The ego, however, is only a part of the personality and attention is given to the unconscious part, or, as identified by Melanie Klein (1960), the split part which forms the inner world of the individual. In studying the life cycle, we speculate that there are situations experienced and feelings engendered which are so painful or stressful to the developing ego that they become subject to the intervention of ego defence mechanisms (Rycroft 1968). Without going into too much detail, there appear to be two principal methods of defence as far as the very early formative years are concerned. One is to take inside and to repress an experience which is felt to be painful or unacceptable. Thus one renders it unconscious, but it remains in one's inner world as a significant determinant of one's personality. This process of introjection begins with the baby's identification of familiar people, familiar patterns of behaviour and feelings associated with these. By introjecting these perceptions and feelings, the infant absorbs them into the developing personality. For example, if the baby introjects the caring, nurturing parts of the carer, this may be reflected at a later stage in life in a giving, open personality. Similarly, if the baby introjects the depriving or rejecting parts of the carer, this may result in a non-giving, withholding personality. As a positive defence mechanism, introjection may help a child cope with separation, or separation anxiety, by providing something of the presence of an absent carer within the child, which may help the child tolerate the crisis.

The other main method of defence is to project on to other people whatever is felt to be personally intolerable. Whatever we fear or are anxious about is inside and is very painful. We may cope by denying and repressing, or we may actually get rid of it by placing it onto someone else. Thus, for example, aggressive feelings that we find intolerable in ourselves are projected on to another, who we now allow ourselves to identify as aggressive. In life cycle theory, the first five or six years of life are deemed most significant because of the child's relationship of inner and outer worlds, because of unconscious processes and of the potential use of infantile defence mechanisms. If the use of such defences make it impossible to tackle life crises realistically, the adult ego may be poorly equipped to cope with later crises. For example, the baby may have very powerful feelings of rage as needs are frustrated if food is not provided when hungry, if movement and the chance to explore is restricted or if the carer is not available when needed. If such feelings of anger are so powerful, they may be quite terrifying to the baby. Anger may, therefore, be a very unsafe emotion to own and express, and crises later in life may be distorted either by an avoidance of anger at all costs or by an undercurrent of anger impeding relationships.

Erikson saw each life crisis as a conflict, characterised by a pull in different directions. The word 'versus' appears in each stage. For example, the first stage is seen as basic trust *versus* basic mistrust. From the outset it should be made clear that Erikson does not assume that the successful resolution of each stage requires absolute goodness, be it complete basic trust, complete autonomy or whatever. Psychological health is not seen as that. Erikson's own words are 'favourable ratio' (p.262), which convey the element of balance in considering the outcome of these crises. For example, the assimilation of some mistrust into one's personality would be vital, otherwise one might have a totally naive, potentially dangerous faith that everything is good and safe.

The various crises which form the life cycle are a process. Thus, if one achieves a favourable ratio of basic trust, one is as well prepared as possible for the next stage. Equally, failure to achieve a favourable ratio is likely to make the resolution of succeeding life crises more problematic.

In the first eighteen months of life, the baby is confronted with the crisis of basic trust versus basic mistrust, which corresponds to Freud's oral sensory stage (Brown 1961) where the mouth is the focus of sensory stimulation. The word 'basic' is not used lightly. It refers to a fundamental sense of trust, of inner confidence in the outer world, that forms the core of one's adult personality. Absence of such basic trust can be a feature of those whose adult personalities are withdrawn in schizoid or depressive states, and this stage of the life cycle assumes considerable importance if we consider our work with people of any age who have particular difficulty forming attachments, making satisfactory relationships or trusting. Can we work effectively with them without specifically trying to help them rebuild a sense of basic trust?

The baby at this stage has to develop a sense of what is good and what is bad by a process of introjection and projection. The desired outcome is a favourable ratio of basic trust with a healthy sense of mistrust to allow future experiences to be evaluated realistically. From a social work perspective, this theory implies that a baby has particular needs which have to be met by parents or substitute carers. We have to try to understand what a baby, without the power of word formation, without formed cognitive thought processes, feels when, for example, the pangs of hunger become distressing or a colic pain upsets or when physical pain is administered by someone. The depth of feeling is not tempered by rationalisation. It is probably a bitter rage and identifies the person associated with the feeling as wholly bad. As Erikson says, 'In introjection we feel and act as if an outer goodness had become an inner certainty. In projection, we experience an inner harm as an outer one: we endow significant people with the evil which is actually within us' (p.240). The bad feelings translate to the world as a bad place, ie not to be trusted. The act of feeding, by breast or bottle, may restore feelings of goodness which are taken in through the mouth and psychologically introjected. Cuddles, holding and physical demonstrations of affection are also very important in conveying to the baby that feeling of goodness which results in the acquisition of basic trust.

Erikson is quite specific that this is not purely a mechanical approach and that the amount of trust acquired in no way depends on how much food is given or how much the baby is held. Trust is created because the parent or carer is sensitive to the child's needs, meets those needs within a consistent framework which begins to have some meaning for the baby and establishes their own trustworthiness. The building of trust depends very much on the quality of the relationship between baby and primary carers. What, therefore, if the carer came through his or her childhood with an unfavourable ratio of basic trust? Here the work of Bowlby (1969) and Rutter (1981) on the formation of attachment is significant. The reciprocal basis of a bond, where, for example, baby offers father/mother/carer rewards just as much as father/mother/carer offers baby, seems to relate closely to Erikson's views on the establishment of basic trust.

Continuity and consistency in terms of helping the baby attach meaning to the outer world also relate to Rutter's research into the number of different carers in a young baby's life. Although the evidence is somewhat limited, Rutter suggests that up to five carers could be involved in the care of a baby without there being harmful psychological effects, provided these carers were responsive and stimulating. The formation of a bond and attachments may well be impeded if the early care of a baby is chaotic and lacking the stability of contact with recognisable people over a prolonged period. Here again we must try to speculate how it must feel to a baby to be left to cry with hunger for a long period with no certainty that food will be provided. In the same way, how does a baby react when there is no recognisably consistent figure to whom to relate or attach? Given the potentially intense feelings, if the world is felt to be an unsafe or untrustworthy place at this stage, there is a strong possibility that it will remain an unsafe place, with consequent inhibiting effects on the individual's ability to tackle subsequent life crises.

The second stage, autonomy versus shame and doubt, coincides with the physical development of muscular control, including the anal sphincter, and Freud's anal stage (Brown 1961). Erikson places the onset of this life crisis in the second year of life, but clearly a baby in the first year displays some kind of autonomy when squirming away from someone or resisting a feed. Thus there is a relationship between all the life crises and it may be true to say that features of each crisis exist before the chronological time for the crisis arrives. The particular nature of each crisis is, however, seen as age related. For example, 'under normal conditions, it is not until the second year that he (the infant) begins to experience the whole critical opposition of being an autonomous creature and being a dependent one' (p.263).

At this stage the crisis is about who controls, and, in the context of toilet training, 'holding on' and 'letting go'. Physically, the infant is becoming more mobile, crawling and walking, and beginning to experience the pleasures of being able to do things and wanting to do things. Anything of value within the house which is within reach becomes vulnerable to the exploring infant. Getting the infant out of nappies and toilet trained assumes significance for parents. Compromise and balance are critical in order to avoid, at one end of the spectrum, the all powerful child who becomes terrified by the lack of meaningful boundaries, and at the other end, the heavily restricted, overly controlled or punished child, who experiences meaningless shame and doubt.

In practical terms, the relationship between child and carer determines so much of the outcome of this stage. The carer who is not stressed about toilet training, who is prepared to wait till the infant seems ready and who is prepared to tolerate the interest in faeces will not unduly inhibit the acquisition of autonomy. The carer who can let the infant explore his or her surroundings, protecting against danger, will also enhance the sense of autonomy. If, however, the infant experiences the pain of punishment, the anger of a carer who clears up the mess or the restriction of having to do things, including the toilet, when other people want, the balance of shame and doubt may be excessive. Shame is the kind of feeling of fear one gets of being completely exposed and of being looked at, the kind of feeling that makes one wish the ground would swallow one or one could be invisible. The risk, according to Erikson, of too much shaming is that the individual may try to get away with things or indeed reacts by defiant shamelessness. Erikson links the origins of doubt to Freud's anal stage of development. The pleasure in the passing of faeces makes the infant aware of the back of the body. If the infant feels shame when those faeces which felt so good to pass are treated with revulsion by the carer, Erikson argues that doubt may be established when that part of the body which cannot be seen by the owner, as it were, attracts such an interest in its control from others.

Holding on at this stage can turn into an obsessional holding on in adult life. This could be a compulsive need to be in control of self or others at all costs. Letting go could be more positive if it is a relaxed feeling of toleration, but could be translated into more destructive activity if it becomes a release of harmful, pent-up emotions. At this stage the infant learns by repeating actions and activities, with boundaries being imposed by carers and by learning from the knocks and bumps of mistakes. The child who is prevented from standing on his or her own feet at this stage, may repress feelings of anger and may become the obsessive adult, the compulsive neurotic, the personality lacking self-esteem. If one were to summarise the aims of the first two life crises, they might be 'the world is an OK place, and I'm an OK person.'

The third stage, described as initiative versus guilt, may broadly be expected to become critical between the ages of four and six years, although one cannot be too rigid, and links with Freud's oedipal complex (Brown 1961). There is often a degree of confusion about the differences between initiative and autonomy and between guilt and shame or doubt. Initiative implies more than autonomy, because it suggests an ability to set something in motion, to make the first move, to plan and to act independently. Because of this element of personal volition and ability, the negative aspect is one of guilt about one's intentions and the actions that one has implemented.

Physically and mentally the child has an energy which enables it to form relationships with others in a more complex way than before. Multiple relationships develop in terms of adults, siblings and playmates. Cognitively, the child is able to begin to reason and deduce, but still carries that part of thinking which could be described as 'magical' in the sense that fantasy and wish fulfilment can make it seem possible to achieve anything. While this may produce good feelings if the results are pleasurable, the feelings may be bad where the results are painful. For example, the death of a parent or carer at this stage, if the child magically assumes some causative part in it, may leave deep anxiety, fear and guilt. Within this particular framework of understanding personality development, this stage is potentially traumatic, as fantasy has to become transformed into reality and the child begins to understand concepts of right and wrong, fair play and deferred gratification and the requirements of social conformity.

Jealousy and rivalry seem to be major features of the conflict at this stage and this is particularly so in those families where a new baby has to be integrated by a brother or sister at this age. Families who foster children may also find that this age presents difficulties for the child of the family or the fostered child. The main arena for the rivalry is seen as the battle for the affections of the parent of the opposite sex, where the fantasy that the son can possess his mother or the daughter her father is, under normal circumstances, doomed to failure. Freud paid particular attention to the concept of sexuality and at this stage the awareness of genitals in boys and the absence of them in girls. If, however, we take a broader, more relationship oriented view, and also acknowledge the cognitive developments in the child's personality, we may begin to understand something of the potential turmoil taking place within the child. This is a transitional time when the child is moving from a very self-centred basis of relating to a much wider basis. The child has to come to terms with different ways of interpreting the world and the possibly intense relationship within the family has to be modified.

Again, the relationship with parents or carers will affect the child's progression through this stage. Psychological health may be maintained if the child is not made to feel that its behaviour is wrong or unduly threatening. Ideally, the child continues to feel the affection of both parents and gradually gives up the desire to possess the parent of the opposite sex and begins to identify with the parent of the same sex. The child is then prepared in this transitional stage to develop wider relationships.

Within our society, this is almost a blueprint for ideal personality development. What happens, however, to the child in care who is deprived of the presence of two parents? What happens to the child in a single parent family? From practice experience it would appear that the life crisis as indicated by Erikson is a critical part of development and that individuals are critically affected by experiences at this stage. There is a relationship-seeking energy at this age which needs to find some kind of outlet in people of the same and opposite sex. In whatever setting the child lives, there are implications for the behaviour of significant adults in helping the child achieve a favourable ratio of initiative, a sense of purpose and awareness of self. Guilt does appear to be unavoidable as there are so many activities that cannot be completed at this age, including being the partner of one's parent, that some guilt must be engendered. This can be exacerbated, for example if a parent of the same sex dies leaving the child with the parent of the opposite sex. Fantasy and reality overlap, creating a potential for either massive guilt or an excess of initiative in the form of extreme risk taking.

These three stages of life crises mark the most critical of the formative stages because of the intensity of experiences and the repression which is needed to help the child cope with everyday events. If a child has a favourable ratio of basic trust, autonomy and initiative, there is a healthy psychological foundation. It is impossible to imagine a child who has not repressed feelings and experiences, and therefore within this model everyone has a potentially neurotic part of their personality. The less favourable the ratio, the more potential repression and it is fair to assume, the less equipped one is to tackle subsequent life crises realistically.

The fourth stage is rooted more in conscious memory and covers the primary school years, industry versus inferiority. Freud called this the latency stage (Brown 1961), because the violent drives and turmoil which characterised the earlier years become dormant at this point pending the onset of puberty. Within our psychosocial framework we tend to find that memory of this period is clearer, and whereas the anxiety provoking experiences of earlier stages are more prone to repression or selective recall, the anxiety of this period is within the conscious part of the ego. The conflict now is about the acquisition of knowledge and skills as a preparation for life in adult society against a feeling of inadequacy or failure. School obviously becomes the focus for much of this conflict, but home life continues to play an important part.

It is usually not difficult to remember teachers and how they made one feel. Nor is it usually too difficult to remember one's own reactions and behaviour. It is all too easy to place a child in an inferior role at this stage, and all children find some way of coping, finding the inner strength or playing the fool or fighting the system, for example. Here one may see that the ability to cope with outside pressures depends on ego strength which derives from a favourable ratio from previous stages. Particularly relevant, but not exclusively, is the result of the autonomy versus shame and doubt conflict. The child who harbours inner doubt or shame has a propensity for feelings of inadequacy and low self esteem and is, therefore, less well prepared for the pressures than the child who has a more favourable experience. Relationships are also widening and peer group identification is becoming a more significant part of personality. There are conflicts inherent in trying to meet the requirements of adults and trying to meet the need to identify with friends and peers. Again, the child who has a sense of purpose and initiative, who is not restrained by the oedipal pressure to cement relationships with a particular member of the family, will be better equipped to find a satisfactory balance.

The onset of puberty, the move into secondary education and adolescence mark the fifth stage of the life cycle, identity versus role confusion. If one considers the fundamental importance of a sense of identity to the individual personality, of being a specific person within an understood environment, one gets an impression of the potential depth of conflict inherent in this life crisis. Such is the fundamental importance that one can begin to appreciate why, at this stage, there is the potential for behaviour to mirror the pattern of earlier conflicts which have not been satisfactorily concluded. For example, a lack of basic trust may inhibit the formation of an identity outwith very narrow, 'safe' surroundings. A sense of shame and doubt may result in behaviour that might be delinquent or repetitive as the adolescent struggles inwardly to establish some satisfactory meaning. Oedipal attachments may once again feature as adolescents wrestle with relationships and attempt to establish a sexual identity. As Erikson says, if there is a 'strong previous doubt as to one's sexual identity, delinquent and outright psychotic episodes are not uncommon' (p. 253).

For every adolescent, this is a time for testing, testing themselves and testing other people in relation to themselves. If one reviews the previous life crises, one can see that a favourable ratio will have established a sense of security, purpose and meaning which form a basis for this part of the life cycle, but which does not imply that such an adolescent will avoid the fights with significant adults which forms part of the testing behaviour. The concern is how the adolescent appears in the eyes of others and how to connect what knowledge and skills which have been acquired to future work or study. Role confusion includes sexual identity, but it also includes, very powerfully, an occupational identity. The absence of employment opportunities may have a significant effect on the developing personality at this stage of life.

Within families there is the potential for conflict. Parents need to understand that the rivalry for mother's affection between father and son, for example, is part of a separation process, a reworking of an earlier unresolved stage. The teenager is in the process of loosening attachments, but if families over-react to behaviour there is a danger that the teenager is expelled or leaves before the natural adjustment has taken place. Psychological health at this stage results in the acquisition of a personal identity with which one is reasonably comfortable, for in some ways the conflicts of this stage are never satisfactorily resolved or completed. Adults are quite capable of behaviour which could be described as adolescent or childish, because of its delinquent or selfish aspect, for example. If, however, one has acquired a comfortable sense of identity, one is prepared for the next psychosocial crisis which is the fusion of that identity with another's.

The sixth stage is described as one of intimacy versus isolation and covers the period of young adulthood which may begin in the teens and last through the twenties. One of the more contentious aspects of this theory centres on genitality and sexual relations, and questions tend to be raised about the importance for psychological health of sexual intimacy. Erikson (1965) attempts to provide a context by describing the ideal of genitality as:

1. mutuality of orgasm

2. with a loved partner

3. of the other sex

4. with whom one is able and willing to share a mutual trust

5. and with whom one is able and willing to regulate the cycles of

    a) work

    b) procreation

    c) recreation

6. so as to secure to the offspring, too, all the stages of a satisfactory development (p.257).

Such a definition raises all kinds of issues, not least about the relative importance of orgasm, heterosexual love and procreation. Theories of homosexuality and sociological concepts of stigma and deviance need to be integrated to this model. If one subscribes to Erikson's view that satisfactory sexual relations serve to make sex less obsessive and make any form of overcompensation or displacement less necessary, it is also important to consider what kind of sublimation, displacement or overcompensation people employ and which may be unhealthy psychologically. Does a satisfactory level of intimacy require an outlet in physical sex?

Another way of looking at what might be a satisfactory ratio of intimacy is to consider the object relations definition of mature dependency (Fairbairn 1952). Very briefly, this suggests that a healthy relationship is based on a capacity to put something of oneself into a relationship and to accept something back from the other person, based on an acceptance in reality of each other as individuals. This requires a degree of trust in others, a sense of autonomy in self and a mature attitude to unresolved parent/child issues. The legacy of previous life crises is therefore as much in evidence at this stage, and studies in marital fit show a tendency for unconscious influences to be at work in determining one's choice of partner. There is, for social work, relevance in the potential correlation between lack of satisfactory experiences in early childhood and the inability in adulthood to form satisfactorily intimate relations with other adults.

It is also possible for heterosexual couples who have apparently achieved a satisfactory relationship to be living in 'quasi' intimacy, which in effect isolates them as a couple rather than as individuals. Shared emotional needs might draw them unconsciously together, and inhibit their ability or desire to share themselves with any other. Such a reaction has particular relevance to the next stage in the life cycle, which Erikson describes as generativity versus stagnation. There is a strong emphasis placed on the adult's need to help provide the next generation and to guide and develop that generation. Although this life crisis includes such a direct reference to the next generation, there is more to generativity than simply having children or wanting to have children. Generativity also includes creativity, which could be artistic or employment based, and concepts of productivity. Implicitly it refers to that concept of adult mature dependency and suggests that there are psychological rewards for adults who can meet other people's needs, who have others dependent upon them. This element of give and take in a relationship is linked to psychological health in adulthood. The adult who is still emotionally dependent, who is 'needy' in relationship terms, may have those needs met by encouraging the dependency of others. Such a relationship is clearly not *mature* dependency.

As an illustration of the life cycle concept, babies are now being born to adults and these babies are experiencing parenting or care from adults whose personalities have evolved through the kind of experiences we have considered. The important question at this stage is how much of the adult personality is based on reality and an honest acknowledgement of past experiences and how much is based on a fantasy. If feelings have had to be repressed in order to cope with the pressures of day to day life, the external part of one's personality which is presented to others may be a gross distortion, superficially fine, but in reality trying to keep in check a lot of troubling feelings. The other consideration is the relative importance of bearing and raising children. Here too the issue of the woman's role in society as opposed to the man's needs to be considered, and personality theory cannot be separated from sociology. The traditional care taking role of women and providing role of men needs to be challenged and evaluated within the concept of this life crisis. Generativity is about using mental and physical energy to meet needs of mind and body, is about having the opportunity to expand one's self, one's ego, and to channel one's libidinal energy. Failure to do so results according to Erikson in a 'pervading sense of stagnation and personal impoverishment' (p. 258). Attitudes to employment, gender and family roles are crucial factors at this stage of adult life.

The final life crisis is seen as ego integrity versus despair and refers to the conflict in old age when the end of one's life becomes imminent, but could reflect a crisis facing those younger people with a terminal illness. If we look firstly at old age, Erikson says, 'only in him who in some way has taken care of things and people and has adapted himself to the triumphs and disappointments adherent to being, the originator of others or the generator of products and ideas - only in him may gradually ripen the fruit of these seven stages' (p. 259). Old age is placed firmly at the top, the culmination of crises of childhood and adulthood, the stage to which adults progress. Ego integrity is about a realistic acceptance of one's past life, an acceptance of one's life as it actually was and an understanding that all events, pleasant or painful, combined to form one's individual self. Ego integrity is about valuing one's individual self.

The favourable part of this life crisis suggests maturity and wise adulthood - progression, and there are important implications for social workers working with elderly people. Not only does it seem vital to avoid the kind of care which encourages child-like dependency and regression, but it also seems vital to work therapeutically towards a fostering of ego integrity. Erikson states quite clearly his belief that if one can achieve a feeling of ego integrity, death becomes less frightening. In the same way, perhaps the younger person, imminently approaching death may need help to integrate past life experiences even though the life cycle is incomplete.

In working with old people there may be a tendency to leave potentially painful experiences alone and not cause upset. This kind of attitude may enhance regression as it has the same kind of basis as the over-protective parent and the dependent child. It may say more about the worker's needs or fears than it does about the old person's potential.

Despair implies that time is now too short. Practically, despair may result in regressed behaviour such as bitter feelings that other people are getting better treatment or pathetically clinging dependent behaviour. Each example in its way suggests that the old person has given up hope of trying other ways to achieve integrity. Despair, according to Erikson, is signified by the fear of death: it could also be signified by a desire for one's life to end. A life that is seen as having had no sense of worth, of purpose or of meaning leaves the individual bitter - 'if only' becomes the predominant thought. Again, societal attitudes towards old age need to be considered. Do we value old people for their experience? A combination of valuing old age and valuing individuals may help promote a sense of purpose in workers that ego integrity is as crucial a part of personality development as any earlier stage of the life cycle.

References

Bowlby, J. (1969), *Attachment and Loss: 1. Attachment*, Pelican.

Brown, J. A. C. (1961), *Freud and the Post-Freudians*, Pelican.

Erikson, E. (1965), *Childhood and Society*, Harmondsworth: Penguin.

Fairbairn, W. R. D. (1952), *Psychoanalytic Studies of the Personality*, London: RKP.

Jacobs, M. (1986), *The Presenting Past*, London: Harper & Row.

Klein, M. (1960), *Our Adult World and Its Roots in Infancy*, London: Tavistock Pamphlet.

Lowe, G. (1972), *The Growth of Personality*, Harmondsworth: Penguin.

Rutter, M. (1981), *Maternal Deprivation Reassessed*, Harmondsworth: Penguin.

Rycroft, I. C. (1968), *A Critical Dictionary of Psychoanalysis*, Harmondsworth: Penguin.

Salzberger-Wittenberg, I. (1970), *Psycho-Analytic Insights and Relationships*, London: RKP.

Segal, J. (1985), *Phantasy in Everyday Life*, Harmondsworth: Penguin.

Storr, A. (1960), *The Integrity of the Personality*, Harmondsworth: Penguin.

Chapter 3

A Psychodynamic Approach to Social Work

Judith Brearley

Social workers are not alone in feeling suspicious about anything that smacks of psychoanalysis. Most professionals are wary of embracing ideas and theories which do not at first sight seem relevant to their pressing day-to-day concerns with practical matters. Social workers in particular have to struggle daily with issues of societal injustice and involuntary clients, and with the demands of investigative work and report-writing. Yet daily we also face such questions as 'Why does this person always become his own worst enemy?' 'How much effort should I put into this apparently entrenched situation?' 'Why does that teenager hate me so much when I am only trying to help?' 'How did that relationship get into such a tangle?' 'What makes our staff meetings and case conferences so conflictual and unproductive?'

These are not questions of the sort which psychoanalysis itself would claim to answer directly, but they are amenable to scrutiny by an approach which draws on ideas developed from psychoanalytic thinking. We call this approach psycho*dynamic*, rather than psycho*analytic*. What follows is an attempt to indicate ways in which a psychodynamic approach might begin to tease out some answers to the kind of questions that social workers have to deal with in their everyday professional lives.

What is a psychodynamic approach?

What exactly is this approach, and how does it differ from psychoanalysis? What is its potential value? How has it been used, and by whom? What might be its limitations?

Social workers require something akin to a map and guide-book as a means of first understanding this psychodynamic approach, and then arriving at conclusions about how they might most appropriately make use of it in practice. This chapter provides such a guide. It has several distinct components: definition and discussion of concepts, debate about contrasting developmental viewpoints, examples of the potential for application of the ideas across a broad range of social work practice, and critical appraisal.

First, then, some definitions.

> A psychodynamic approach implies recognition of the psychological forces motivating human behaviour and of the importance of feelings in the client's life and in the worker/client relationship (Hornby 1973).

> Psychodynamics is the study of the motivated and meaningful life of human beings, as persons shaped in the media of personal relationships which constitute their lives and determine how their innate gifts and possibilities will develop, and how the "maturational processes" develop in the "facilitating environment" of other human beings (Guntrip 1977).

> The term . . . (psychodynamic) . . . refers to those theories that derive from Freud, which stress the importance of unconscious mental processes and which involve acceptance of such central psychoanalytic concepts as transference and resistance (Yelloly 1980).

> My concept of dynamic psychology incorporates any type of psychological knowledge or insight which is concerned with the processes occurring in the mind - both conscious and unconscious. It further acknowledges the importance of the biological, cognitive and affective influences on human behaviour - both singly and in their interaction - as well as recognising that the context for such behaviour is always its social environment. It finally includes a recognition of conflict between the various aspects of individual personality and different persons as an inherent feature of human life with its potentialities for good and ill. Such a loose definition of dynamic psychology is intended to encompass in addition to the classical Freudian psychoanalytic theory its various derivatives regardless of how far some of these may have departed from the original (Butrym 1981).

In my own view, psychodynamic thinking is seen as predominantly concerned with certain key relationships, namely, those between:

— self and significant other people
— past and present experience

— inner and outer reality

with simultaneous focus on both the actual relationships and those built up internally from experience, and with special emphasis placed on the *processes* of these relationships and interactions.

It is clear that the psychodynamic approach owes a very great deal to psychoanalysis. Despite overlaps in terminology and concepts, the two approaches are, however, essentially different in the way they have developed. Many useful insights about the person derive from psychoanalysis but are now part of the repertoire of all those in the caring professions, who have modified or extended them for their own purposes. Psychoanalysis itself has not remained static; 'Psychoanalysis starts with but does not end with Freud' (Mitchell 1986). From a social work point of view, the developments in analytic thought in the fifty years since Freud's death are exciting because they tend increasingly to approach and mesh with some of the central concerns of current social work practice, and with other forms of psychological enquiry, especially, for example, child development research. Previous hostility and lack of dialogue are now replaced by collaborative thinking.

Psychoanalytic concepts of relevance for social workers

For Freud and almost all later theorists, *the unconscious* is the central concept, on which most other ideas about mental functioning are based. The idea was already familiar in the 19th century, but Freud was the first to chart its territory, discover how it worked and investigate it systematically. Freud regarded mental life as being made up of several portions: consciousness as the sum total of everything of which we are aware; preconsciousness as the reservoir of everything we can remember; and the unconscious as that vastly greater area of mental life where all our more primitive impulses and repressed images and their associated emotions are stored and whence they continue to influence our behaviour. Freud inferred the existence of the unconscious on the logical grounds that some of our activity is not consciously initiated, but flows out of us as if it comes from 'another'. As is sometimes said, 'I must have been beside myself to do that!' Such behaviour, which is often self-destructive, must have a source. Freud pointed out the illogicality and irrationality of the unconscious, its allusive, distorted quality, the fact that it is not located in time or place, and is communicated symbolically rather than in words. All these characteristics are, of course, familiar to us through dreams.

Freud saw the development of character in an individual as the result of a three-cornered struggle between the demands of parents and other family members, of impulses from the unconscious, and of the *superego*. This superego, loosely equated with 'conscience', is the aspect of childhood acceptance of adult authority and ideals which has been taken into the self, mainly at an unconscious level. These competing forces within an individual's mental life may be resolved by a variety of techniques, some successful, others less so, such as sublimation, reaction-formation, and symptom formation, known collectively as *defences*.

A key to the understanding of defences is the concept of *anxiety* and its nature. Anxiety is ubiquitous in human nature. It is at times intolerably painful, and it seriously affects a person's ability to function normally. The greater the degree of anxiety in relation to the person's tolerance and ability to manage it, the more will there be a need to construct defences against it. A very young child whose security is threatened when his mother goes away shows by desperate crying how vulnerable to panic and terror he is. Individuals as they grow through life develop a repertoire of defensive strategies to protect themselves and manage their more painful experiences. It is important to bear in mind that anxiety and defences against it operate not only at an individual level but also in marital relationships, in families, in groups and in institutions.

Some memories can be easily recalled, even though 'quite forgotten', whereas the memory of other experiences seem buried, split off and completely inaccessible. This second type of forgotten memory - the dynamic unconscious - is our main concern. It is inextricably linked with the notion of *repression*. This term describes the process whereby certain feelings, ideas or experiences are pushed into hiding and disowned because they are too painful, shameful or threatening to be acknowledged consciously at the time. Such objectionable feelings, eg irrational distrust or over-dependence, do not simply disappear, but remain in the psyche, almost as a foreign body. They are liable to resurface later in coded form in emotions, behaviour and relationships, especially between spouses, parents and children.

Another fundamental concept fits in with this scheme of ideas - *resistance*, the name given to those forces in a person which prevent or censor ideas entering conscious awareness because they are so totally incompatible with the person's view of themselves. It is the threat of arousal of unacceptable feelings which may bring about a client's unwillingness to engage in any exploration of potential change.

Denial is one of the most commonly encountered defences, and one which is relatively easy to perceive in operation. All of us want to keep unpleasant reality at bay, and there are times when a temporary buffer is needed against the pain of a well-nigh intolerable realisation. The loss by death of a spouse, child or parent is a clear example of such a situation, as is the diagnosis of a feared illness. Practically everyone in these situations will react at first by saying, 'No, it's not true. I don't believe it! This can't be happening to me.'

There is then often a delay before other feelings of distress emerge. The denial proves useful as a cushioning device, at least for a short time.

These aspects of Freud's theory were built on in different ways by Anna Freud and by Melanie Klein. Kleinian ideas have proved the more accessible, have led to much further debate and seem to have more relevance for social work practice, and therefore will be emphasised here. An exceptionally clear account of these ideas is provided by Salzberger-Wittenberg (1970), who demonstrates through the use of rich case material how social workers can utilise them in practice.

Klein (1959) described two psychological 'positions' whose origins can be traced back to the earliest months of life, each with their own characteristic anxieties and ways of responding. The first position begins to develop at the age of two to three months, and is described as the *'persecutory* or *paranoid-schizoid position'*, in which very primitive and intense anxieties about being left alone with terror, of not surviving or of falling apart hold sway. These are persecutory anxieties, and the defences against them are said to be splitting and projection. Noonan (1983) calls this the 'either/or' phase. The personality is split into parts, with the negative aspects projected outwards, onto other people.

Splitting arises from the existence of utterly contradictory feelings that seem impossible to countenance simultaneously, and which are therefore kept in separate compartments. The very young baby cannot yet understand that the mother who feeds and cares is also at times the one who has to go away and therefore is the one who neglects. The mother is therefore divided into a good and a bad figure, one idealised, the other hated. This process can be seen in action when a baby suddenly shifts from a quite blissful state to one of rage and despair, or in adults who polarise their experiences in extreme fashion. Social workers often experience themselves on the receiving end of this process when, for example, a client describes their work in glowing terms whilst at the same time scathingly criticising the GP or Health Visitor. (The roles could just as easily be reversed.) It is as if the client is unwittingly attempting to drive a wedge between the various agencies involved, and, unless there is a good degree of self-awareness on the part of the workers, the manoeuvre often succeeds, to the detriment of the work. Mattinson and Sinclair (1979) describe such processes in graphic detail.

Projection occurs when a feeling or characteristic which in reality belongs to the self is first externalised and then ascribed to another person; 'the pot calling the kettle black'. Not only negative qualities are projected; within a marriage for example, as Pincus (1976) has demonstrated, any desirable traits may be regarded as the sole prerogative of an idealised partner.

Introjection is a complementary process in which feelings (both good and bad) belonging to the external world come to be incorporated into the self.

Klein's second position develops at a later stage of infancy when the child discovers that the good and bad figures from his early months are different aspects of the same person - his mother - and comes to believe that he is in danger of magically destroying the person he loves the most. This stage leads to feelings of guilt and depression and is accordingly called the *'depressive position'*. Winnicott (1984) more helpfully refers to *'the development of the capacity for concern'* which implies a greater degree of maturity. In this, the 'sometimes' phase as Noonan (1983) calls it, the inevitable conflict between love and hate for the same person is not bypassed by the 'either/or' strategies of splitting and projection, but rather by tolerating the ambivalence involved, and *working through* the realistic sadness and grief towards a sense of reparation. There is recognition and acceptance that significant other people may sometimes let us down, but that this is not an ultimate disaster. The nature of the anxiety associated with this phase is concerned less with our own survival, and more with a fear of being destructive rather than creative in relationships. The depressive position, like the paranoid-schizoid position, is never totally worked through, and relics of it will always persist in the form of anxieties, especially ambivalence and guilt, which may come to the fore at different stages, such as during adolescence and at mid-life. These are times when the consequences of failure to tolerate the painful feelings involved may be discerned in such phenomena as drug-taking, promiscuity, unresolved grief and even suicide.

Defences are often viewed critically, or seen as pathological, but they can frequently act as helpful, even vital coping mechanisms. In effect, they represent the best solution to the problem that could be found at the time. Because they served such an important purpose they are valued by their owner and not easily relinquished, even when later they prove dysfunctional and cause extra problems. This is partly because of lack of confidence that there is anything to put in their place.

Whenever people meet, their feelings for each other always seem to be affected not only by the immediate occasion but also by association with past experiences, both good and bad. To the extent that this happens, most often unconsciously, the past is being revived and relived in the present. Freud called this phenomenon *'transference'*, and the concept remains a central one in psychodynamic thought, useful in all forms of relationship work. The starting point is early experience, rarely a single trauma, usually a repeated or pervasive series of interactions, as for example when a parent constantly disparages the efforts and achievements of a child. The impact of such experience then leaves residues, expectations and fantasies which in turn affect later relationships quite profoundly. In this example, the person so treated in the past is likely to perceive with particular sensitivity any critical comments, and is more liable to interpret reactions of others as put-downs, so shaky is his or her confidence and self esteem. Furthermore, these expectations and interpretations will influence others in subtle ways, through behaviour which elicits from them the very response most feared.

Social workers are often puzzled and discomfited by responses from clients which seem unwarranted; all the worker's best efforts may be met with resentment and exploitation. As Temperley (1980) suggests: 'I am afraid we have to recognise how tragically identified that client is with his own mother, and how he is likely to waste and abuse the worker's goodwill as his mother did his own. The failure as I see it, of much social work training, to prepare workers for this kind of negative treatment, seems to me a recipe for a life of professional masochism.' She goes on to discuss the massiveness of *negative transference* to which social workers are subjected, working with clients none of whom wanted to see them, and how she was struck by the way social workers took such treatment from clients 'without adequate apology, and without daring to value themselves sufficiently to name the client's behaviour as aggressive or even questionable' (pp.46-47).

Two related ideas help us to find a constructive way through this apparent impasse. Extending some of the concepts mentioned above, Kleinians speak about *projective identification*. To quote Temperley again, this is 'an *unconscious* mechanism whereby experiences which are felt to be unmanageable are disowned, largely by eliciting those experiences and emotions in others . . . The more disturbed we are, the more we will be using it' (p.49). This helps to make sense of some of the very irrational transactions that go on in marriages and families. It is also an important factor in the helping relationship itself, and if we can gain insight into what is happening between worker and client we can at the same time begin to understand at a much deeper level what the problem is really about. This is achieved by making use of the *countertransference*, those intense feelings and reactions elicited and stirred up in the worker by the client's story and behaviour. Monitored carefully to screen out what is personal to the worker, these reactions provide a valuable clue to what the client most wants to communicate. A practice example may clarify these processes. A GP was visiting a terminally ill patient. Both the man and his wife were stoically cheerful, but the doctor experienced a powerful feeling of unbearable sadness, which led him after some reflection to explore with the couple in a sensitive way the losses they were anticipating but had hitherto been unable to voice.

Finally, *the reflection process* is worth discussion as it relates closely to the above concepts, and is often encountered in social work supervision. A good illustration of this reflection process in operation, pointed out by Mattinson (1975), is when a student (or worker) behaves out of character in supervision. What seems to happen is that the student may have been seduced or manipulated into the client's way of feeling or thinking, and then in supervision re-enacts this viewpoint as if it is his own. More commonly, the student becomes so confused about what is going on in a family that in an attempt to convey what is hard to explain he unconsciously mimics aspects of his clients' behaviour. Another example of the reflection process is provided by the student who leaves an interview unusually burdened with anxiety or distress, as if those feelings have been dumped on him by the client, and who then in turn attempts to leave these feelings with the supervisor. Such transactions are very complex, involving as they do many of the processes outlined in this section. The value of understanding them, through positive use of the supervisor's counter-transference, is that it prevents the supervisor simply blaming the student for over-identification, and helps both parties to see with greater clarity the strength and nature of the client's problem.

Psychodynamic views of development

The main risk for those interested in psychoanalytic concepts but unfamiliar with the adaptive nature of the psychodynamic approach is holding on to outdated ideas based on Freud alone. Any theoretical approach which professes the crucial significance of relationships cannot itself behave as a closed system and ignore work which refines, supports or challenges its basic tenets. Freud himself was well aware of the problem, as he wrote to Jung as early as 1909: 'Your surmise that after my departure my errors might be adored as holy relics amused me enormously, but I don't believe it. On the contrary, I think my followers will hasten to demolish as swiftly as possible everything that is not safe and sound in what I leave behind'. Guntrip (1977), describing Freud as a fearless thinker whose mind was forever on the move, suggests that the question to ask is not so much 'What did Freud say?' as 'What has Freud's work led on to?'

The classical Freudian view proves least helpful when we come to explore ideas of human development. Many social work students are still being taught a narrow syllabus based on Freud's original schema of oral, anal and genital stages, and their grasp of the more useful family systems concept of the Oedipus complex tends to be a bit shaky. Some mention of the developmental ideas of Klein has already been made: it is uncommon for social workers to be familiar with these except through the growing number of discussions applying them to current issues (Mattinson 1988, Menzies-Lyth 1988, Pearson et al. 1988).

Fortunately it is becoming rare for students not to have some acquaintance with Erikson's (1965) conceptualisation of developmental stages. This encompasses the whole life cycle and firmly places individual development in family, social and cultural contexts, stressing the relationships between these.

Erikson's work has been discussed in its own right elsewhere in this handbook, as has the work of Bowlby.

For a time Bowlby was in danger of being misinterpreted because, like Freud, he revised his ideas quite radically over the years, and there was always a delay before the newer findings were well-communicated to students. However, up-to-date thinking on his attachment theory (1988) is now finding its way into the curriculum, and its scientific validity is increasingly acknowledged.

Similarly, Winnicott's ideas are relatively familiar, and are highly valued, especially perhaps by those working with children and teenagers or in residential settings. Since his death twenty years ago many of his papers have been republished in more accessible form, (1984, 1986) and several very good commentaries have been written (Davis & Wallbridge 1983, Clancier & Kalmanovitch 1987, Phillips 1988). His ideas about transitional objects, playing, the false self, the anti-social tendency, primary maternal preoccupation and the 'good enough' mother are all extremely fruitful concepts for social work practice.

I believe that the ideas of all the above-mentioned theorists, taken together, go a long way to providing us with a coherent psychodynamic framework of development. There are, however, at least two important omissions, namely, the ideas of Ronald Fairbairn, and those of Daniel Stern.

It is ironic that Scotland's great psychoanalytic thinker should be such an unfamiliar figure in his own country. Now, over 100 years after his birth, Fairbairn is increasingly acknowledged here and in the USA as a founder of the British 'object relations' approach, and for the originality and applicability of his ideas. Sutherland's (1989) psychobiography 'Fairbairn's Journey into the Interior' provides the most accessible exposition of his work.

Fairbairn (1952) offers a fundamentally different view of human motivation from that of Freud. Whereas Freud talked of drives, instincts and a pleasure-seeking libido striving for satisfaction through the media of various erotogenic zones, Fairbairn believed that what persons require and seek most assiduously is emotional contact with others. The infant is oriented to other people (its 'objects') from the very start, and this pressing urge to seek and maintain relationships continues throughout life. These ideas, based on the concept of a central ego seeking to relate itself with objects where it may find support, are congruent with Bowlby's, and both would postulate adaptive biological genetic reasons for this need to interact. Fairbairn emphasises that the unconditional loving care first of mother, then of father and others is essential, and that the child's love must be similarly received. In other words, the child needs to be loved and enjoyed for himself. If these conditions are not met, then survival, development and maturity are all threatened. To become a real and effective self, an individual has to be in satisfying relationships. This theme of the centrality of the human encounter, both in the growth of the person and in therapeutic relationships, is fundamental in Fairbairn's thinking, and has been amply confirmed in Bowlby's researches.

Fairbairn sees the infant as a 'whole', as having an intact ego with innate potential for growth from the very start, rather than as the product of a number of elements which eventually cohere into an ego. Splits in this intact self occur as a result of bad experience, eg if the mother is inconsistent in her care or does not respond to the child's love. Through processes of internalisation, the earliest experiences of relationships set a pattern which shapes future expectations of involvement. Bowlby's concept of 'internal working models' echoes this.

There are gaps in Fairbairn's thinking; he gives little detail about the transitional stage between infantile dependence and mature dependence. Also his terminology is unfortunate, as 'object relation' sounds extremely impersonal, and is better thought of as 'internalised relationship with a significant other person'. His ideas are however receiving increasing attention as a way of gaining more in-depth understanding of marital problems, schizoid factors in adult personality, and the nature of the therapeutic encounter.

Stern (1985) challenges some traditional assumptions about developmental sequences and tasks. He is concerned to integrate with psychoanalytic insights the enormous research advances of the last few years in observational and experimental work on infant development.

Stern, like Fairbairn, places the self at the very centre of his enquiry. He says that we all have a real sense of self, and of other, that profoundly influences all our social experiences, and provides a basic organising perspective for all interpersonal events. He assumes that some senses of self exists long before self-awareness and language. He is concerned to understand both normal social development and pathology, and to refine our awareness of developmental processes, with their alternating periods of rapid change (quantum leaps) and of relative quiescence. He identifies four different senses of self, each defining a different domain of self-experience and social relatedness: first the sense of an emergent self, which forms from birth to age two months; the sense of a core self, at two to six months; the sense of a subjective self, forming between seven to fifteen months; and a sense of a verbal self which forms after that. These are not successive phases that replace one another, rather they coexist once formed, and continue to function throughout life.

Stern questions the notion of developmental phases devoted to specific issues or tasks, such as orality, autonomy, and trust. Instead he sees these as issues for the entire lifespan, relevant at all points. He hypothesises that it may be more useful to locate clients' problems in one of the domains of self-experience than to see them as originating at a specific stage.

Further applications of psychodynamic understanding in social work

Work with families

Will & Wrate (1985), presenting their integrated model of family therapy, acknowledge several specific contributions from psychoanalysis, whilst at the same time expressing strong reservations about the use of a purely interpretative technique as a model of therapy. Psychoanalytic therapy (and to a lesser extent psychodynamic counselling) rests on the patient's ability to develop a transference relationship, whereas in family therapy and also in most forms of social work, this ability is neither a prerequisite nor does it usually facilitate the different tasks. In family therapy, the family members should be more involved with each other than with the therapist. In social work, the client is generally preoccupied with the reality problems which brought him to the agency and the contact may be short-term and compulsory. All this does not mean that transference reactions are not present, or that they do not require to be understood, rather that they are not fostered or acted upon. Even so, Will and Wrate suggest that psychodynamic insights may greatly enrich the way the worker perceives and understands the situation, thus allowing a more profound assessment. Awareness of feelings being defended against by family members, and understanding of projective identification aid work on the communication processes. 'Psychoanalytic object relations theory not only provides a highly sophisticated model of transactional patterns within families, but also provides a depth of understanding that cannot be derived from a "behavioural" systems model of family functioning alone' (p.6).

Child abuse: social work supervision and case conferences

Child abuse situations provide a wealth of evidence of primitive emotions and irrational transactions in operation. The inquiry into the death of Kimberley Carlile (London Borough of Greenwich 1987) contains many salutary descriptions of the ways in which such feelings and processes surface in destructive behaviour and relationships, not only in the family but also in and between the workers and their agencies. A particularly interesting section of the report, on supervision, makes recommendations in terms of psychodynamic principles. The following quotations speak for themselves:

> Supervision enables practitioners to know themselves . . . There is considerable evidence from all disciplines of workers struggling to contain feelings of anger or denial . . . The second function of supervi-

sion ... is its need to help the social worker recognise the effect achieved by the emotions being beamed out from the family. Many emotions and reactions are contagious. .... A social worker needs to have his antennae in working order to pick up the signals of child abuse (pp.192-3).

A vivid account of counter-transference at work in a case conference is given by Bacon (1988). This looks at the processes whereby professional workers, concerned to help a child and his family, ended up by resisting getting too close to them and by rejecting them. The case was one of clear-cut emotional abuse with indications of both physical abuse and neglect, yet all colluded in the decision not to place the family on the child abuse register. What were the complex hidden reasons for this hostility to registration? Social workers' avoidance of a painful reality was one factor; registration would make more conscious and explicitly shared what had previously been kept on the edge of awareness of individual workers, and it would also put pressure for direct work to be done with the child, a threatening and disturbing task, since he was described as possessing murderous rage towards caretakers. The second factor concerned collusive identification on the part of the professionals with the parents in their projection of badness onto the child, who was rejected and punished, and who then in turn actually became destructive and unlovable. By failing to be honest with the parents, the workers denied them their 'bad' parts (ie deprivations, hurts), and withheld from them any conviction that such painful areas of themselves could be contained, worked with, and modified.

Feminist psychotherapy

Since the mid-seventies, the Women's Therapy Centre in London has been refining its understanding of women's psychological development and the significance of gender identity, and its responses whether by individual work, therapy groups, workshops, couple counselling and training events. In evolving their theory, Eichenbaum and Orbach (1983) put forward two reasons for finding the work of the object relations theorists, particularly Fairbairn, Winnicott and Guntrip, helpful and relevant to their specific concerns. There were clinical echoes between those writers' observations and their own case experience in the area of women's therapeutic needs, and secondly there was shared emphasis on the basis of personality formation being located within a relational context. Psychodynamic concepts permeate their approach, and this is especially clearly seen in the therapy groups, where issues about receiving enough nurturance and taking time from others tend to surface as key themes. Mother-daughter transferences onto the therapist are very common, and provide a way of working through the vulnerability, pain and anger that members bring from their life experiences.

Organisational consultancy

As a result of a partnership between psychoanalysts and social scientists at the Tavistock Clinic and Institute since the 1940s, our understanding of institutional dynamics and of ways of bringing about change in organisational life has developed dramatically. Menzies-Lyth (1988) has written a great deal on this subject, much of it detailed accounts of her own interventions in hospitals and residential settings. Of particular interest is her work in the cot unit of an orthopaedic hospital, where the damaging effects of separation experiences on very young children were significantly reduced by a combination of strategies. These included physical alterations (putting down carpets to reduce noise, closing doors to limit comings and goings and to establish the boundaries of the unit), shifts in attitudes of various types of staff, including social workers (redefining the unit of care as the family and not just the child), and far-reaching changes in nursing practice (encouraging nurses to respond to signs of distress in a child and to see this as a normal reaction to an abnormal setting, rather than giving false reassurances or treating anger or upset as naughty). My own experience in this type of work has confirmed for me the validity of a psychodynamic approach with groups as diverse as industrialists, civil servants, clergy, multidisciplinary teams and staff groups in small voluntary associations.

Unemployment

It may seem surprising that a topical social problem with such evident structural and political dimensions should be addressed here. Yet the interface of emotional reactions, family relationships and the wider social context has been repeatedly stressed as a central concern of psychodynamics. In 'Work, Love and Marriage: the impact of unemployment', Mattinson (1988) explores by means of detailed case examples the neglected subject of the underlying meanings of people's work in relation to their marriages. Unconscious motivation in the choice of work is seen in the way in which people try, often successfully, to use their job to lay old ghosts. One example given is that of an airport apron manager who had always needed to keep inner chaos at bay and to fend off the pervasive childhood experience of a father who always 'rubbished' him. He found success in this through his task of parking aircraft immaculately to the great approval of his boss. A change of boss in this case precipitated breakdown. Mattinson then links such issues with marital dynamics, showing how the specific nature of the job may play a significant role in maintaining the status quo of the marriage, eg work in the off-shore oil industry could be used to keep an optimum degree of distance between the couple. What is disturbing about the findings is how powerfully social forces can resonate with an individual's inner fantasies, and together upset a precarious balance in the marriage. Divorce, psychiatric illness and suicide attempts are not uncommon responses to redundancy. This book does not talk about clients in isolation from the helping agencies, and it has some thought-provoking material about the emotional responses of social workers to these situations.

Conclusion

This chapter has clarified some of the concepts and terms used in the psychodynamic approach to social work. The essence of this approach is that it recognises the importance of psychological processes - between self and 'significant other' people, between past and present experience, and between inner and outer reality.

Tension between people's internal and external worlds is particularly crucial for social workers. Probably the major single reason why social workers have traditionally been so hostile to ideas based on psychoanalysis - and hence have neglected to test out their potential more widely - is their failure to resolve this tension. The origins of this failure, suggests Butrym (1981), lie in the absence of consensus about the nature of social work and its main objectives and tasks. Two basically opposing schools of thought can be discerned among social workers' views about assessment and intervention: one view emphasises environmental factors to the exclusion of emotional factors; the other - just as extreme - stresses the leading role of emotions and relationships but seems to underestimate the importance of the environment. Despite the lip service that the proponents of each view may pay to the other, the polarity remains unresolved.

The reality is more complex. Very many clients' problems are rooted in poverty and disadvantage. Gross inequalities of access to health care, housing, education and employment undoubtedly exist, and it is important to seek remedies through political action rather than helping individuals to adjust to their misfortune. But structural explanations throw little light on why some people abuse their children while others in similar social circumstances do not. Neither can political measures meet the needs of couples in marital conflict or children facing successive foster home breakdowns. Thus, concludes Butrym, social workers cannot confine themselves exclusively either to their clients' inner problems or to their environment. They must not only do both, but also work at the interface and address the interaction between them. In short, they must resolve the tension between inner and outer reality.

Social workers are increasingly pressured to deliver tangible services in a cost-effective way, as 'packages of care'. In doing so they may come to regard the world of feelings and relationships as an irrelevant intrusion - or, at best, an optional extra. Again a balance between inner and outer reality has to be struck; practical measures cannot be accurately targeted unless there is also a good understanding of their emotional significance to clients.

In assessing the relevance of psychodynamic ideas for social work, one important distinction should be borne in mind, that between its great value in *understanding* human behaviour and its more limited application as a *method of intervention*. The psychodynamic approach can be of immense value in helping social workers to understand what is going on in their clients' lives and in their own relationships within the social work team. It can also, as Jacobs shows elsewhere in this handbook, inform the counselling process in some very profound ways. However, it is not - and should not be confused with - psychotherapy. Greater clarity about the boundaries between psychodynamics and psychotherapy - and psychoanalysis from which many of its insights have been drawn - would have avoided much fruitless and acrimonious debate about the uses of psychodynamics in social work.

Finally, much more needs to be done to improve the way psychodynamic thinking is taught as part and parcel of the social work curriculum. Its principles should be as applicable to teaching methods as to practice. Learning has to be *both* at the experiential *and* at the cognitive levels. It can only be fully grasped by combining academic understanding with professional and personal experience. It will make demands on the self-awareness and emotional resources of students, teachers and practitioners. The realisation of the full potential of psychodynamic approach requires that it is conveyed in a fashion that brings to life the tension - and the resolution - between inner and outer reality. For this to happen adequate support and informed supervision are needed to enable the ideas to be translated into awareness and practice.

Acknowledgement

Grateful thanks are due to Don Bryant for his valuable help in clarifying and expanding many of the ideas in this chapter.

References

Bacon, R. (1988), Counter-Transference in a Case Conference: 'Resistance and Rejection in Work with Abusing Families and their Children', in Pearson G. et al. (eds) *Social Work and the Legacy of Freud*, London: Macmillan.

Bowlby, J. (1988), *A Secure Base: Clinical Applications of Attachment Theory*, London: Routledge.

Butrym, Z. (1981), 'The Role of Feeling', *Social Work Today*, 13, 11.

Clancier, A. & Kalmanovitch, J. (1987), *Winnicott and Paradox*, London: Tavistock.

Davis, M. & Wallbridge, D. (1983), *Boundary and Space*, Harmondsworth: Penguin.

Eichenbaum, L. & Orbach, S. (1982), *Understanding Women*, Harmondsworth: Penguin.

Erikson, E. (1965), *Childhood and Society*, Harmondsworth: Penguin.

Fairbairn, W. R. D. (1952), *Psychoanalytic Studies of the Personality*, London: RKP

Guntrip, H. (1977), *Psychoanalytic Theory, Therapy and the Self*, London: Hogarth.

Klein, M. (1959), 'Our Adult World and Its Roots in Infancy', *Human Relations*, 12 and in Segal, H. (ed.) (1988), *Envy and Gratitude*, London: Virago.

London Borough of Greenwich (1987), *A Child in Mind*, The Report of the Commission of Inquiry into the Circumstances Surrounding the Death of Kimberley Carlile.

Mattinson, J. (1975), *The Reflection Process in Casework Supervision*, London: Institute of Marital Studies.

Mattinson, J. & Sinclair, I. (1979), *Mate and Stalemate*, Oxford: Blackwell.

Mattinson, J. (1988), *Work, Love and Marriage*, London: Duckworth.

Menzies Lyth, I. (1988), *Containing Anxiety in Institutions*, London: Free Association Books.

Mitchell, J. (ed.) (1986), *The Selected Melanie Klein*, Harmondsworth: Penguin.

Pearson, G., et al. (eds) (1988), *Social Work and the Legacy of Freud: Psychoanalysis and its Uses*, London: Macmillan.

Phillips, A. (1988), *Winnicott*, London: Fontana.

Pincus, L. (1976), *Death and the Family*, London: Faber.

Salzberger-Wittenberg, I. (1970), *Psychoanalytic Insight and Relationship*, London: RKP.

Stern, D. (1965), *The Interpersonal World of the Infant*, New York: Basic Books.

Sutherland, J. D. (1989), *Fairbairn's Journey into the Interior*, London: Free Association Books.

Temperley, J. (1979), 'The Implications for Social Work Practice of Recent Psychoanalytic Developments', *Change and Renewal in Psychodynamic Social Work* Group for the Advancement of Psychotherapy in Social Work.

Will, D. & Wrate, R. (1985), *Integrated Family Therapy: A Problem-Centered Psychodynamic Approach*, London: Tavistock.

Winnicott, D. W. (1986), *Home Is Where We Start From*, Harmondsworth: Penguin.

Winnicott, D. W. (1984), *Deprivation and Delinquency*, London: Tavistock.

Yelloly, M. (1980), *Social Work Theory and Psychoanalysis*, New York: Van Nostrand.

Chapter 4

A Structural Approach to Social Work

Ann Davis

Introduction

Qualifying social workers must be able to:

— develop an awareness of the inter-relationship of the processes of structural oppression, race, class and gender

— understand and counteract the impact of stigma and discrimination on grounds of poverty, age, disability and sectarianism

— demonstrate an awareness of both individual and institutional racism and ways to combat both through anti-racist practice

— develop an understanding of gender issues and demonstrate anti-sexism in social work practice

— recognise the need for and seek to promote policies and practices which are non-discriminatory and anti-oppressive.

(CCETSW 1989, para 2.23)

This paragraph from the CCETSW document which outlines the requirements and regulations for the Diploma in Social Work (Paper 30) places structural issues firmly on the social work agenda for the 1990s. It suggests that all social workers need, during basic training, to develop an understanding of the economic, social and political forces which structure contemporary British society. What is more, it suggests that they will be required to demonstrate that they can practice in ways which are explicitly informed by a knowledge of the structures shaping the lives, choices and opportunities of people who become social work clients.

Specific reference to the importance of social workers understanding and actively challenging oppression, discrimination and stigma suggests that an analysis of inequality in contemporary Britain is a critical starting point for social work training. Such an analysis necessarily includes the distribution of power as well as economic resources and the way in which that distribution impacts socially on individuals, groups and communities.

This is material which has been traditionally dealt with on most social work courses as part of the 'input' from 'the social sciences'. It has been part of courses labelled as sociology, politics, sociology of welfare or social policy. The content of such courses has varied enormously and what students do with that content in terms of their practice has largely been left to chance. This lack of connection between structural analysis and the everyday practice of social work has resulted in the marginalisation of structural issues on most social work courses.

> Ignoring the structurally common components of clients' situations, the mainstream social work literature has focussed primarily on methods and techniques of working with individuals and groups. Social work methods are presented as tools which the social worker needs to 'fix' situations (Davis in Loney et al. 1987, p.87).

However, the agenda that has been set by CCETSW for the 1990s suggests that this approach is no longer adequate. Students are now being asked to demonstrate that they have acquired a knowledge of the forms inequality takes, what oppression means, and how it operates in respect of individuals and groups within society. Students are also being required to develop a practice which challenges oppression and other manifestations of inequality and disadvantage in their work with clients.

Such requirements are bound to open up debate amongst social work educators. Putting structural issues at the heart of practice poses a major challenge to the way in which social work education has traditionally been designed and delivered. As Jordan and Parton (1983) and Davis (1987) have noted, the history of social work in the UK shows it to be a profession primarily concerned with those who are the most powerless in our society. Yet its methods, techniques and 'theories' have in the main been characterised by a disregard of the issues raised by systematic structural differentiation in respect of race, gender and class. Indeed, since the 1950s a number of critics of social work have suggested that this absence of concern with the structural has been a deliberate, depoliticising strategy. Such a strategy is designed to keep practitioners' hearts and minds focussed on individual pathology and their methods and techniques uncontaminated by the realities of the society in which they are operating (see for example Wootton (1959), Bailey and Brake (1975), Simpkin (1979), Corrigan and Leonard (1978).

Because of the strength of this tradition, the newly launched emphasis on structural approaches is bound to stir up discomforting debate within social work education. Part of this discomfort will stem from the wider political climate in which the debate is taking place. Since the late 1970s government has been promoting greater inequality in society as one of the major means of attaining economic growth. Pond (1989) and Walker and Walker (1987), amongst others have shown that the results have been an increase in those living in poverty alongside an improvement in the income and wealth of the richest 10% in society. A social work profession which addresses inequality as a central issue in this economic and political context is bound to find itself subject to official criticism, scrutiny and ridicule.

As Nellis has noted, over the last decade the personal social services and those employed in them as social workers have become 'emblematic of the "dependency culture" Thatcher is seeking to eradicate' (Brown and Sparks 1989, p.104). It is little wonder that 'there have been few, if any, positive images of social work in the press or in government statements during the Thatcher years' (p.9). In Nellis' view this is because social work has been seen as part of the problem government has with welfare policy rather than part of the solution. A professional education and training programme which questions the manifestations of inequality in Britain is likely to reinforce this view.

In responding seriously to the challenges which CCETSW's statement poses and developing programmes which address structural issues, at theoretical and practical levels, social work educators are likely to find themselves in difficult territory - professionally and politically.

This chapter has been written in order to begin to chart this territory. It is concerned to explore what may be involved in breaking with tradition and working with structural approaches. The chapter therefore briefly considers:

— the major structural context in which social work is currently operating

— the way in which an analysis of this context can be used to inform practice

— one possible approach which is being developed to deliver the agenda which CCETSW has set.

The structural context of social work

The starting point for building an understanding of the structural context in which social workers are operating is a consideration of inequality in Britain. The reasons are succinctly outlined by Pond:

> The distribution of economic rewards between different groups in the population and different parts of the country, is an important determinant of the nation's economic and social structure. Economic and social

inequality are inextricably intertwined, and the distribution of income and wealth, the extent of poverty and privilege, have their effects on living standards, life chances and opportunities. Individuals' health and well-being are influenced by their position in the labour market, income and access to economic resources. Thus, class differences in health have persisted, despite an overall improvement in national standards.

Moreover, inequalities in wealth have political implications, providing the wealthiest individuals with access to economic, social and sometimes political power. For this reason, inequalities can become self-perpetuating, having an influence on the institutions that reinforce the class structure (Pond in Hamnett et al. 1989, p.44).

An understanding of the social structures in which social workers operate involves an examination of the way in which power and economic resources are distributed, the characteristics of that distribution, the interests it serves and the part played by welfare services in the processes of distribution. This is a matter of both absorbing the evidence which exists about change in this area and understanding the range of interpretations which are being generated to explain this evidence.

The analysis that has emerged over the last decade presents a picture of 'a growing divide between those able to enjoy the property and share owning democracy . . . and the growing ranks of the poor who are excluded from it' (Lister in Walker and Walker 1987, p.140). This polarisation has in the view of some commentators resulted in the creation of a permanent 'underclass' of the poor. This group is not only characterised by their exclusion from the opportunities afforded by prosperity. When the ranks of the 'underclass' are examined they consistently display particular patterns related to class, gender, race, age and disability and regional difference. For example, black people and other ethnic groups are more at risk of high unemployment, low paid employment and poor social security rights. They therefore appear in disproportionate numbers in groups living in poverty in British society (Oppenheim 1990).

It is officially estimated that between 1979 and 1987 the increase in real income for the total UK population measured over 23%. However, for the 10% on the lowest incomes there was a fall in income in real terms of 6.7% and for the 10% above them a fall of 1.1% (Halsey 1987). Amongst this 20% at the bottom of the income ladder, women, black people, older people and people with disabilities and long-term health problems were over-represented. The increase in people in work and in households with children in this low income group has been a marked feature of the last decade. This reflects in part the impact of government employment policies. The increase in low paid, unregulated and unprotected employment has gone hand in hand with social security regulations which have placed pressure on people to remain in such employment. As a consequence more employed people with children are finding themselves living in poverty.

Widening regional divisions in respect of unemployment rates and low paid occupations have also been noted as a result of a decline in manufacturing industry, growth in service industries and growth in unemployment. Members of ethnic groups are disproportionately affected by unemployment as the result of changes in the economic cycle. Within the ranks of the low paid the over-representation of women and black people is a consistent feature (Campaign for Work 1990; Brown 1985; Oppenheim 1990).

Evidence has emerged over recent decades of a widening gap in the distribution of life and health in Britain (Townsend and Davidson (1982), Whitehead (1988)). This evidence points to the way in which members of lower occupational classes systematically experience shorter lives and greater severity of ill health and disability. Summarising the situation, Whitehead states 'the health of the lower occupational classes has actually deteriorated against the background of a general improvement in the population as a whole' (Whitehead 1988, p.266). In areas such as housing and education the Church of England's report on inner cities (Archbishop of Canterbury 1988) has revealed how the distribution of poor quality and inadequate resources reinforces the lack of power, life chances and opportunity amongst particular sections of society.

The distribution of living standards, which reflect the distribution of wealth, income and welfare goods and services has been buttressed by government economic and social policy. This policy has sought to increase the use of private and occupational welfare provision while reducing the scale and scope of state welfare. As Titmuss pointed out, such social divisions in welfare provision result in a marked stigma for those groups reliant on state welfare for basic income and services and serve to reinforce socially existing economic inequalities (Titmuss 1958).

This evidence of systematic and deepening inequality is critical for social work because those people who become social work clients are, in the main, drawn from those groups that have been increasingly excluded from mainstream society. 'Social work remains, as it was in the nineteenth century, primarily a service for the poor and destitute. Despite its professional aspirations in the post-war period, it is a service of last resort' (Davis in Loney 1987, p.84).

The way in which social work agencies are organised reinforces the individualisation of despair and anger amongst dispossessed people. Social workers' attempts to 'normalise' their clients' lives or 'rehabilitate' individuals and families take little account of the way in which material and social deprivation structures choice and opportunity. Such attempts fail to challenge the way in which inequality, buttressed by ideologies about family and individual responsibility, operates to control and constrain those who become social work clients. As a consequence, social work intervention can reinforce the negative, stigmatising images of people in need which have been enhanced by current welfare policy.

Social workers in training must, therefore, learn to unravel the reinforcing way in which structural contexts interact with the organisation of social work. To do this it is essential that students have an opportunity to learn about the way in which their society is structured and debate the structural analyses which are on offer.

Analysing structures

In seeking an analysis of structural context which aids the development of a challenging practice, social workers will find that there are currently two contrasting approaches on offer within the literature. Their roots are in a set of political and professional debates which have characterised social work education from its inception. They both seek to address, rather than ignore, structural issues. They therefore provide a starting point for the work which we need to undertake in social work education in the 1990s and beyond.

The first approach promotes the view that social workers should understand the structural status quo and practice in a way which is not directed at undermining it.

Martin Davies' book, *The Essential Social Worker: A Guide to Positive Practice* (1985), exemplifies such an approach. He views social work as a 'by-product of an unequal and imperfect society' (p.235) - created by the state to provide 'humane safeguards for its most vulnerable citizens' (p.1). In operating as it does at the interface of the individual and society, Davies asserts that 'the essence of social work is maintenance, maintaining a stable, though not static, society, and maintaining the rights of and providing opportunities for those who in an unplanned, uncontrolled community would go to the wall' (p.234).

Davies' work spells out in some detail an approach to practice based on a 'theory of maintenance' in which social workers are 'maintenance mechanics oiling the interpersonal wheels of the community' (p.31).

This is a consensus approach to analysing structural inequalities in society and the role of social work in relation to such inequalities. As such it sets specific limits on the way in which practice should challenge structural inequality. Davies argues that the existence and survival of social work is dependent on two conditions. First, that social workers retain a 'broad respect for the political and economic viability of their society and its underlying political philosophy' (p.32). Second, that the 'state itself . . . must retain a broad commitment to a fair, just and humanitarian society, in which the rights of each individual, and especially of each most vulnerable citizen, are given due consideration' (p.32).

Given these two conditions, social work practice should not be directed at challenging the structural status quo. This does not mean that social workers should not raise questions about the direction and distribution of resources and the discrimination which their clients may experience. Advocacy is part of the 'tools' needed for the job. However, such activities should not be confused with the kind of political activity which any citizen might decide to take. The scope of professional intervention must be channelled along the given organisational channels, bearing in mind the state's mandate for social work.

A contrasting approach to analysing the structures in which social work operates is to be found in that stream of social work literature referred to as 'radical social work'. As Clark and Asquith's discussion (Clark and Asquith 1985, p.105) of the characteristic features of this movement shows, the label 'radical' covers a wide range of political, professional and personal positions (see for example the social work texts by Corrigan and Leonard (1978), Bailey and Brake (1975), Simpkin (1979) and Langan and Lee (1989)). As a consequence it cannot be unproblematically summarised but it does promote a number of core ideas.

It is an approach which does not accept Davies' account of the nature of the state. For radical social workers the state is seen as serving particular dominant interests and cannot play a neutral, humanitarian role with respect to vulnerable people. Consequently, any maintenance role undertaken by social workers with respect to state welfare policies will perpetuate inequality and its associated oppressions, disadvantages and stigma. Radical social work texts argue that social workers need to understand the nature of state power and the role of social work as an element of state control and oppression, and to construct an approach to practice which is underpinned by this understanding. Such practice must be directed at challenging and changing structures which oppress. It should be directed at transforming the relationship between service users and providers. It should consistently seek to empower users by transferring power to them.

In working out the practice implications of this approach practitioners will find that the radical social work literature has, until recently, failed to take into account the range of oppressions which operate within contemporary British society. In the view of Langan and Lee the early emphasis on class inequality in radical social work texts and practice led to a failure 'to recognise the systematic denial of power to women and black people' (Langan and Lee 1989, p.9). Consideration of inequality arising from sexuality, disability and age has also been neglected.

Recent texts (Dominelli (1988), Dominelli and McLeod (1989), Langan and Lee (1989)) have begun to address some of these limitations. They provide a 'radical' or conflict analysis of inequality in relation to anti-racist and feminist social work practice. In doing so they argue for an understanding of the way in which oppression, located as it is in a society structured by conflicts of interest, operates in a number of different dimensions which simultaneously affect the individual. Prioritising such oppressions is not seen as the way forward to developing and applying structural understandings of society to social work practice. Instead, this analysis of structure which argues for both challenge and change must be developed in a way which takes account of the range of social inequalities which characterise British society. The practice which is developed in the light of this analysis must be responsive to the voices and views of oppressed groups.

These two broad approaches which offer a contrasting analysis of, and ways of working with structural issues, provide different starting points for social workers in training and practice. The first, in arguing for maintenance within given conditions, promotes a consensual view of practice in which recognition of the discrimination suffered by vulnerable groups is dealt with through advocacy within organisational and political givens. The second, in arguing for change of existing structures which perpetuate inequality promotes an adversarial view of practice which simultaneously seeks to alleviate and transform the conditions in which oppressed clients find themselves.

As starting points both these approaches are necessarily outlined at a level of abstraction which needs to be worked out in detail if they are to inform the way in which social work education delivers on anti-discriminatory and anti-oppressive practice.

Hardiker and Barker (1988) have pointed out that attempts to view a situation as a social worker *solely* in structural terms can be totally incapacitating in relation to working out where and how to intervene. They suggest that it is necessary to 'disaggregate different levels of analyses to avoid reductionist explanations and misdirected interventions' (Becker and McPherson 1988, p.106).

The different levels they outline are:

1. *Structural*, ie an understanding of inequalities and how they are reinforced through social class, gender, age, disability, ethnicity and regional difference.

2. *Organisational* in terms of needs and resources and their distribution in relation to personal difficulties and way in which social work intervention accesses people to available resources.

3. *Interactional or psycho-social* in terms of the way in which private difficulties can be understood as influenced by structural as well as personal forces.

Such an approach to working through the levels which comprise a structural approach to practice does not promote either a consensus or a conflict analysis of social structure. Both can be accommodated within this framework. The task is for the student in training and those working with them (in practice and in educational establishments) to work out their own starting position in discussion and debate.

Delivering a structural approach to social work practice

The challenge faced by practice teachers and social work educators who engage with the structural approach is how to make it accessible to social workers in training. Such approaches have often been dismissed in the past on the grounds that their level of generality was too far removed to be of 'practical use' to social workers. The language of many structural texts - be they sociological, political or practice-based - has been a barrier to social work students searching for alternatives to the traditional practice texts.

In thinking through the delivery of a structural approach in social work training at Birmingham University I have been working with a colleague, Roger Evans, on an introductory course for social workers which is organised around a personal and political approach to inequality. Our starting point has been to make the introduction to a structural approach a personal one. This is shared and then extended and reflected on through the use of sociological and social policy material on inequality, power, oppression and stigma.

We start with our own and the students' biographies and ask them to consider their lives in relation to some of the prime sites of structural difference - gender, race, class, age, disability and sexuality. Each site is covered in a pair of sessions. The first session is experiential - we ask students to reflect on, through discussion and exercises, the way in which their own biography has been shaped by the social inequality under consideration.

For example, in the session on gender the exercise set for small groups of students as a way of opening up their personal experience of gender inequality is as follows:

Complete the following sentence (as it relates to your own gender) as many times as you like:

As a man I am expected to . . .

As a woman I am expected to . . .

Share your answers with the rest of the group and record your answers for feedback in a whole course discussion.

Repeat the exercise in relation to the following sentences:

As a woman I want to . . .

As a man I want to . . .

Our experience to date suggests that students are puzzled, discomforted, challenged and exhilarated by these sessions. They lose the distancing comfort of academic approaches which leave their personal lives unexplored. They are also unable to use the lives of others, ie their clients, in making their responses. In opening up these areas for themselves students learn a lot about how explosive and distressing these topics are for individuals for a wide range of reasons. The questions raised by students in these experiential sessions also reveal another critical area for practice ie their rights as individuals in social work training not to disclose to the institution or its educators facts about themselves which may have unknown repercussions on the way they are assessed. This is the stuff that clients experience daily in their contacts with welfare organisations, and so early opportunities are provided for considering issues of oppression and stigma in welfare services.

Each experiential/discussion session is followed by a teaching input which explores each site of inequality and provides empirical and theoretical material in relating it to the structures which characterise British society.

Course assessment draws on both strands of the course so that students are required to write essays in relation to the personal as well as the political.

This approach appears to provide a way of making direct connections on a social work course between social science teaching on inequality and issues of practice, values and politics. It is an approach which seems to us to have a potential for practice teaching in these areas. The way in which students learn about oppression and inequality is not just by an exposure to where and how their clients live with it, but also by reflecting on the similarity and differences of their experiences as social workers and citizens. Such reflections should be part of learning within both educational institutions and agencies if students are to be expected to work towards the expectations laid on them by CCETSW for social work in the 1990s.

References

Archbishop of Canterbury's working party on deprived urban areas (1985), *Faith in the City*, Church House publishing.

Becker, S. and McPherson, S. (eds) (1988), *Public Issues, Private Pain: Poverty, social work and social policy*, Insight.

Bailey, R. and Brake, M. (eds) (1975), *Radical Social Work*, London: Edward Arnold.

Brown, C. (1985), *Black and White Britain: The Third PSI Survey*, Aldershot: Gower.

Brown, P. and Sparks, R. (eds) (1989), *Beyond Thatcherism: Social Policy, Politics and Society*, Milton Keynes: Open University Press.

Campaign for Work (1990), *Racial Disadvantage and the Economic Cycle*, Research Report 2, 5.

CCETSW (1989), *Requirements And Regulations for the Diploma in Social Work*, CCETSW.

Clark, C. L. with Asquith, S. (1985), *Social Work and Social Philosophy*, London: Routledge & Kegan Paul.

Corrigan, P. and Leonard, P. (1978), *Social Work Under Capitalism*, London: Macmillan.

Davies, M. (1985), *The Essential Social Worker: A Guide to Positive Practice*, Aldershot: Gower.

Davis, A. (1987), 'Hazardous Lives: a view from the left' in (Eds) Loney, M. et al. *The State or the Market: Politics and Welfare in Contemporary Britain*, London: Sage.

Dominelli, L. (1988), *Antiracist Social Work*, London: Macmillan.

Dominelli, L. and McLeod, E. (1989), *Feminist Social Work*, London: Macmillan.

Hamnett, C. et al. (eds) (1989), *THe Changing Social Structure*, London: Sage.

Halsey, A. H. (1987), 'Social Trends Since World War II', *Social Trends*, 17, London: HMSO.

Hardiker, P. and Barker, M. (1988), 'A window on child care, poverty and social work' in Becker, S. and McPherson, S. (eds) *Public Issues, Private Pain: Poverty, Social Work and Social Policy*, Insight.

Jordan, B. and Parton, N. (eds) (1983), *The Political Dimension of Social Work*, Oxford: Blackwell.

Langan, M. and Lee, P. (eds) (1989), *Radical Social Work Today*, London: Unwin Hyman.

Lister, R. (1987), 'There is an alternative' in Walker, A. and Walker, C. (eds) *The Growing Divide: A Social Audit*, CPAG.

Loney, M. et al. (eds) (1987), *The State of the Market: Politics and Welfare in Contemporary Britain*, London: Sage.

Nellis, M. (1989), 'Social Work' in Brown, P. and Sparks, R. (eds) *Beyond Thatcherism: Social Policy, Politics And Society*, Milton Keynes: Open University Press.

Oppenheim, C. (1990), *Poverty: the Facts*, CPAG.

Pond, C. (1989), 'The changing distribution of income, wealth and poverty' in Hamnet, C. (ed.) *The Changing Social Structure*, London: Sage.

Simpkin, M. (1979), *Trapped in Welfare*, London: Macmillan.

Titmuss, R. (1958), *Essays on the Welfare State*, London: Unwin Hyman.

Townsend, P. and Davidson, N. (eds) (1982) *The Black Report*, Harmondsworth: Penguin.

Walker, A. and Walker, C. (eds) (1987), *The Growing Divide: A Social Audit*, CPAG.

Whitehead, M. (1988), *The Health Divide*, Harmondsworth: Penguin.

Wootton, B. (1959), *Social Science and Social Pathology*, London: Allen and Unwin.

Chapter 5

Theory, Concepts, Feelings and Practice: The Contemplation of Bereavement Within a Social Work Course

Gerard Rochford

The subject of this paper is how to relate theory to practice by contemplating personal experiences of loss. I am not proposing that the approach I take is appropriate to all teaching. I would say, however, that in some areas of social work education and training theory can only be related to practice by using a model of experiential learning which engages the thinking and the feelings of the students concerning their inner lives and the hypothesised inner lives of those with whom they have shared their intimate personal and professional time. It is my view that teaching students how to relate theory to practice using an experiential model not only brings the subject to life in a way that purely didactic and cognitive teaching fails to do, but provides a cognitive framework in such a way as to keep alive the relationship of theory to practice as a continuing and internalised process. Theory and technique which are taught *and then* applied by solely cognitive processes will always feel somewhat stiff for the practitioner and be perceived as false and manipulative by the client, as having something done to them rather than engaging in a joint task, and will thus re-enact and reinforce their already crippling experiences of powerlessness, victimisation and alienation.

Selection

If you use an experiential model of teaching there are issues around student selection that need to be addressed. The selection process must replicate some features of the course, partly so that students will learn what kind of cognitive but more especially *affective* work will be demanded of them, (them selecting us), but also for us to assess their ability to make their feelings available for cognitive work without undue risk or frustration to themselves. In this sense the work of the course begins in the applicants' personal statement, and is elaborated at interview in a way which makes the acceptance of a place a sufficiently informed consent of a particular kind, namely that a good deal of self-enquiry will be demanded of them.

We are familiar with applicants whose personal statements contain nothing personal and where interviewers are unable to reach the applicants' personal feelings about major life events and their work with clients.

And we know too applicants with a powerful desire to help, but whose life events have swamped them with feelings which are all too readily amplified by the experiences and feelings of clients, raising the issues of anger, guilt, and reparation, the potential problems of counter-transference, its value but also its dangers.

Within the two years of a course the one could not be sufficiently reached nor the other sufficiently healed, nor can it be our task with students to attempt this. Being cut off from feeling or flooded with feeling should lead to an applicant being turned down, though selection errors undoubtedly occur at these boundaries.

Between these extremes there are those with sufficient freedom of feeling around not only normal but in some cases tragic life events to make them available to the cognitive task relating to theory, the practice task relating to work with clients, and the encompassing task of turning self, client, theory and practice into a functioning whole.

The recently wounded would-be healer on the mend may be asked to re-apply. The 'cut-off' whose control and fears of their own feelings are likely to lead to a purely intellectual grasp of theory and a controlling and phobic response to clients' feelings would not be.

We may work readily, therefore, with both the unscarred and the sufficiently healed, though I do feel, to paraphrase Winnicott (1971), that although it can be said that if you have been wounded yourself you have greater sympathy with wounded people (though this is not always the case) somehow it would always have been better if we had not been wounded, (though all of us have).

The tutor's and the supervisor's task

I am talking here about educating students to work with feelings where the resource is the self and the techniques reside in the responses you make to the person in the room - the therapeutic interview. To develop this resource tutors have a legitimate interest in the students' feelings in so far as these are likely to manifest themselves in professional encounters.

Not only tutors but also supervisors have a legitimate interest in students' feelings.

It is possible, however, to identify shifts of focus, although both tutor and supervisor have the same field of vision which encompasses the thoughts and feelings of student and client, flowing within and between them. Both tutor and supervisor seek to promote a helpful response which is based on and leads to further elaboration of cognitive and empathic understanding and subsequent responding. The focus for the tutor may be more towards the student, and for the supervisor more towards the client. From time to time it will become clear that a student is in need of psychotherapy or counselling. This, in my view, should never be offered by the tutor or supervisor.

Somewhere in there lies a boundary, between education and grandiose ambition, between the legitimate *need* to see the student's feelings, and voyeurism, and between being tutor or supervisor and being a counsellor or therapist. Any strict separation between being a tutor and being a counsellor/therapist would no doubt be unhelpful (Fleming and Benedek 1983) but separation there must be. I would suggest that it is in some ways easier for the supervisor, since the focus and priority is the current work with clients for which the supervisor is often accountable.

Personal analysis and self-reflection

To focus upon the student's feelings per se is both legitimate and vital. I do hold, with Freud (1957), that no personal work with clients goes further than my own complexes and internal resistances permit. In psycho-analytic education and training the cognitive, personal, and practice tasks have four clear and separable (though not separate) arenas, namely theoretical seminars, case presentations, the personal analysis and the treatment of cases under supervision.

In social work, to make a contribution to the task of applying theory to practice, from the particular theoretical and clinical tradition of psychoanalysis, obviously requires a considerable modification of such a model, especially in that most crucial aspect, the personal analysis.

The theoretical seminar, the case-presentation and the direct work with clients under supervision, all have their counterpart in social work education and training. The personal analysis does not.

Yet some of the process and purposes of the personal analysis have to be present if social workers are to work with distressed feelings and if the contribution of psycho-analytic theory to social work education is to be meaningful and more than an intellectual exercise. To do this we have to provide students with 'situations and experiences which facilitate' some of the process and purposes of a personal analysis so that the students' 'own experiencing becomes an object of study' and so that they are able 'to anchor the fleeting phenomena of experience in the cognitive framework of concepts and theory', to value self-enquiry, see the need and practical value of it, and to have the confidence to 'generalise from their own experience' (Fleming and Benedek 1983). Part of this process is about converting sympathy to empathy so that a permeable boundary is kept between your feelings and the client's, a boundary none the less for being permeable and a closeness none the less for having a boundary. A client's grief will make you sad. But it is their grief and your sadness.

It is, I hope, accepted that empathy, by which the distressed feelings presented by the client and the feelings generated and available to the social worker, can be the medium in which work is done without loss of identity - that empathy is both an essential quality and also an educable resource. This can be achieved by making the student's own experience a primary object of *study*, in such a way as to make the empathic and the cognitive work together (Fleming and Benedek 1983). This must be done in time to prepare the student for placements and for work. And it must be done in a way which enables the student to internalise a process, a skill *and a commitment* which they will take further with them (Winnicott 1971). This is most vital because, to paraphrase Fleming and Benedek (1983), the social worker may be confronted by any client in any period of their professional life with one or other vulnerable area in their own personality and will be presented with changes caused by ageing, fatigue, illness or other external events which increase the social worker's vulnerability to the challenge of a client's demands. The achievement of the sort of educative process I advocate has been well put by Winnicott (1971) - whereby it becomes possible for a serious person to maintain a professional standard even when undergoing very severe and personal strain in private life. This also concerns avoiding burn-out and underlines the need for supervision throughout one's professional life.

This can only be achieved if students are educated to set up within themselves a free but disciplined communication between thoughts and feelings, the past and the present, the conscious and the unconscious of themselves and of the client in the room.

In which experiences and with which theory can we meet with the students for this task? I would suggest that the experience of loss may be especially relevant to the integration of theory, feelings and practice, where the theory to be understood is psycho-analytic theory.

The experience of bereavement: theory, concepts, feelings and practice

It appears from applicants' personal statements, and from interview material, that a major feature of motivation to do social work is the working through of the experience of loss, both normal and exceptional.

Looking at two recent intakes, from 38 students, ten had suffered the death of their father during childhood or adolescence and a further four had lost their mother, three had suffered the death of a close friend, one had lost a child, at least one had had an abortion, three had been divorced, one twice, and two had been close to persons committing suicide.

The experience of loss and grief is especially fitted for the teaching of theory and practice and for the educative process of putting a cognitive framework to personal experiences and feelings.

The prevailing theoretical perspective is psycho-analytical, a fact of special aptness. The case which first drew Freud to his life's work was a young woman whose symptoms were shown in response to her father's illness and death. Freud comments: '. . . her symptoms . . . correspond to a display of mourning, and there is certainly nothing pathological in being fixated to the memory of a dead person so short a time after his decease; on the contrary it would be a normal emotional process' (Freud 1910). It was this patient who called analysis 'the talking cure' and years later Leared said of the bereaved 'All they need really is to be able to talk about what has happened, in order to give full expression to their grief' (Leared 1977).

The theme brought forth a stream of classic literature, Freud's *Mourning and Melancholia* (1957), Klein's *Mourning and its Relationship to Manic-Depressive States* (1948), Bowlby's work on *Attachment and Loss* (1975), Marris' *Loss and Change* (1974). A ground base is the idea that mourning is a necessary process in normal healthy living. Glancing back to what I said about applicants rejected, they are often blocked grievers or those for whom the experience of loss is still too raw.

The classic psycho-analytic account of response to loss is Freud's (1957) *Mourning and Melancholia*, mourning being a healthy response to loss of a loved one, melancholia or depression being its pathological form.

The features of depression are described by Freud as follows:-

> The distinguishing mental features of melancholia are a profoundly painful dejection, cessation of interest in the outside world, loss of the capacity to love, inhibition of all activity, and a lowering of the self-regarding feelings to a degree that find utterance in self-reproaches and self-revilings, and culminates in a delusional expectation of punishment. This picture becomes a little more intelligible when we consider that . . . the same traits are met with in mourning.

Freud goes on to distinguish two forms of melancholia; one in which the lost object is evident but the response not that of healthy mourning, the other in which we cannot see what is lost and it is reasonable to assume that the sufferer cannot consciously perceive it either. He summarises the main distinction thus: 'in mourning it is the world which has become poor and empty; in melancholia it is the ego itself'. This may be relevant to post-natal depression in which the experience of birth seems to have been not that of adding another life but of emptying out a part of oneself. This suggests a powerful identification between the woman and infant, a projective identification by which the infantile part of herself is projected into the foetus and there identified with. She is then 'emptied' at birth and transformed into a demanding and helpless infant, a further stage in the projective identification.

The characteristics of mourning

The characteristics of mourning following Bowlby (1961) are usually organised according to stages developmentally described and consistent with those theories which relate present coping processes to early, particularly infantile, experiences. The concept of stages tends to encourage the view that progress is orderly, the stages discrete and that they must all be entered and passed through 'cleanly'. Perhaps also the concept of stages encourages impatience in the family, friend, neighbour or counsellor who look for progress, and fails to capture the ambivalence of feeling, the to-ing and fro-ing, which seems to pervade the experience of bereavement. Maybe the word 'stance' is closer to the tentativeness of the desire to move on and the fear of betrayal which pulls you back.

The stances of a bereaved person will include many of the following features:

> *Shock*, numbness, dazed withdrawal; denial, disbelief, a feeling of isolation, of being in a dream, of being childlike, of detachment; over-activity or physical collapse. The funeral often marks a transition: loss of religious faith may be experienced. The funeral also takes on the process of idealisation, only the good is remembered (Jacques 1955). It is to be noted that denial is predicated upon some level of acceptance, a later stance. All stances have the others beneath and around them, varyingly accessible to empathic work.

> *Yearning* and protest, pining, weeping and anger; pangs; illusions, misperceptions, dreams and hallucinations of the lost one; psychosomatic symptoms of anxiety and fear, panic, sleeplessness, palpitations, dryness of the mouth; self-neglect. The bereaved may still disbelieve

and deny death, speaking as if the dead person were still alive and imminent, trying to get close, to a chair, a bed, a grave; make nostalgic journeys yet showing fear of other haunts which are now dangerous, places which were previously entered, as it were, on the spouse's arm. The impulse to recover, retain, restore the lost one is also a search for reality and the disappointment of the search, as reality insists upon its truth, can engender in the bereaved person a more relaxed sense of *internal* presence. Perhaps the most disturbing feeling of all is the feeling of triumph, 'I am alive and he is dead'. There are thus disturbances of thought, feeling and perception, which are attended or followed by feelings of foolishness, shame, frustration and anger.

Despair, apathy and a feeling of emptiness or meaninglessness signal belief in the death. Bitterness, irritation and hostility to others may emerge with, usually muted, expressions of guilt and anger. The bereaved person senses the world as a dangerous place, withdraws and becomes disorganised, aimless. There is a giving up of associations with the lost one, while retaining one chosen 'version' of him, for example a photograph.

Re-organisation, acceptance and adaption follow. The bereaved person re-emerges, rebuilds social relationships, restores herself. The sense of mourning as a duty is relinquished, an act that may require the 'permission' of a trusted person. It is now possible to reminisce about happy and unhappy times, with an appropriate sense of the lost and the retained. The reality of reminiscence replaces the unreality of denial. The 'good enough' survivors replace the 'resented, intrusive' substitutes.

There are no feelings unique to the loss through death of a loved one. The processes of denial, search and realisation, the ambivalence of feeling, the contradictions of thinking and the errors of perception are the familiar experiences of reflective consciousness as we stand amid what was, what is, what we would like and what ought to be. These processes in particular occur not only within the bereaved but within the dying and within those who, in whatever capacity, share intimately the experience of the dying and the bereaved.

Theory and practice approaching a bereaved person

The psychoanalytical perspective has at least three implications for those, whether family members, volunteers or professionals, who respond to the bereaved. First, bereaved persons cannot be understood except in the context of two resonating sets of relationship, the primary ones of their infancy and the later adult relationships.

Second, bereavement induces a process which in its manifestation and in its internal feel is in some sense a repetition of the separation anxieties of infancy and the attendant guilt as represented in the statement 'my badness drove her away'. Third, an enabling offer cannot be made to a bereaved person except by reaching into our own losses, both of infancy and of adulthood. Hence the special gifts that may be offered by those who have themselves grown from their own mourning, who can approach the bereaved from their own creative wounds. The proper assumption for practice has been put by Freud with nice severity: '. . . although grief involves grave departures from the normal attitude to life, it never occurs to us to regard it as a morbid condition and hand the mourner over to medical treatment. We rest assured that after a lapse of time it will be overcome, and we look upon any interference with it as inadvisable or even harmful' (Freud 1957). I take interference to mean anything which tends to suppress the expression of grief, including drugs commonly prescribed to bereaved persons.

The appropriate therapeutic stance is indicated both implicitly and explicitly by various writers. Klein (1948) says that the normal working through of mourning relates to the way in which the person first deals with this process in infancy. When the good person (mother) has gone she becomes bad and this gives rise to the ambivalence of love and hate. One way of coping with loss is by internalising the lost person. The paradoxical effectiveness of this process, stressed by Bowlby (1975), is that the ability to tolerate separation-anxiety is a sign of deep attachment. Similarly, in bereavement, deep attachment leads to a corresponding deep loss, but also to the greater likelihood of restitution, as Pincus so movingly illustrates (1974). Deep attachment leads to healthy mourning as the strength of the remembered good person is retained and drawn upon, and as emotion is withdrawn from the really dead person. This parallel process, of letting go and of harvesting, eventually allows the bereaved person to talk with equanimity about both the good and the bad. The reality of the death and the reality of memory both assert themselves. Just as the anger and hatred against the dead revive and spring from infantile feelings, so also the infantile sense that badness drove the mother away can be seen in the bereaved person's guilt and sense of responsibility for the death, 'if only I'd looked after him better', 'if only I'd made him go to the doctor'. Some share of the ambivalent feelings of the bereaved towards the self and the other, will also be felt by friends, neighbours, relatives, helpers and counsellors, however well intentioned and however actually helpful. The irrationality of this may be a further source of guilt later, as the bereaved person recalls this time with some shame. Substitutes for the lost one may expect both thanks and resentment.

It is Parkes' (1975) view that prolonged or delayed mourning is usually attributable to excessive guilt and/or pronounced ambivalence in the relationship to the deceased. Kubler-Ross (1970) sees the somatic symptoms of the bereaved as a failure to work through guilt, and its attendant unconscious punishment. The starting point for Pincus (1974) was to 'explore whether .. . various responses to bereavement might best be understood or even predicted by focussing on the particular relationships which made for unique family patterns'. The extent to which the relationship had been enhancing or depleting, whether the one was engaged with or lost in the other, interdependent or dependent, will find expression in the extent to which losing the other is being lost oneself. The internal representation of these relationships in the survivor will determine whether or not the taking in and giving out of what was good and bad was achieved without depletion, an experience which can then be drawn upon for the work of the restoration of the self in relationship with survivors.

It is clear that an enabling response to bereaved persons requires sensitive and 'risky' use of self, particularly the ability to live within ambivalence and not be tempted to 'reason' with contradictory feelings.

Just as we may understand the neurotic as someone who, due to constitutional, personal and social-environmental forces got stuck within a developmental process which most people travel through so also with particular responses to bereavement. Theoretical understanding of bereavement draws together the reciprocating knowledge of the normal and the abnormal experience, and of adult and child experience. This perspective requires us to listen not only to carefully designed research investigations but also to the analysis of practice experience and the anecdotes of the wise. For even an anecdote, honestly told, is valid data when theory is concerned with a universal phenomenon.

For both theoretical and practice reasons adult loss by death of a loved one cannot be split off from other losses experienced in the life-cycle. The loss of infancy, childhood, adolescence, youth, friends, lovers, hopes and the breast's security, all resonate within us. Whether the later versions of these experiences give rise to some internal restoration or further crippling depletion is heavily dependent on early experience, leading to investment of the self *in* others, (over-involvement), *for* others, (the helping response), or *with* others (love).

Working with the experience of loss

Encouraging a psycho-analytic approach to the students' personal losses introduces them to the way of understanding adult relationships and experiences by reference to early primary relationships, and to their abiding primitive and infantile feelings.

It has the power to arouse in them the recognition that loss in its manifestation and its internal feel is in important ways a repetition of the separation anxiety of infancy. And it does this in a way which values their personal experiences for their own sakes and as professional resources. In terms of practice it hopes to arrive quickly at the realisation that an enabling offer to persons with distressed feelings can only be made to the extent that we have reached into our own, holding them as separate from the client's but as a resource none the less.

The potential this theme has for facilitating access to feelings is matched by its suitability for cognitive work.

It introduces students in an experiential way to stage theory both in the general way of examining the evolution of their own dependencies, independencies and interdependencies and for many of them the micro-stages of mourning and grief work.

It introduces them through their feelings to a whole array of key concepts - denial, detachment, projection, identification, guilt, the desire for magical restoration, the flight into health, gain from illness, triumph, regression, despair and perhaps most important of all - ambivalence, important not only because ambivalence is of the essence of grief but because it introduces the paradox of understanding *cognitively* the powerful processes of *irrationality*.

It gives some access to the defence mechanisms through self-reflection in a way which also enables students to question but also to *value* their defences, having been protected by them. This helps them not to be provoked by the defences of clients, not to see them as walls to be attacked but perhaps maintained and even when pathological, only to be eased away painfully, gently and truthfully. It helps them to acknowledge bad feelings in others and not to take flight in unhelpful re-assurance or change of subject. It teaches them the emptiness of euphemising social work encounters in order to save, that is waste, people's feelings.

In terms of its relevance to client groups the contemplation of loss and grief has considerable power for entering the worlds of others.

For example, though there are many more, (abortion, loss of a limb, divorce) in residential child care the theme of loss is both background and foreground to childrens' experience, where private griefs are compounded by public responses.

A recent study of List D girls (1985) shows from a sample of 80 girls that 50 had lost a parent either from death or desertion, and among the remaining 30, 17 had one parent with serious illness. Similar figures were found among 100 List D boys.

Working with families of handicapped children involves the loss of the perfect unrealised child reverberating down the years, at the anniversaries, and at the many lost rites of passage.

At the other end of life, anyone working with the elderly or in hospitals has to enter the world of grief and must therefore be enabled to do this without being overwhelmed by their own resonating feelings.

The formal task

By addressing loss in lectures and tutorials I have, I believe, identified a theme which unites teacher and student together in mutual experience. By requiring all students to write about bereavement, relating personal and professional experience to concepts and theory, they can discover that one way of acquiring knowledge is not by taking it in but by unlocking it - so they can say, with Freud's patient, 'I've always known it but never thought it', discerning that some forms of unknowing come not from being empty but from being resistant to, or split off from, yet-to-be released feeling which has a habitation but no name.

The format of an essay also, *and importantly*, leaves students in control of what material they are willing to expose, while at the same time putting them close to feelings and experiences which they can reflect upon but may not wish to write about or share with tutors, though it is important for them to be able to share with someone.

It is part of the journey towards mature hope so tellingly mapped by Searles who argues that any realistic hope must be grounded in the ability to experience and survive loss. Furthermore he suggests that hope comes into being when one discovers that despair can be shared with a fellow human being, thus fostering a feeling of relatedness rather than of alienation. This experiencing of loss and despair leading to hope is also part of the maturational process traversed by every therapist in the evolution of their own personal feelings in relation to patients with whom they become deeply and sustainedly involved (Searles 1979, pp. 484, 502).

The risks that students take and the hard cognitive work they undertake convinces me it is a journey into darkness well worth the illumination.

References

Bowlby, J. (1961), 'Process in Mourning' in *Int. Journal of Psycho-analysis*, 41.

Bowlby, J. (1975), *Attachment and Loss*, Harmondsworth: Penguin.

Fleming, J. & Benedek, T. F. (1983), *Psychoanalytic Supervision*, New York: International Universities Press.

Freud, S. (1910), *Five Lectures on Psycho-Analysis, Lecture I*, S.E. Vol. XI, London: Hogarth.

Freud, S. (1957), *The Future Prospects of Psychoanalytic Therapy*, S.E.11. London: Hogarth. (from 2 above)

Freud, S. (1957), *Mourning and Melancholia*, S.E. Vol. XIV, (1917) London: Hogarth.

Jacques, E. (1955) 'Social systems as a defence against persecutory and depressive anxiety' Ch. 20, in Klein, M., Heimann, P., Money-Kyrle, R. E. (Eds) *New Directions in Psycho-Analysis*, London: Tavistock.

Klein, M. (1948), 'Mourning and its relation to manic-depressive states', in *Contributions to Psycho-Analysis*, London: Hogarth.

Kubler-Ross, E. (1970), *On Death and Dying*, London: Tavistock.

Leared, J. (1977), in *Sharing the Pain*, Age Concern, 23.

Marris, P. (1974), *Loss and Change*, London: Routledge and Kegan Paul.

Parkes, C. M. (1975), *Bereavement: Studies of Grief in Adult Life*, Harmondsworth: Penguin.

Petrie, C. (1985), Girls in a List D School. Unpublished thesis, University of Aberdeen.

Pincus, L. (1974), *Death and the Family*, London: Faber.

Searles, H. F. (1979), 'The Development of Mature Hope in the Patient-Therapist Relationship'. Ch. 21, p.484. *Countertransference and Related Subjects*, Madison, Connecticut: International Universities Press.

Winnicott, D. W. (1971), *Therapeutic Consultations in Child Psychiatry*, London: Hogarth Press & The Institute of Child Psychiatry.

Some of the material appeared previously in:

Rochford, G. (1985), 'Bereavement' from *Developing Services for the Elderly*, Research Highlights in Social Work No. 3. London: Kogan Page/Jessica Kingsley.

Chapter 6

Towards Social Theory for Social Work

Pauline Hardiker and Mary Barker

... to practice without theory is to sail an uncharted sea; theory without practice is not to set sail at all (Susser).[1]

Without a social theory the social worker is at the mercy of a thousand discouragements (Marshall).[2]

Introduction

In this chapter, we discuss the general theme of discipline knowledge for social work. Other chapters in this volume present specific theories from the social sciences (eg loss and bereavement; attachment theory) and models of social work intervention (eg behavioural; counselling).

An identifying characteristic of social work is the great range of human situations addressed; this encompasses not only people's predicaments but also their social situations. The work requires a breadth of discipline knowledge, derived not only from the social sciences, but also from other bodies of knowledge (eg law, psychiatry, and philosophy). Furthermore, social workers need to be sufficiently familiar with them to make informed choices, to keep up to date with advances and to discard redundant theories. This is a tall order indeed. Practitioners, therefore, often adopt a pragmatic stance, claiming to use whatever approach appears to work in a particular case. However, social workers are rarely as arbitrary as this implies; their practices are influenced and constrained by their agencies, by the nature of the cases, and by changing ideas of the role of the state in welfare.[3]

For example, social workers practice from an agency-specific location, so child abuse referrals are processed through a variety of legal and administrative systems and are assessed in different ways, eg neglect, incest, family dysfunction.[4] As Hardiker, Exton and Barker[5] suggest in relation to preventive child care:

> Problem definition and assessment is not a simple, objective measure but a complex process which involves values, principles, agency policies and procedures, the current legal position and the perspectives of social workers and their managers. Similar situations may or may not lead a client to seek help, a social worker to open a case file, a court to make an order (p.112).

Furthermore, child-abuse assumes different forms in relation to the nature of injuries and patterns of parenting. These perceived variations also shape the types of interventions chosen. Very serious physical injuries may involve police, courts and probation officers, whereas less serious ones may be processed through community facilities and self-help groups. Finally, child abusers differ in respect of their age, gender, socio-economic status, race, ethnicity and neighbourhood, ie typically, social inequalities.[6]

The poverty lobby suggests that the parenting of many young, working-class mothers, living in deprived communities, may be too-readily labelled as child abuse instead of being recognised as adequate coping in stressful circumstances.

It has been suggested in this introduction that, in spite of the wide range of discipline knowledge available to social workers, they are rarely in a position to choose whatever theory or approach they please. Frameworks for practice are shaped by the nature of problems referred, circumstances of families, and agency functions and resources.

Social theory for social work

Where can one look for principles and frameworks of knowledge which will help social workers to find a way through this range of discipline knowledge? One way in which this is attempted on the Leicester MA in Social Work course is through a sequence we have called 'Social Theory for Social Work'. It is studied in the final academic block of this two-year post-graduate course, when students have already received teaching in many of the contributory disciplines, and in social work theory and methods. They have also completed two practice placements and their practice study. They are, therefore, relatively well-versed in both theory and practice.

It is probably best to convey the nature of this sequence through the use of an exercise, taken from the social theory course. This example concerns approaches to child abuse (though any field of practice could have been selected, and the analysis offered is intended to be transferable).

Exercise

The students are asked to think of a *general statement* about child abuse and to write it down (working individually)

Students are then handed the following *list of statements* about child abuse (taken from the literature or illustrating a commonly held view) and asked to compare them with their own individual statements. It is anticipated that most of the students' statements will have parallels in the list, and that there may even be clusters of typical responses (eg bonding and family systems):

1. Fatal battering has been shown to occur where young, unstable, deserted and unhappy women associate with young, *psychopathic* and criminal men (Smith, et al, p.575).[7]

2. Neither parent has had any experience of a normal loving home and I think they need a *sustaining and nurturing* experience themselves to enable them to cope with the demands and stresses of their own small children (Court, p.x).[8]

3. By definition, however, the child that has been abused has demonstrably not *bonded* with its abusing parents (Beckford Report, p.97).[9]

4. Mr X is *repeating* patterns of abusive parenting which he experienced in his own family.[10]

5. This episode of abuse reflects some of the ways in which this child is *scapegoated* within her family.[11]

6. This child's *'failure-to-thrive'* has partly arisen because his aversive temperamental attitudes have shaped his interaction with Mr and Mrs X who found him difficult to parent.[12]

7. The *relationship between the parents* is problematical. Mr and Mrs X wish to avoid conflict because they fear their marriage will break down. Mrs X opts out of the family and Mr X becomes over-involved with his daughter. This abuse maintains the pattern.[13]

8. *Boundary roles within this family* have weakened external and internal inhibitory mechanisms which might have protected the child against abuse.[14]

9. This family is *socially isolated* in the neighbourhood.[15]

10. J's *delinquency* is a symptom of the abuse she has experienced in her family.[16]

11. The *infant-mortality rate* in this deprived district is two and a half times higher than that in 'leafy suburbia'.[17]

12. *Mr X's assault* on his daughter is the cause not the symptom of this family's difficulties.[18]

13. *Welfare agencies* have under-reacted or over-reacted to the signs of physical injury notified to them.[19]

14. The problem of child abuse should be addressed at a *much earlier stage* in the community, eg education programmes, self-help and parent-craft groups.[20]

15. The identification of *risk groups* by the Area Review Committee is sexist, racist and discriminates against vulnerable working class families.[21]

16. The Child Protection Register *polices problem populations* and dangerous families.[22]

Note: It is important to remember that this exercise is presented as a teaching device not a comprehensive theory of or approach to child abuse; otherwise, the presentation over-simplifies and caricatures perspectives which are normally appropriately more complex. The exercise has also been used with groups of practice teachers.

Review

In discussion, the students are asked to identify some of the assumptions underlying the statements (which may be implicit or explicit), and the different theoretical frameworks they represent.[23]

This exercise is quite 'mind-bending' for anyone who attempts it, as we rarely, if ever, attempt to write down the full range of possible explanations or approaches to any particular social work situation.[24] The students are then asked to contribute to the discussion the statements about child abuse that they themselves wrote down, and to try to identify the assumptions underlying those. Often, their own statements add even more to the range of views, eg child abuse as a rediscovered problem-definition; the relationship between sexual abuse and adult psychiatric difficulties.

The discussion leads into an analysis of the exercise, in which an attempt is made to look for themes/frameworks/concepts which underlie this diversity, and help social workers to make more sense of the whole. This approach is demonstrated in the next section, and again is related to the exercise on child abuse, for the purpose of illustration. The following themes are discussed:

1. Identifying concepts and theoretical traditions.

2. Value positions and ideologies.

3. Explanations and interventions.

Themes and frameworks of social theory

1. Identifying concepts and theoretical traditions

The statements listed above are derived from the authors' reading and understanding of the literature on child abuse (which is less than exhaustive). A first stage in learning about social theories for social work is the ability to recognise particular concepts and theories. This may not be easy for social work practitioners, who have sometimes internalised them so that they are 'taken for granted' and not questioned. For instance, many of the statements use the concept of parenting as crucial to the understanding of the problems (eg numbers one to six). Bonding is identified in the third statement, and boundary roles in the seventh and eighth. Risk groups are suggested in statements fifteen and sixteen. Such concepts are significant tools in increasing understanding and achieving a common discourse, and readers are invited to identify others.

Sometimes the theoretical approach underlying such concepts is relatively clear. For example, a psycho-dynamic approach is evident in the second statement, and a behavioural one in the sixth. A sociological view is implied in the eleventh, and organisational theory in the thirteenth. Again, readers should be able to identify others.

It will be obvious that the same concept may be used in different theoretical approaches. For example, parenting may be understood in psycho-dynamic ways (statements two and three), or in behavioural terms (the sixth statement). Intergenerational patterns of parenting may be analysed in terms of cycles of deprivation (the fourth statement) or the persistence of the patriarchal family (the twelfth).

In the same way, units of analysis (eg the family) may be considered from different perspectives, such as cultural (number nine) or systems (number eight).

Identification of such theoretical underpinning can give pointers to social workers in the way of further study. For instance, behavioural methods are often used in 'common sense' ways, but a better grasp of principles and techniques can achieve much more. The concept of 'bonding' has gained wide acceptance and usage, but is often misused, and the term has widely differing meanings and implications.

2. Value positions and ideologies

Another framework for understanding social work and social policy is in terms of the value positions which underlie actions and choices. Fox[25] compares two schools of thought represented in child care legislation,

policies and practices: 'kinship defenders' and 'society-as-parent protagonists'. The 'kinship defenders' see the natural or biological family as being the
best environment for almost all children. They emphasise class and economic
variables, rather than parental inadequacy and culpability, as factors associated with poor standards of care. For example, Holman[26] stressed the link
between child separation and poverty, advocating more supportive services
to enable good parenting to take place. The 'society-as-parent protagonists',
on the other hand, place great importance on the need to defend children
against neglectful and abusive parents, by the beneficient interventions of
state welfare. Rowe and Lambert,[27] for instance, emphasised the psychological need of children for early placement in secure, permanent substitute
families, in preference to long-delayed reclamation by their parents. In our
exercise, statements two, eleven and fifteen can be seen as examples of the
'kinship defender' position, whereas numbers one, three and twelve might
represent the views of the 'society-as-parent' view. Readers may be able to
see similar links in other statements. Of course, any of these statements may
be appropriate to individual cases, and there is overlap between the two
perspectives, but realisation of the social values underlying policy trends and
actions may remind us of other important objectives. It also helps us to
unpack over-generalised phrases such as 'best interests', 'the welfare of the
child' and 'parents' rights', which may camouflage great differences in
interpretation and preferred action.

The concept 'ideology' suggests yet another way in which some of these
theory-practice links can be explored.[28] By ideology, we mean a set of ideas
and beliefs, which is systematic enough to convey an underlying attitude to
society, shared by members of a social group. Ideologies may be difficult to
identify because they are often implicit and taken for granted by those who
hold them. However, they may have a profound effect on choices and
decisions, sometimes representing the interests of one social group (eg
parents) as against others(eg lawyers), and carrying considerable emotional
weighting.

The statements about child abuse may be analysed in terms of the
ideologies which seem to underpin them. For instance, the first example may
represent a judicial ideology, which emphasises legal rights and duties, and
due punishment for offenders. It draws attention to the deviance which may
underlie serious child abuse, which might lead to a punitive disposal. A
welfare ideology, on the other hand, would focus on the needs of the families
concerned, and the ways in which they could be helped (possibly through
therapeutic and resource-based interventions). Statements two to ten exem-
plify this attitude. Number fourteen, however, calls attention to possibilities
of addressing child abuse through community participation and empowerment, in accordance with a developmental ideology. Proponents of this

viewpoint would be concerned with poverty and disadvantage, and would consider the possibilities of changing systems rather than people. Statement thirteen carries this approach further towards a radical view, in suggesting that the actions of state institutions may themselves be part of the problem.

Ideologies are complex and multi-dimensional, and it is not suggested that they can be adequately studied in such simple ways. However, an attempt to understand the ideological basis of trends in policies and practices is another way of breaking through the assumptions and stereotypes which may determine action. It may also increase the range of alternative approaches considered.

Some strongly held ideologies are sustained at the cost of vulnerable social groups. For example, powerful ideologies about family privacy, parental rights and patriarchy have probably maintained some forms of child abuse, and limited access to sources of help. Sexual abuse is a prime instance. From some feminist perspectives and also research evidence,[29] families are not safe places for many women and children, and alternative living and relational forms are circumscribed through social and economic policies, limited day care resources, housing legislation and familial ideologies.

Good questions to ask ourselves, in seeking to understand any pervasive social problem, are 'whose interests are being served?' and 'are the interests of one social group being met at the expense of others?'. Some social problems persist because all of us have social and psychological investments in maintaining them. (Exercises to increase students' understanding of the relevance of values and ideologies in social work are included in the appendices to this chapter).

3. Explanations and interventions

The literature on child abuse is currently entering a relatively 'scientific' phase, in which strong links are made between explanation and intervention, and some very exciting helping approaches have been initiated.[30] For example, behaviour modification programmes are devised to change the behaviour of parents who abuse their children through over-chastisement or lack of cuddling; boundary roles in families may be redefined and clarified in order to alter power balances between father/daughter and husband/wife, respectively, thereby reducing the risk of incestuous liaisons.

However, we should be aware that different social science disciplines tend to use different levels of analysis to explain social problems. Characteristically, psychology is concerned with the study of individuals and small groups; sociology with social institutions and social processes; and social policy with political economy and welfare organisations. These levels of analysis suggest different units of intervention: parents or parent-child dyads; families and social networks; social legislation and welfare agencies.

As referrals normally come to social service departments in terms of individuals and families, it is, perhaps, understandable that theories which are directly concerned with these units of intervention often seem more relevant and applicable, eg play therapy and family casework. However, other social sciences direct us towards other units of intervention, such as schools, communities or agency procedures.

Sometimes, a further connection is made, in that work with individuals is considered as 'social control' and work with communities as 'social change'. However, it is important to recognise that the unit of intervention should not necessarily determine the objectives of the work.[31] Work with individuals can include social change objectives, eg helping them to have a better appreciation of their social situation and how they can work towards influencing it (conscientisation). Conversely, work directed towards communities may be more concerned with dampening social protest than with empowerment of residents. Examples may be drawn from the field of child abuse. For instance, work with parents and children may appropriately take the form of family work, or of a unitary systems approach[32] which would identify a wider range of targets. Work with adolescent girls may be directed towards re-socialising them into traditional gender roles or towards empowering them to choose another lifestyle outside the nuclear family.[33] Possibilities of addressing child abuse at a community level (eg through education programmes, self-help groups, or social policies in relation to poverty and housing) should also be kept in mind.[34]

Review

In this section, we have explored some ways in which relatively tight links are made between causal explanations and types of social work interventions. These links may derive from specific theoretical approaches, eg behavioural and family systems, or from particular units of analysis, eg child, parent, neighbourhood. It was also argued, however, that the unit of analysis should not necessarily determine the objectives of the intervention.

Our earlier discussion on values and ideologies may also help us to clarify some of these issues because it reminds us that social work relies on other sources of understanding besides social science disciplines. Understanding is based on an amalgam of ideas, beliefs, interests and hunches which may indicate a particular attitude or approach on the part of the social worker. For example, a behavioural or family systems intervention suggests a welfare ideology, whereas a community support project points to a developmental ideology.

As any social worker knows, practice is never as abstract as these arguments imply, because our profession is an art as well as a science. England[35] refers to the importance of skills such as the use of self, intuition, meaning and subjectivity in the art of social work. All these dimensions: values and ideologies, skills in the use of self and intuition, may help us to understand ways in which social science knowledge should inform social work practice rather than take it over.[36] The next section explores some of the ways in which a psycho-social approach brings these several sources of knowledge and understanding together.

Theorising the psychosocial

Social work is more than applied sociology, applied psychology or social policy and administration, though, as we have seen, it relies on and borrows heavily from these disciplines. First, social workers necessarily use psycho-social terms such as coping, functioning, self-determination, loss and change, 'good-enough' parenting, rather than relying on terms central to other disciplines such as personality, role, social institution, and poverty. Second, social work is a purposeful and value-based rather than solely conceptual exploration. Therefore, if they were not already to hand, social workers would need to create such terms as person-environment fit, person-in-situation, psychosocial functioning. These equations may be informed by psychodynamic, behavioural, social-ecological or critical theories, but they still amount to 'more than' their theoretical underpinnings.

Such psychosocial perspectives are sometimes adopted in the child abuse literature. For example, O'Hagan[37] argues that 'social work categorisations' are needed to address the varieties of child sexual abuse and differential indications for intervention; these categorisations relate to child protection, family and social context, and resources. Joan Court's report on the Beckford family was informed partly by psychodynamic ideas but was also based on a broad psycho-social perspective which considered communication, stresses, environmental resources, accounts and values.[38]

It has been suggested, though, that social workers also need to move beyond theoretical conceptualisations (even those of a psychosocial variety). This is one reason why the term 'practice theories' is so useful. Hardiker and Barker[39] illustrate these in relation to child protection work. For example, social workers rely on many faculties in assessing family situations: thinking, feeling, empathising, observing and doing. This enables them to locate their purposes in relation to clients and to agency functions. For example, they may try to understand these in the following ways:

— *clients' situations*: relationships, feelings, needs which cannot be met, handicapped and handicapping families

- *workers' roles and agency functions*: the pain of working with families who have experienced abuse, problems of involvement and detachment, anxieties around statutory intervention
- *the inalienable elements in social work*: working with shades of grey rather than 'cut and dried' situations or responses; trying to decide whether to enable a family to split up or stay together; determining who is the client; being brokers in lesser evils (eg preventing the need for more intrusive interventions).

These examples illustrate ways in which social workers rely on many sources in their attempts to understand and work with painful human predicaments. However, a psychosocial approach (like any other) can be exploitative, even damaging. Practitioners must secure a clear value base, knowledge frameworks and practice skills if they are to be 'altruists under social auspices' (Timms and Timms).[40] The papers in this book on models of understanding human development and social work intervention provide further directions for the pursuit of professional competence, ethically based.

The next section raises more general issues of the functions of theory in social work. Again, many of the examples will be drawn from the field of child abuse.

Some functions of knowledge in social work

It is not only the substantive nature of knowledge which differentiates one form of explanation or understanding from another in social work; the functions of knowledge vary also. Social theory identifies at least three functions of knowledge in social work:

1. Enlightenment in the liberal education tradition

2. Boundary-defining

3. Metaphorical and semantic

1. Enlightenment

The liberal education tradition serves an enlightening function when it enables us to understand and explore some ways in which 'things are not what they seem'. This is sometimes referred to as a 'romance' phase in learning and most of us will be able to recall such experiences in our lives.[41] But enlightenment must function rather more profoundly than this in professional education, and some clues are now suggested.

i. HUMBLING

In the grand literature and discourses of the humanities and the sciences, knowledge should help us to locate ourselves in the universe. Pearson et al[42] illustrate this succinctly:

> The theory of the unconscious as Freud . . . described it, is one which insists that 'the ego is not master in its own house'. This, he suggested, was the 'third blow' to human narcissism that had been delivered by science: the first having been Copernicus's revelation that the earth was not the centre of the solar system, and the second Darwin's assertion that human beings were of animal descent.
>
> In this sense, Freud's work was a continuation of the humbling experience of modernity and rational enquiry - whereby the process of scientific enlightenment stripped humankind of its naive illusion that it stood at the centre of the universe' (p.21)

Sadly, social science literature does not always appear to facilitate this humbling function, perhaps because, 'all seekers after truth believe that the truth will set them free'. (PH can remember the time when sociology seemed to fulfil this promise, though it no longer does so, for her). Ashdown and Clement Brown[43] understood these issues profoundly:

> It seems obvious that such a service calls for wide and liberal training so that the psychiatric social worker may see what she is doing in perspective, against a background of historical change and social movement, and *may escape the insidious error that 'wisdom shall die', or was born, with her own or any other generation* (p.228) [Our italics].

This is a reminder that our own struggles in learning and even inspirations may only bring us to the early stages of the understanding of those who have gone before.

ii. NON-DOGMATIC

The history of social work illustrates some ways in which it has been besieged by different 'isms': biologism, Freudianism, behaviourism, genericism, Marxism, anti-sexism, anti-racism. Though social work, like any other practice, changes in different generations, any profession monopolised by one ideology is a type of dogma. Social theory should enable teachers, practitioners and students to think through complex issues rather than *starting* arguments with 'isms', which may too readily function as thoughtstoppers. Professional education should enable social workers to locate and identify the frames of reference and value-bases through which we all think and write; this should dissolve dogmatism, especially if efforts are made to read literature with which one is not sympathetic.[44]

iii. NO UTOPIA

There are no safe hiding places in social work, whether these are sought in methods, client groups, settings, theories or value positions. This is a very conservative statement and, if misinterpreted, encourages paralysis and negative attitudes. This is hardly the intention! An illuminating exposition of this stance can be found in a paper written by an Australian welfare administrator:[45]

> . . . social control is about private pain as well as public issues. Social workers are more than control agents in the name of the socio-economic status quo, they are part of those social processes that protect themselves, their clients and the community from excessive anxiety and distress and intolerable discomfort.

> Unfortunately, not all personal pain is political . . . And sometimes we are subject to what is a confidence trick of significant appeal, that of politicising all personal pain for our *own protection* (p.67).

Whether one's *orientation* is personal or political, casework or social policy, another non-Utopian function of social theory is to grasp ways in which social work - even at its best - can only achieve modest goals. Freud[46] understood this in relation to psychoanalysis:

> . . . much will be gained if we succeed in transforming your hysterical misery into common unhappiness (p.393).

Any social worker who claims to have 'cracked' child abuse after completing a short training course or even a life-time's career in practice has failed to grasp some of these messages. Any social theorist or politician who fails to appreciate that some human predicaments brook of no solutions is also being utopian.

2. Boundary-defining

Though the parameters of social work are permeable and loosely-defined, social theory functions to locate the boundaries of permitted and required practice in every age.[47] For example, Gordon[48] traces the history of welfare services in relation to child abuse and family violence in America in different eras: child-saving, reform and economic amelioration, psychiatry and familialism and (latterly) anti-family ideologies. This meant that child abuse itself was defined in different ways, from cruelty, neglect and poverty through to family dysfunction and patriarchal violence. Parton[49] also traces some ways child abuse was rediscovered as a social problem in this country in the 1970s. This is a reminder that problems in child care are ever with us, but that these have historically been defined in different ways. Social workers are part of these changing problem-definitions, but their practices can be better understood if they are located in relation to social and historical changes.

Thus, social theory informs rather than determines practice by outlining some of the boundaries of the activity; this lays bare some of the choices available to practitioners (such as family support or freeing for adoption). Moreover, if interventions in child abuse are increasingly based on statutory orders,[50] social workers may not be wholly free to reverse the trend, though an understanding of the issues raises some lessons for practice; work to empower parents has to be embraced much more seriously in these circumstances.

Hardiker, Exton and Barker[51] explored some of these boundary-defining functions in relation to preventive child care:

> . . . social work practice has to be understood in the context of client careers, agency objectives and social policies, ie that the methods and resources used have little meaning unless they are contextualised in this way (p.225).

Another way of describing this function is to point out that there will always be a hiatus between theory and practice, ie that an understanding of the social, historical and personal reasons for the construction of social problems and welfare responses does not necessarily provide the practitioner with pointers to direct interventions.[52]

> The fact of . . . the social origin does not preclude treatment on an individual basis. The reverse is true; treatment on an individual basis [must] proceed at the same time that the theory suggests that the 'ailment' and ultimately the 'cure' is extra-individual (p.141).

Jacoby is explaining here how an understanding of some of the structural sources of, say, child abuse and risk registers need not prevent practitioners helping individual families caught up in these processes. Different understandings and interventions can coexist because they are different forms of activity. We may add that, not only should understandings not preclude interventions, these activities should interact in social work practice informed by social theories.

3. Metaphorical and semantic

Social scientists sometimes read social work language too literally, which is surprising, given their 'critical' functions. The main section of this paper, which outlined a range of different explanations for child abuse, was an exercise in the literal use of language, ie that child abuse may relate to bonding, family systems, social isolation, etc. It is important not to leave the literal argument here, though, because concepts should not be reified (ie assumed to have a concrete form). The first stage in understanding the metaphorical functions of social theories is to prefix knowledge-statements with the words, 'as if'. Supervisors of social workers frequently invite them to hypothesize about a referral, using a range of 'as if' statements. No explanation should ever monopolize a practitioner's repertoire.

A further stage in metaphorical work involves an understanding of the broader purposes which language serves in practice.[53] This was alluded to briefly in the discussion of psychosocial perspectives above, because the person-society connection can be explored through a variety of theories: psychodynamic, behavioural, feminist and sociological.[54] The suggestion here is not that any type of theory serves equally well a particular social problem, such as child abuse, but that social theory for practitioners needs to go further than explanation and understanding. For example, it was seen earlier that a range of social science disciplines may analyse child abuse and ways in which it is controlled. But what purposes are social workers fulfilling that they need to find explanations of such circumstances? The purposes derive from the remit of social workers in contemporary Britain, which is to assess *needs* and to help *reintegrate* people engaged in abusing interactions into civil society. Needs may be explained psychologically or socially, but they have to be represented psychosocially. Families caught up in these situations have problems in coping with child abuse, whether the main reasons lie with them in their situations or with the intrusions of social controllers, or both.

Social theory should provide a language which speaks for 'child abusers' as persons, rather than as deviants, to the powerful social control agents who make decisions.[55] This is one dimension of preventive child care, when social workers are engaged in delabelling vulnerable families or negotiating removal of names from a Child Protection Register. Scientific language alone is not adequate in these circumstances; we have to speak metaphorically about 'good enough parenting', coping under stress, providing 'adequate protection' for pre-school children, listening to stories about how other parents handle similar difficulties. If social workers fail to hold on to these psychosocial equations when they speak for families in courts and case conferences, they are no longer fulfilling social work purposes.

Conclusion

This paper explored selected social theories and some functions of knowledge in social work. An exercise illustrating different ways in which psychosocial equations can be worked out was outlined, and others may be found in the Appendix. The brief for this chapter was manifestly ambitious and calls for several books rather than a brief paper! Nevertheless, we hope we have conveyed some of the ways in which we continue to struggle with these eternal issues and try to make social theory illuminating rather than paralysing for ourselves, our students and practice teachers.

This book for practice teachers is transparently welfare-oriented, ie the papers illustrate different helping and needs-based approaches. This is, of course, the structural space which social work still inhabits in contemporary Britain. It is important to remember that this 'space' straddles much larger social institutions, such as the judicial system, a welfare state which is being fundamentally restructured and also those oases of social transformation in which social changes are taking place. Social work has to address structural realities, such as punishment in the community; the new Children Act; the move to private and voluntary-based welfare; growing inequalities in health care; disease, ageing and disabilities; homelessness and poverty. Though needs-based helping approaches are relevant as never before, the challenge lies in making psychosocial equations which firmly address the structural realities of our changing society.

Acknowledgements

We are grateful to Professor Noel Timms and our academic colleagues at the Leicester School of Social Work for their generosity in guiding us through a labyrinth of literature. Students, social workers and practice teachers have moved us on in our understanding of many of the themes outlined in this paper. We also appreciate - as ever - Mrs Barbara Freer's efficiency, help and goodwill in the production of numerous drafts of this paper.

Appendix I

EXERCISES USED IN TEACHING
SOCIAL THEORY FOR SOCIAL WORK

Some of the exercises which the authors and their colleagues have used with students and practice teachers are described below.

I. Summary statements

i. The statements listed under the heading *Explanations of Child Abuse* in this chapter illustrate some of the ways in which different concepts or theories are used to explain a social problem. The same approach can be used to explore *other social problems*, eg delinquency, mental handicap, schizophrenia, poverty, homelessness, single-parenthood, disability and ill-health, ageing, drug abuse; try it. This kind of exercise tests the participants' actual knowledge (we did not know all the theories listed until we undertook some research and a mini literature review), and teaches them about types and functions of explanation.

ii. Write down in one sentence *the gist of a case* or a statement regarding the 'story' it conveys. This exercise often works to produce materials of a psycho-social nature.

iii. Write down in one sentence *a current dilemma* in your practice. This exercise often produces materials which illustrate some ways in which problems of practice are partly problems of theory. For example, dilemmas commonly reflect the following issues:

  — identifying values and purposes (social protection, change efforts, etc)
  — deciding on the unit of intervention (individual, family, neighbourhood, agency) or who is the client?
  — unravelling social work processes: assessment, intervention, evaluation
  — choosing between different theories and/or methods

iv. Examine a new referral and explore *a range of hypotheses* which may be relevant to an assessment.

II. Exploring different value positions

Select a child care case of your own (or, if this presents difficulties, use one of the case summaries from the authors' research, which are given as Appendix II (Sylvie and Gemma) and Appendix III (Anthony)). Then read the article by Fox,[25] summarised earlier in this chapter and in the chart given as Appendix IV. Consider the services offered by the social services departments, and the interventions of the social workers, in terms of the two value positions, 'kinship defenders' and 'society-as-parent protagonists'. In what respects were these value positions demonstrated? Did either position dominate?

This exercise often works well as a group task.

III. Alternative ideologies

Select a case involving delinquency or criminal justice (or use the case of Kes, (Appendix V), if other social work material is not available). Write a social inquiry report or an assessment using one or more of the different ideologies of deviance, such as:

— classical justice
— diversionary justice and radical non-intervention
— welfare: helping models (eg psychodynamic, behavioural, crisis theory, community social work and liberal reform)
— the New Right
— Marxist

An example of the use of this exercise is given in Appendix VI, Alternative Ideologies. This is an attempt by a Leicester student to construct four different social inquiry reports, following four different ideologies, in respect of an offender, Paul.

This exercise can also be carried out by a group.

Exercises II and III should serve some of the following purposes:

i. Enable participants to learn the content of different approaches

ii. Illustrate the ways different value positions and ideologies shape (not determine) the structure and content of assessments, choices of intervention, and types of evaluation

iii. Explore means of making assumptions and ways of thinking explicit

iv. Locate the boundaries of knowledge frameworks in social work. Although in classroom exercises one may have the privilege of indulging in endless explorations of different theoretical positions, where actual case material and practice examples are used the choice of ideology will invariably be limited. For example, radical non-intervention will be almost impossible for a very grave offence: a 'kinship defender' option will be limited in some cases of child abuse

These exercises always work best if participants use materials from their own practice or (if this is not possible) vignettes of practice from research and students' placements (such as those attached). We are always struck by ways in which we could not make up actual social work cases if we tried. This appears to be because of the combination of contingencies which converge on 'people in trouble', the cumulative nature of stresses in their lives, and the relative absence of protective mechanisms to enable 'good enough' psycho-social functioning.

CASE MATERIAL: SYLVIE AND GEMMA

Sylvie was brought up in a repressive home, by parents of Afro-Caribbean origin who belonged to a strict religious sect. When she was 15, she ran away from home and was received into care when her parents refused to have her back. She was pregnant and was placed in a purpose-built hostel, which included small flats where residents could look after their own children if they wished. Before and after the birth of her baby, Gemma, Sylvie was adamant she wanted her adopted and made no preparations for her care. However, after a visit from her own mother, Sylvie asked for time to make up her mind and at her request Gemma was received into care and placed in a local short-term foster-home. The social worker and hostel staff supported her in her wish to build an independent life for herself and, meanwhile, to reach her own decision about Gemma's future. During the next two and a half years, the following resources were mobilised:

1. Income support.

2. Facilities for her to have Gemma with her at the hostel, full-time or part-time, with staff back-up.

3. Continuation of short-term foster care for Gemma with full access.

4. Payment of registration fees and fares for Sylvie to take a CSV course, to train for community service.

5. Negotiations with the housing department leading to an offer of a council flat for Sylvie and Gemma, backed up by a rent guarantee from the social services department as she was under 18.

6. Offer of day-nursery and part-time care facilities if Sylvie chose to have Gemma with her.

Sylvie did well in care, finding and keeping a job against the odds, and eventually moving into her own accommodation. She was encouraged to visit Gemma, to have her for weekends, and to make plans which gave her the option of having Gemma, but there were long periods when she dropped out of contact with her completely. In practice, she avoided contact, while not being willing to consent to long-term plans for her. Much work was undertaken with Sylvie, her mother and the foster-mother to try to reach an agreed plan, but to no avail, and eventually the social worker recommended that Gemma should be 'freed for adoption', by application to the County Court, under new legislation. Sylvie visited the prospective adopters several times, got on well with them and did not appear in court to oppose the application. The social worker concluded:

All necessary resources were made available to facilitate Gemma's rehabilitation to her mother. It was a very painful piece of work - any social worker would feel absolutely ridden with guilt about taking a big step like freeing for adoption. It has not been easy, but I am very satisfied with the outcome. I feel in my heart of hearts that I did everything to the best of my ability to try to rehabilitate the child with her mother and then to find suitable prospective adopters.

CASE MATERIAL: ANTHONY

Background

Anthony was a member of a reconstituted family, his parents having divorced and remarried, and the four parents were in waged work. There were personal and family difficulties during Anthony's last year in school. He had some involvement in glue-sniffing, was admitted to hospital following an overdose (?a suicide attempt) and was subsequently seen by a community psychiatric nurse. Anthony became involved in offending during his final six months at school (burglary, criminal damage, threatening behaviour and assault).

During this time, Anthony called at the SSD duty office. He talked about difficulties at home and in school, and requested help in finding alternative accommodation. His request was dealt with on an advice/liaison basis.

Three months later, Anthony was remanded (S.23) into the care of the local authority; he had been expelled from school, was charged with several offences of burglary and assault and his parents were unwilling to have him home. At this stage, the Social Services Department undertook a social work assessment, which explained the offences in terms of Anthony's adolescence, when he was finding school difficult, mixing with undesirable colleagues and rebelling in the home situation. A six months' supervision order (S.7/7) was recommended to the court on the grounds that Anthony's offences were related to his needs. Anthony was requesting help, and the Social Services Department could offer a package of support which would address his problems in the context of his family and his plans for employment. Some outstanding offences were dealt with by the Crown Prosecution Service and Central Intermediate Treatment Team which liaised to pay off costs, etc. During the period of the supervision order, Anthony moved 'in and out of care'.

Appendix IV

SUMMARY OF: L. M. FOX: TWO VALUE POSITIONS IN CHILD CARE, *BJSW 12*, 3, 265-290

Issue	Kinship defenders	Society as parent
Primacy of child's welfare as guiding principle	Supported	Supported
Need for child removal in some cases	Supported	Supported
Need for broad preventive policies	Supported	Supported
Differ re:		
1. Importance of *blood tie* and natural family	Emphasised	Not emphasised
2. Effects of uncertainty and *multiple parent* figures	Not emphasised	Emphasised
3. Emphasis given currently to *prevention* and rehabilitation	More needed	Sometimes too much
4. Success of *adoption*	Reservations	Emphasised
5. Nature of *fostering*	Inclusive: exclusive	Adoption and fostering - not nec. mut. excl.
6. Effectiveness of *state intervention* in child care; adequacy of court, professional decision-making	Sceptical	More confident
7. *Existing balance* between natural parents, statutory agencies and substitute parents	Weighs against natural parents	Weighs too much in favour of natural parents
8. Awareness of *class* transactions in child care	Emphasised	Not emphasised
9. Concepts of *cause/remedies* re unsatisfactory parenting	Structural inadequacy	Personal
10. *Examples of groups* and schools of thought supporting positions	CPAG, Holman, Heywood & Walton, BASW: Tunstill 'Equality for children' et al	BAAF, Rowe, Kellmer, Pringle Tizard, Goldstein

CASE MATERIAL: KES

Kes is 16 years old and subject to a two-year Supervision Order by the Social Services Department, plus 90 days IT condition, for theft offences. An 18 hours Attendance Centre Order, for Taking and Driving Away and a 120 hours Community Service Order, for burglary, followed.

Background

1. Family

Kes was born and raised in a large city and was the eldest child of his mother's second marriage; he has a half-brother, two half-sisters and two younger sisters.

His home background appeared to have been stable until his father died of cancer three years ago. This was a tremendous shock to the whole family; Kes's mother never seemed fully to recover in health and strength, and she died a year later. Kes moved to live with his half-sister (who became his legal guardian) and brother-in-law. The household also contained his two younger sisters and a nephew. The family lived on a council estate. The brother-in-law was unemployed and the family received housing and income support.

2. School

After moving from the local middle school to a nearby large comprehensive school, Kes found it difficult to settle and his school career 'deteriorated' in his final two years (ie after his father's death).

He was involved in theft from the school, bullying and was eventually suspended. Kes then attended an Intermediate Treatment Centre, but was dismissed for disobedient behaviour.

Kes was then placed at a remedial unit, but was suspended from there for disobedience.

Kes finished his educational career without academic qualifications.

3. Waged work

Kes began a Youth Training Scheme with a Neighbourhood Project, but was dismissed after two months for 'disruptive behaviour'. Kes has been unemployed since and receives income support.

4. Social background

Kes's father had been in unskilled employment and the family lived on a large council estate, where Kes still lives with his sister.

He has two main hobbies: carpentry and raising pigeons. He had developed these interests with his father. He is a member of his local peer group.

Poverty affected Kes in countless ways: clothing, language, housing, family relations, unemployment, restricted access to a variety of services and resources, etc.

5. Circumstances of the various offences

i. Theft

Kes stole goods (to resell) from his school, and said he did this because he was 'broke'.

ii. Taking and Driving Away

This offence was committed with his mates, 'for a laugh'.

iii. Burglary

Kes acted as lookout for his mates from his bedroom window, for which he was given £2.

Kes appeared to have a total disregard for his offending, and dismissed it as unimportant and insignificant.

> 'He claimed that he cared neither for the kudos from his peers nor the labels given him by society'.

Notes

Though for professional purposes further details about Kes's life and situation plus some picture of the dynamics between the various participants in the interventions would be required, there should be adequate data available to you here for this exercise.

Work on the different ideologies that could be used in understanding Kes's case (either profiles for your own use, or possibly an 'alternative social enquiry report'). Examine implications for assessment, intervention and evaluation.

Suggested ideologies

1. Help/welfare

eg grief, transitions, loss and change

the culture of poverty

family forms

needs

attachment

life stages

2. Classical justice
>   punishment for the offences
>
>   due process
>
>   rights

3. Diversion
>   radical or minimal intervention
>
>   avoiding net-widening, etc

4. Community development
>   subculture or youth culture
>
>   community social work (varieties)
>
>   radical social action/social policy
>
>   needs and rights

5. Others
>   eg Marxist, Fabian,
>
>   The New Right

ALTERNATIVE IDEOLOGIES

Paul

These 'accounts' were devised by a Leicester MA / CQSW student in the early 1980s. It is important to remember that this was a teaching exercise, so that they illustrate 'caricatures' of different approaches to writing social inquiry reports.

Essential information

Paul - aged 18 years

Previous offences:

    1978 - theft - fine

    1979 - theft, indecent exposure (2 year supervision order)

    1981 - assault - bound over

Present offences:

1. Offence of theft - stole cakes to the value of £40 from the back of an open delivery van.

2. Offence of theft - entered depot and stole crate of lager to the value of £15.

3. Offence of deception and fraud - stole cheque left out for the milkman; altered it and cashed it.

Treatment model

A. Personal/social circumstances

1. Paul's mother and father split up when he was 12 years old; Paul presently lives with his mother and stepfather. From my investigations, it appears that Paul has never enjoyed the benefits of a secure and emotionally satisfying family life. His mother explained that her first marriage was marked by disagreement and violence and that her present relationship with Mr Green was going through similar difficulties. It became apparent that Paul has always been witness to these distressing circumstances and one may speculate that the environment necessary for his healthy emotional development has never been present through his childhood. I am of the opinion that Paul has, in many ways, brought himself up unassisted; the father to whom he still holds an attachment, left home whilst his mother, working full-time, appears to have devoted most of her attention to her second husband and Paul's stepsisters.

2. Paul's achievements to date reflect the career of a deprived and disturbed young man. He is of low intelligence and achieved little at school; he is illiterate and has few interests or friends. He has lost numerous jobs through lack of commitment, concentration and poor timekeeping. Two years ago he came to the notice of this department for indecent exposure, interpreted at the time as evidence of an immature and inadequate personality.

B. Offences and circumstances

Paul's past offences have occurred during periods of personal crisis and these are no exception. After a major dispute, he was thrown out of his house. Paul had no money and nowhere to live. One may imagine that for a man of such limited ability this was a most distressing experience. The offences of theft and deception, superficially may be viewed as an attempt to meet his immediate needs for food and money. I am of the opinion, however, that they are symptomatic of the more complex, unconscious conflicts that are causing Paul such distress.

C. Recommendation

It is submitted that this disturbed young man needs immediate intensive help if he is not to continue offending. A two-year probation order would provide the opportunity for therapeutic counselling to help Paul to work through his feelings about his childhood and self-image. It will be possible to supplement this with practical assistance, with literacy skills and help in seeking employment.

Liberal reformist

A. Offender's personal/social circumstances

Paul lives in the family home, which is a three-bedroomed terraced house adjacent to a large chemical factory. The house is rather overcrowded and, understandably, Paul spends most of his time away from it.

Unfortunately, Paul lives in an area with few recreational facilities for young men of his age. Consequently, most of his time is spent frequenting the less desirable cafes in the area. The problem is further exacerbated by lack of employment opportunities. Paul has had several jobs, but the educational system has left him ill-equipped to perform most work satisfactorily, and consequently he has rarely succeeded in holding down a job for longer than a few months. As a result, Paul has no money, plenty of free time but nothing to do with it. It is not surprising that there are many pressures in this area to seek alternative avenues for excitement and adventure, and inevitably these are usually criminal activities.

B. Offences and circumstances

Paul explained that this offence was committed with the co-accused when they were feeling bored and frustrated. They had both recently become unemployed and were 'at a loose end'. He informed me that they stole the cakes and beer 'for a laugh' and there was no intention to gain materially from the offence.

C. Role of lay and official controllers

The fact that St Marks is a predominantly middle-class and prosperous area hides the fact that there are large numbers of discontented working class youths who are not catered for by mainstream youth clubs. Over the last few years, a largely delinquent subculture has developed in the area which seeks entertainment through petty theft and vandalism. It is an indictment of the existing youth service and education facilities that these young men have been pushed into defining their own areas of entertainment.

D. Recommendation

The court will wish to impress on Paul that his delinquent activities cannot be tolerated by the community. It is suggested, therefore, that a Community Service Order may be the most appropriate disposal in this particular instance, affording him the opportunity to provide a beneficial service to his community, whilst occupying his time and reintroducing him to the work habit.

Radical non-interventionist

A. Personal and social circumstances

There is nothing unusual or exceptional about Paul. He went through normal schooling, which he attended throughout but never excelled at. He has tried several jobs, but has not settled in any. As with many his age, he is now unemployed, but he continues to look for work. Paul lives at home with his family and spends most of his time associating with friends of his own age and interests.

B. Offences and circumstances

These offences are very typical for Paul's age group and largely occurred because the opportunity presented itself. In fact, it is fair to say that these offences are commonplace throughout society and rarely come to the attention of the court. Paul is not an accomplished criminal and in no way is a threat to society. The offences were committed more due to a lack of forethought and perception than through any over-riding malicious intent.

C. Role of lay and official controllers

This is Paul's fourth court appearance for what is again another relatively trivial offence. I am concerned that this contact with the judicial system will only have the effect of reinforcing Paul's self-image as a criminal and push him further along a delinquent career. Paul comes from a working class family, he is poorly educated and has little money. His mode of dress and attitude to authority figures is consistent with many his age, but also makes him susceptible to special treatment by the police. These offences may more appropriately have been dealt with by a warning or a formal caution rather than once again processing Paul through this labelling process.

D. Recommendation

Paul is a normal, well adjusted 18-year-old. The only factor that distinguishes him from other young men is that he has been caught for trivial offences that are typically committed by most boys at some time or other. However, it is of concern that Paul has not drifted out of delinquency at this age and I attribute this to the previous disposals by the court. Accordingly, it is suggested that the court impose a sentence which intervenes as little as possible in Paul's life, such as a small fine or conditional discharge.

Marxist (Revisionist)

A. Personal and social circumstances

Paul is a human casualty of the contradictions within capitalism. He is working class, unskilled and unemployed. In times of recession, he has no active role to play in capitalist society other than as a member of the reserve army of the unemployed, depressing wages and discouraging strike action. Because society fears the violence and destructiveness of discontented youth, Paul has been bought off by inadequate YOP programmes and a breadline wage, just enough to keep him quiet and passive, but low enough for him to be an example to the workforce. Paul is the detritus of capitalist society, uneducated, unskilled and without opportunity - in short, an expendable unit of production.

B. Offences

Paul's offences of theft are logical in the context of a society which values property above all else. Paul's place at the bottom of society means that it is only by theft that he is able to appropriate goods. Unfortunately, it is clear that Paul is politically naive and at this stage is unable to differentiate between stealing from those who exploit him and stealing from those of his own class.

C. Role of official and lay control

Although materially insignificant, Paul's offences have been considered seriously because he is working class. The working class must ensure that social order is maintained and that the workers can only gain reward by selling their labour. The police actively espouse this ideology and Paul, by challenging the social order, has been singled out for punishment.

D. Recommendation

Paul is aware at some level that he has been exploited, controlled and dehumanised throughout his life. At present, however, he is politically uneducated. Most disturbing is his association with neo-fascist elements and his placing of blame for his problems with the ethnic minorities in the area. I have offered Paul the opportunity of weekly voluntary meetings in order to raise his political consciousness and increase his feelings of class solidarity.

Bibliography

1. Susser, M. (1968), *Community Psychiatry: Epidemiologic and Social Themes*, New York: Random House, v.

2. Marshall, T. H. (1946), 'Basic training for all types of work'. In (Nuffield College), *Training for Social Work*, London: Oxford University Press, 1

3. Hardiker, P. and Barker, M. (eds) (1981), *Theories of Practice in Social Work*, London: Academic Press; Briar, S. and Miller, H. (1971), *Problems and Issues in Social Casework*, New York: Columbia University Press; Loewenberg, F. M. (1984), 'Professional ideology, middle range theories and knowledge building for social work practice'. *British Journal of Social Work*, 14 (4), 309-322.

4. Hardiker, P. and Barker, M. (1985), 'Client careers and the structure of a probation and after-care agency'. *British Journal of Social Work*, 15 (6), 599-618.

5. Hardiker, P., Exton, K. and Barker, M. (1989), *Policies and Practices in Preventive Child Care*, Research Report to the Department of Health.

6. Frost, N. and Stein, M. (1989), *The Politics of Child Welfare: Inequality, Power and Change*, London: Harvester Wheatsheaf.

7. Smith, S. M. (1975), *The Battered Child Syndrome*, London: Butterworth; Smith, S. M., Henson, R. and Noble, S. (1974), 'Social aspects of the battered baby syndrome'. *British Journal of Psychiatry*, 125, 568-582.

8. Court, J. (1985), 'Independent social worker's report, 8th September 1981'. In, *Beckford Report*, vi-xi. This statement illustrates some of Kempe's theories.

9. London Borough of Brent (1985), *A Child in Trust*, [The report of the panel of inquiry into the circumstances surrounding the death of Jasmine Beckford]. The following books illustrate different explanations of bonding, from psychoanalytical to social learning theories: Sluckin, W., Herbert, M. and Sluckin, A. (1983), *Maternal Bonding*, Oxford, Blackwell; Bowlby, J. (1988), *A Secure Base: Clinical Applications of Attachment Theory*, London: Routledge; Kempe, R. S. and Kempe, C. H. (1978), *Child Abuse*, London: Fontana.

10. This statement is often associated with a crude cultural transmission theory (Keith Joseph), but intergenerational patterns can be explained in various ways: ethological, psychodynamic, behavioural, cognitive, structural and patriarchal: see Corby op cit, also: Rutter, M. and Madge, N. (1976), *Cycles of Disadvantage*, London: Heinemann; Quinton, D. and Rutter, M. (1988), *Parenting Breakdown: The Making and Breaking of Intergenerational Links*, Aldershot, Avebury.

11. Vogel, E. G. and Bell, N. W. (1968), 'The emotionally disturbed child as the family scapegoat'. In, G. Handel (ed), *The Psychosocial Interior of the Family: A Source-book for the Study of Whole Families*, London: George Allen and Unwin.

12. Iwaniec, D., Herbert, M. and McNeish, A. S. (1985a), 'Social work with failure-to-thrive children and their families. Part I: Psychosocial factors'. *British Journal of Social Work*, 15 (3), 243-259; Iwaniec, D., Herbert, M. and McNeish, A. S. (1985b), 'Social work with failure-to-thrive children and their families. Part II: Behavioural social work intervention'. *British Journal of Social Work*, 15 (4), 375-389.

13. Bentovim, A., Elton, A., Hildbrand, J., Tranter, M. and Vizard, E. (1988), *Child Sexual Abuse within the Family: Assessment and Treatment*. A rather different family systems

approach is illustrated in Dale, P., Davies, M., Morrison, T. and Waters, J. (1986), *Dangerous Families: Assessment and Treatment of Child Abuse*. London: Tavistock.

14. Finkelhor, D. (1984), *Child Sexual Abuse*, New York: Free Press.

15. There are a variety of theoretical explanations for the socially patterned nature of child abuse. The social isolation view derives from Garbarino, J. and Gilliam, G. (1980), *Understanding Abusing Families*, Cambridge, Mass., Lexington Books, based on social ecology; Gelles, R. and Cornell, C. (1985), *Intimate Violence in Families*, Beverly Hills, Sage, explain abuse in relation to culturally-sanctioned patterns of physical chastisement; Gil, D. (1979), *Child Abuse and Violence*, New York: AMS Press, analyses ways in which societies and families are structurally violent; the NSPCC presents evidence of a social-epidemiological and social-pathology kind. These theories explain the links between social class and abuse in different ways.

16. A good example of this type of link being made can be found in an excellent paper by a paediatrician: Lynch, M., 'The consequences of child abuse'. In, K. Browne, C. Davies and P. Stratton (eds) (1988), *Early Prediction and Prevention of Child Abuse*, Chichester, Wiley; 'Treatment model' explanations of female delinquency are critically debated in recent feminist criminology, Morris, A., (1987), *Women, Crime and Criminal Justice*, Oxford, Blackwell; Worrall, A. (1989), 'Working with female offenders'. *British Journal of Social Work*, 19 (2), 77-94; Carlen, P. and Worral, A. (eds) (1987), *Gender, Crime and Justice*, Milton Keynes, Open University Press.

17. Black Report (1980), *Inequalities in Health*, (Report of a Research Group chaired by Sir Douglas Black). London: DHSS; Westergaard, J. and Resler, H. (1975), *Class in a Capitalist Society: A Study of Contemporary Britain*, London: Heinemann; Whitehead, M. (1987), *The Health Divide: Inequalities in Health in the 1980s*, London: Health Education Council.

18. *Feminist Review Collective* (1988), *Family Secrets: Child Sexual Abuse*, London: Special Edition, 28, Sprite.

19. Dingwall, R., Eekelaar, J. and Murray, T. (1983), *The Protection of Children: State Intervention and Family Life*, Oxford, Blackwell; and types of agency response: Aldrich, H. E. (1979), *Organisations and Environments*, Prentice Hall; Benson, J. K. (1982), 'A framework for policy analysis', in, D. Rogers and D. Whetten (eds), *Inter-organisational Coordination*, Iowa State University Press; Cook, K. S. (1977), 'Exchange and power in networks of interorganisational relations'. *Sociological Quarterly*, 18, 62-82.

20. Browne, K., Davies, C. and Stratton, P. (eds) (1988), *Early Prediction and Prevention of Child Abuse*, Chichester, Wiley; see also, Chandler, S., Stone, R. and Young, E. (1989), *Kidscape: Keeping Yourself Safe, A Programme for Nursery Aged Children*, Corby, Pen Green Family Centre.

21. Parton, C. and Parton, N. (1988), 'Women, the family and child protection'. *Critical Social Policy*, 24, (Winter), 38-49; Ahmed, S., Cheetham, J. and Small, J. (1986), *Social Work with Black Children and their Families*, London: Batsford, BAAF; Hardiker, P. and Curnock, K. (1984), 'Social work assessment processes in work with ethnic minorities - the Doshi family'. *British Journal of Social Work*, 14 (1), 23-47; Equality for Children (1983), *Keeping Kids out of Care, Crisis and Consensus in Child Care Policy*, London: NCOPF, et al; Holman, Bob (1988), *Putting Families First*, Basingstoke, Macmillan Educational. Frost and Stein op cit.

22. Parton, N. (1985), *The Politics of Child Abuse*, Basingstoke, Macmillan; Parton, N. and Small, N. (1989), 'Violence, social work and the emergence of dangerousness'. In, M. Langan and P. Lee (eds), *Radical Social Work Today*, Unwin-Hyman; Rojeck, C., Peacock, G. and Collins, S. (1989), *The Haunt of Misery: Critical Essays in Social Work and Helping*, London: Routledge; Spitzer, S. (1975), 'Towards a Marxian theory of deviance'. *Social Problems*, 22 (5), 638-651.

23. Stainton Rogers, W., Harvey, D. and Ash, E. (1989), *Child Abuse and Neglect: Facing the Challenge*, London: Batsford, Open University. See especially Brian Corby's excellent theoretical review (Chapter 2).

24. Curnock, K. and Hardiker, P. (1979), *Towards Practice Theory: Skills and Methods in Social Assessment*, London: Routledge.

25. Fox, L. (1982), 'Two value positions in child care'. *British Journal of Society Work*, 12 (3), 265-290; Freeman, M. D. A. (1983), *The Rights and Wrongs of Children*, London: Frances Pinter. Further value positions, laissez-faire and children's rights are also developed in Harding, L. (1990), *Perspectives on Child Care Policy*, London: Longman.

26. Holman, R. (1976), *Inequality in Child Care*, London: Child Poverty Action Group; Holman, R. (1988), *Putting Families First: Prevention and Child Care*, London: Macmillan Educational.

27. Rowe, J. and Lambert, L. (1973), *Children Who Wait*, London: Association of British Adoption Agencies.

28. Hardiker, P. (1981), 'Heart or head: the function and role of knowledge in social work'. *Issues in Social Work Education*, 1 (2), 88-111; and Hardiker and Barker, op cit, Chapter 7; and Smith, G. (1977), 'The place of 'professional ideology' in the analysis of 'social policy''. *Sociological Review*, 25 (4), 843-865 for an exploration of these ideologies.

29. Feminist Review Collective (1988), *Family Secrets: Child Sexual Abuse*, London, 28; Dobash, R. E. and Dobash, R. (1980), *Violence Against Wives: A Case Against the Patriarchy*, London: Open Books; Pahl, J. (1985), *Private Violence and Public Policy*, London: Routledge and Kegan Paul.

30. Browne, et al, op cit; Glaser, D. and Frosh, S. (1988), *Child Sexual Abuse*, Basingstoke, Macmillan, BASW; Walker, C. E., Bonner, B. L. and Kangman, K. L. (1988), *The Physically and Sexually Abused Child: Evaluation and Treatment*, Oxford, Pergamon Press.

31. Cockburn, C. (1977), 'The Local State: Management of Cities and People'. London: Pluto Press; Cowley, J., Kaye, A., Mayo, M. and Thompson, M. (1977), *Community or Class Struggle?* London: Stage 1; Leonard, P. (1984), *Personality and Ideology: Towards a Materialist Understanding of the Individual*, London: Macmillan; Rein, M. (1970), 'Social work in search of a radical profession'. *Social Work* (US), 15 (2), 13-28.

32. Herbert, M. (1988), *Working with Children and their Families*, London: Routledge, Leicester BPS.

33. Hudson, A. (1985), 'Feminism and social work: resistance or dialogue?' *British Journal of Social Work*, 15 (6), 635-655; Hudson, A. (1989), 'Troublesome girls: towards alternative definitions and policies'. In, M. Cain (ed), *Growing Up Good: Policing the Behaviour of Girls in Europe*, London: Sage.

34. Smale, G. et al (1988), *Community Social Work: A Paradigm for Change*, London: National Institute for Social Work.

35. England, H. (1986), *Social Work as Art: Making Sense of Good Practice*, London: Allen and Unwin.

36. Timms, N. and Timms, R. (1977), *Perspectives in Social Work*, London: Routledge and Kegan Paul.

37. O'Hagan, K. (1989), *Working with Child Sexual Abuse*, Milton Keynes, Open University Press.

38. See 8.

39. Hardiker, P. and Barker, M. (1986), *A Window on Child Care Practices in the 1980s*, Leicester University School of Social Work: Research Report; Hardiker, P. and Barker, M. (1988), 'A window on child care, poverty and social work'. In, S. Becker and S. Macpherson (eds), *Public Issues, Private Pain: Poverty, Social Work and Social Policy*, London: Social Services Insight Books.

40. See 36.

41. Towle, C. (1954), *The Learner in Education for the Professions*, Chicago, University of Chicago Press; Harris, R. J. (ed) (1985), *Educating Social Workers*, Leicester, Association of Teachers in Social Work Education.

42. Pearson, G., Treseder, J. and Yelloly, M. (1988), *Social Work and the Legacy of Freud: Psychoanalysis and its Uses*, Basingstoke, Macmillan.

43. Ashdown, M. and Clement Brown, S. (1953), *Social Service and Mental Health: An Essay on Psychiatric Social Workers*, London: Routledge.

44. For example: Rojeck, C., Peacock, G. and Collins, S. (eds) (1989), *The Haunt of Misery: Critical Essays in Social Work and Helping*, London: Routledge.

45. Green, D. (1976), 'Social control and public welfare practice'. In, P. J. Boas and J. Crawley (eds), *Social Work in Australia: Responses to a Changing Context*, Melbourne, Australia, International Press, 62-70.

46. Breuer, J. and Freud, S. (1985), 'Studies in Hysteria', in *The Standard Edition of the Complete Psychological Works of Sigmund Freud*, 2. (London: Hogarth Press, 1955).

47. See Bailey, J. (1980), *Ideas and Intervention: Social Theory for Practice*, London: Routledge and Kegan Paul; see also Heywood, J. S. (1978), *Children in Care: The Development of the Service for the Deprived Child*, Third edition. London: Routledge; and Packman, J. (1981), *The Child's Generation*, Oxford, Basil Blackwell and Martin Robertson.

48. Gordon, L. (1988), *Heroes of their own Lives: The Politics and History of Family Violence*, London: Virago Press.

49. See 22; Dingwall, R. (1986), 'The Jasmine Beckford Affair'. *Modern Law Review*, 49 (3), 489-507.

50. Parton, C. and Parton, N. (1988/9), 'Women, the family and child protection'. *Critical Social Policy*, 24, 38-49.

51. See 5.

52. Jacoby, R. (1975), *Social Amnesia: A Critique of Conformist Psychology from Adler to Laing*, Boston, Beacon Press.

53. Philp, M. (1979), 'Notes on the form of knowledge in social work'. *Sociological Review*, 27 (1), 83-111; Novak, M. W. and Axelrod, C. D. (1979), 'Primitive myth and modern medicine'. [Special book review of E. Kübler-Ross, 'On Death and Dying']. *Psychoanalytic Review*, 66 (3), 443-449.

54. Leonard, P. (1975), 'Explanation and education in social work'. *British Journal of Social Work*, 5 (3), 325-333; Webb, D. (1981), 'Themes and continuities in radical and traditional social work', *British Journal of Social Work*, 11 (2), 143-158.

55. See 53.

Part II

MODELS OF SOCIAL WORK INTERVENTION

Chapter 7

Behavioural Social Work

Barbara L. Hudson

This chapter is intended to remind the fieldwork teacher of the most important concepts and procedures associated with the behavioural approach.

First some definitions:

- *Behavioural social work* refers to the use within social work of
  procedures based on learning theories. The procedures are used to
  analyze and to change behaviour and their focus can be ourselves,
  our colleagues, our clients, or other people whose behaviour affects
  our clients.
- *Learning theories* form a body of theory about how behaviour
  changes as a result of experience, how behaviour is learned,
  maintained and unlearned. This body of theory has been built up
  by way of scientific experimentation and it is constantly being
  modified as new findings emerge. Learning theorists do not pretend
  to be able to explain everything about human behaviour: they do
  not make claims that cannot be substantiated by empirical research.

Learning theories are not intellectually compatible with competing psychological theories. For example, one cannot both believe that agoraphobia is a
set of learned behaviours that can be unlearned *and* that agoraphobia is a
symbolic representation of early childhood fixation; nor that bed-wetting is
a failure of learning *and* that it is a 'symptom' of something else.

An outline of learning principles

Learning theories comprise respondent, operant and social learning theory.
This is not the place to go into the details of the experimental evidence which
supports them - except to emphasise that they are not armchair theories and

they are not based on clinical anecdote in the way that Freudian theory and its derivatives are.

Respondent learning theory

This is also called classical or Pavlovian conditioning or learning. Respondent learning involves behaviours over which we normally have little or no control, such as salivation, eye blink and other reflexes, sexual arousal and feelings of anxiety and anger. These constitute responses to stimuli. In some circumstances - for example, blinking at a flash of light or a startle response to an unexpected loud noise - these responses are described as unconditioned, that is, not learned; and the stimuli are described as unconditioned stimuli. If an unconditioned stimulus is regularly associated with a neutral stimulus, the neutral stimulus will come to elicit the response by itself. After this has happened, the neutral stimulus has become a conditioned stimulus and the response has become a conditioned response. Watson and Rayner's (1920) case study of Little Albert is a (fortunately) rare example of this process demonstrated with a human subject.

> Little Albert was startled (unconditional response) when a loud noise sounded behind him (unconditioned stimulus).
>
> He played with a pet rat (conditioned stimulus) just before the loud noise (unconditioned stimulus).
>
> He began to get startled (conditioned response) when he saw the rat (conditioned stimulus).
>
> Loud noise = unconditioned stimulus. Startle at loud noise = unconditioned response.
>
> Rat = conditioned stimulus. Startle at rat = conditioned response.

In poor Albert's case *stimulus generalisation* also occurred. He developed a startle response to stimuli resembling the rat: other furry creatures and white cotton wool, for example. Fortunately for Albert, such conditioning can also be unlearned - repeated experiences of the conditioned stimulus (the white furry thing) without the unconditioned stimulus (the loud noise) usually result in what is known as respondent extinction. This process can be helped along if the person produces a competing response, such as relaxation, whenever he experiences the disturbing stimulus. The same is true for unlearning the results of a related process called *higher order conditioning*. In higher order conditioning a conditioned stimulus has been paired with yet another stimulus (for example, white fur coat with lady next door, resulting in fear of lady next door even without her coat).

Operant Learning Theory

Operant learning is also called instrumental or Skinnerian conditioning or learning. Operant behaviours, unlike respondent behaviours, are mainly affected by consequences in the environment. Operant behaviours are called 'operant' because they operate on the environment to produce consequences. They closely parallel what we call 'voluntary' behaviour, but that does not mean that each operant behaviour is thought out and decided on in advance - indeed, we may well be unaware of our operant behaviours and their consequences. Operant learning can take place 'unawares' as well as on a conscious level.

The pairing of a behaviour and a consequence (a reinforcer or a punisher) is the core of operant learning. The key processes of operant learning are positive and negative reinforcement, extinction and punishment.

Positive reinforcement. Whenever Mary has a tantrum her mother gives Mary a sweet. We may deduce that tantrums are being reinforced by the giving of sweets. The process is called positive reinforcement and the sweets positive reinforcers. (Of course we can't be sure. The reinforcer may be something else - Mother's attention, perhaps. The way to find out is to look at what happens if the presumed positive reinforcement ceases.)

A reinforcer is an event or thing that increases the probability of the behaviour that precedes it. A social worker saying uh-huh every time a client mentions her relationship with her mother is a positive reinforcer for this behaviour if the behaviour increases in frequency during the course of their conversation and decreases if the uh-huhs cease.

Negative reinforcement. Negative reinforcement also increases the probability of the behaviour that precedes it. (Think of 'reinforcer' as meaning strengthener.) In negative reinforcement, it is the *ending of something* that increases the preceding behaviour. Something unpleasant is escaped or avoided or terminated after the operant behaviour has occurred. Mother dislikes seeing the children fighting (aversive stimulus) - Mother yells at them (operant response) - children's fighting stops (termination of aversive stimulus; that is, negative reinforcement of Mother's behaviour). Mother yells next time the children fight and we may hypothesise that operant learning by Mother has occurred.

Punishment. A punisher is an event or thing that decreases the probability of the behaviour that precedes it. It might be a critical comment, a fine, or a slap. As with other operant processes, learning by punishment can take place unawares.

Extinction. This process has the same general effect as punishment, that is, lowering the frequency of a behaviour. If a behaviour has been maintained by a particular reinforcer and that reinforcer ceases to arrive then the behaviour will decrease. But first it will increase - this is known as the extinction burst. The parents who had been rushing up to Mary's room whenever she called out to them in the evenings, taking her orangeade and biscuits and reading her stories, decided to ignore her. For the first few nights the yelling got much worse, but they held out, and it gradually decreased and ceased altogether.

In addition to describing these basic processes, operant learning theory offers a considerably body of knowledge about the effects of timing of reinforcement and punishment, the side effects of the different kinds of consequences, and the role of antecedents in learning and performing operant behaviours.

Social learning theory

Modelling (also called imitative or observational learning) is the process at the basis of social learning theory. Learning occurs when one person observes the behaviour of another person (the model). What is acquired is information about the behaviour and about its consequences; and this type of learning is much faster than operant and respondent learning. The performance of modelled behaviour on the part of the learner is facilitated if: the learner sees the modelled behaviour being reinforced; the model has status and power; the model is moderately similar to the learner; the learner practises the behaviour soon after seeing it; the learner's new behaviour is reinforced.

A famous experiment by Bandura (1965) illustrated aspects of this process. Nursery school children were shown films in which an adult attacked a large plastic doll, punching it, hitting it with a mallet, kicking it, and throwing balls at it, each action accompanied by a distinctive phrase, such as 'Pow, boom, boom'. In some films, the model was punished for his aggressive behaviour, in some he was rewarded, and in the others there was no consequence. The children were then taken separately to a room with toys including the same doll. Those who had seen the model punished were much less likely to imitate the model's aggressive behaviour. When all the children were offered incentives for copying the model, however, this latter group imitated the aggressive responses almost as much as those who had seen the model being rewarded: it was clear that all of them had learned the responses by observation and that incentives encouraged the performance of the responses they had learned.

Social learning theory brings in cognitive aspects of learning. Modelling involves a process that the psychologist cannot observe directly; the theory suggests that the learner observes, stores information, anticipates outcomes. Social Learning Theory enlarges the picture provided by the other learning theories, providing a more complicated account of human behaviour. It includes the concepts of 'single trial' learning (learning from one example only), the use of symbols (learning from what is heard or read), attention, memory, and *expectations* of reward or punishment, success or failure. On a more philosophical note, social learning theory emphasises the idea of people acting on their own environment as well as being acted upon (reciprocal determinism).

Following on from the analysis of modelling, social learning theory also focuses on the effects of *anticipated* outcomes on behaviour, the notion of foresight, and the processes by which people achieve self-regulation of behaviour.

More recently, the cognitive theories have been further developed, notably by Beck (1976) who identifies the unconstructive beliefs which, in his view, lead to depression and which he considers can and must be altered in order to treat the condition (see Dryden in this volume for further details). Seligman and his colleagues (Seligman 1975) studying the development of the mental set they designate 'learned helplessness' and working originally from an operant model and in the animal laboratory, have also contributed to our understanding of the cognitive aspect of people's functioning. Learned helplessness is characterised by apathy and difficulty in learning that one can do something to improve one's lot. It is brought about by the experience of uncontrollable trauma and people can be helped to get over it by experiencing mastery - even if they have to be almost forced to undertake easy tasks. Later work by this group (Abramson et al 1980) suggests that who develops learned helplessness and in what circumstances depends on individual beliefs about the uncontrollable experience, in particular, whether the person puts it down to personal inadequacy and if so, whether he thinks this inadequacy is chronic or temporary, and whether he sees the circumstances as unique or not unique.

After this quick trip through learning theory principles let us look at what these principles cash into in terms of social work methods. The behavioural approach is a very clear instance of theory informing and guiding practice. I shall present some key features of the behavioural approach, describe its procedures and give a brief overview of areas relevant to social work where there is evidence of its effectiveness.

Salient features of the behavioural approach

1. The behavioural approach is based on a scientific theory of behaviour. It has no place for untestable hypotheses, for unprovable and undisprovable speculations about how to help people.

2. Students must not take for granted that some procedure works unless they get some evidence of their own. They should try to make every

piece of work into a mini experiment. Is there actually a change in the problem - have unwanted behaviours decreased or wanted behaviours increased? Has a new skill been learned?

Before setting up an intervention plan the student should first look up the published evidence (not published anecdotes!). But nothing can be taken on trust. As the intervention proceeds the student must monitor progress: and must not carry on unless she or he gets some evidence that the intervention is helping this particular client. If the evidence suggests otherwise, then the student must be encouraged to think again.

3. In order to evaluate the work, it is necessary to specify in advance what it is the student is trying to change; and the goals must be clear. A baseline is needed - a measure of the state of affairs before intervention. It is necessary to measure before intervening, during intervention, and after intervention. This is the very simplest kind of mini experiment (there are more sophisticated kinds). From this short account I think it can readily be seen why it is that behavioural social workers try to focus on observable events. They do this because observable events are accessible and can be precisely defined.

Now some key questions often asked about the behavioural approach.

1. The question of causation. Behavioural theorists recognise three sets of causes. First, genetic or biological causes, such as injuries, the effects of drugs, infections, handicap, inborn personality differences. Second, historical causes - to do with the person's learning history. For example, a child may learn aggressive behaviour by observing a violent parent; some phobias and fetishes have been traced back to early experiences. Third, contemporary causes of behaviour: the factors in a person's current environment that regularly precede particular behaviours (antecedents) or follow the behaviours (consequences). These are the causes that behavioural workers focus on.

Antecedents: Being taunted by other children can trigger feelings of aggression. Being offered drugs may precede drug-taking. Your wife says you don't measure up to her ideal lover (that could precede either a row or a marvellous sex session - depending on your learning history!)

Consequences: Tantrums that are followed by sweets and cuddles are likely to continue. Sexual advances that are punished or ignored are not.

In some cases, it may be necessary to look also at covert antecedents and consequences, the thoughts and feelings that precede and follow the behaviours in question.

Behavioural workers focus on contemporary causes of behaviour rather than on historical causes for one very good reason: you can't change the past, but you may be able to modify current events.

2. 'Insight'. It's preferable to use the term 'psychological awareness' in this field. We are interested in teaching clients the principles of the behavioural approach and how to identify and alter the contemporary causes of their own and others' behaviour. 'Beat the System and programme your own behaviour'. This can go to the lengths of teaching clients quite formally, hoping that this might act as a form of prevention of future difficulties. Awareness for its own sake - particularly of historical causes of behaviour - may, of course, be valued by some people; and such awareness can sometimes be very reassuring. So we may share our guesses about historical causes, though this is not central to our work with clients.

3. The client-worker relationship. Drawing on research, behavioural social workers agree that certain worker behaviours are crucial: behaviours that are judged by clients to express empathy, warmth and genuineness. Also, in group work, the encouragement of client behaviours that are summed up as 'group cohesion'. So behavioural workers try to increase these. At a more individualised and specific level, we use friendly comments and the like to try to help clients feel less anxious or less guilty; to make them feel they are valued or that they have done well. We also try to indicate affinity with the client, and give the impression of confidence and competence because these things help us to operate more surely as a model for the client.

A good working relationship is not a substitute for the behavioural core of the work: using learning principles to analyze problems and to work out a careful behavioural programme for each individual. The relationship is necessary, but not sufficient. It sets the scene for effective helping. The student certainly doesn't have to put on a different hat when doing behavioural work, except in two respects: being willing to be more directive or structured and make concrete suggestions for action: and developing more interest in charts and graphs and evidence and doing less speculating - instead, learning to develop hypotheses with the client about what to do to help - and to test the hypotheses out together.

Assessment

This is a distinct phase in behavioural work. It is the key to successful intervention. It gives the information that determines exactly what techniques should be tried.

After a general 'getting to know you' assessment, the behavioural worker and the client proceed to a detailed description of current problems and the selection of initial target problems. These problems need to be defined very precisely and they should be much more circumscribed or 'modest' than is perhaps usual in social work. Thus, goals like 'decrease number of tantrums and increase time spent in co-operative play' or 'lower anxiety ratings and travel unaccompanied anywhere in town three times a week' are the order of the day rather than 'improve self esteem' or 'overcome agoraphobia'. Selection of target problem (behaviour to be modified) will usually require a compromise between what is the client's most pressing problem and what looks feasible.

Baseline

How often does the behaviour occur now? This information will be needed later in order to check whether the intervention technique that has been instituted is actually having an effect. Sometimes it is easy to get a baseline; the baseline may be zero: not up before midday for the last five years, no sexual intercourse for the last year. Or it can be more awkward to get a baseline: talked about delusions on average four times a day over a three-week baseline period; screamed an average of 30 minutes a night over two weeks. With behaviours you can't measure in a concrete way, you may need a simple rating scale, for example, 0-10 as a rating of anxiety in a specific situation. Whatever measuring device is used, the student must write the measurements down. During the intervention period, the student should use the same measures at regular intervals.

Behaviour analysis

Having defined the behaviour clearly it is necessary to identify what happens before and what happens afterwards. This is sometimes known as the ABC of the behavioural approach. A is the antecedent, B the behaviour and C the consequence. For example, the behaviour of interest is refusing to do what mother says (the goal being to increase the number of times the child does what mother says without making a fuss); the antecedents are a request or direction from mother; the consequences are mother gives up and lets child do what he wants or bargains with child. This analysis might lead the worker to decide as a first shot to try to arrange a change in the antecedents and consequences. The worker rehearses mother in making requests clearly and firmly and helps her to work out new, effective consequences for obedience and disobedience.

Another example, with respondent behaviour in mind: the problem behaviours are feeling anxious when alone out of doors and avoiding going out; the antecedent is going out or approaching the street or supermarket; the consequences are avoiding anticipated anxiety and receiving a lot of fuss from husband. In this case, the worker might decide to institute a programme of rapid exposure to the feared situations and also attempt to bring in the husband as a co-therapist to help his wife with her exposure programme and provide more appropriate consequences, that is, praise for effort. Note these are just examples - no assumptions about particular problems can be made without an individualised and detailed analysis.

Intervention techniques

Based on Operant Learning Theory

Positive reinforcement. This means devising a programme of positive reinforcers which should follow the behaviours as quickly as possible. Note that it is important not to assume that any thing or event is a positive reinforcer for an individual without checking that it does in fact increase the behaviour it follows. Positive reinforcement should at first be delivered every time the desired behaviour occurs, and later should be thinned out so that the behaviour is reinforced less and less frequently. This is the best way to ensure that a newly learned behaviour is resistant to extinction. Where it is necessary to use 'concrete' reinforcers, such as sweets, these should be paired with 'social reinforcers', such as praise, and the concrete reinforcers gradually withdrawn.

Chaining means teaching the person one part of a chain of behaviour then another and then another until the chain is complete. This method is particularly useful for teaching new skills that have first been broken down into a list of separate behaviours occurring in a set order. Chaining is a very common component of work with people with learning difficulties who need to learn ordinary skills of daily living such as dressing, or eating with a spoon, or using public transport.

Shaping (also called successive approximations) means reinforcing a behaviour somewhat like the desired behaviour and then raising the standard for reinforcement and so on, step by step, until the person has got it perfect. This is another effective way of teaching skills, such as social skills. For example, in training a social work student in 'active listening' the teacher might begin by reinforcing simply looking at the speaker, then require other non-verbal signs of attentiveness and concern, and then perhaps some verbal encouragement.

Points systems, which may be used with children and teenagers, include the familiar star chart and the token economy. They are a means of providing immediate reinforcers (the star on the chart or the token) which are later exchanged for back-up reinforcers which it would be difficult to deliver at the time the wanted behaviour occurs. Points systems often also include a negative punishment system - loss of points for unwanted behaviours. They are most appropriate for child behaviour problems in the age group seven to twelve approximately.

Contracts between clients may be part of behavioural, marital or family therapy (the other components are often communication training and problem-solving training - see below). People agree in writing to change their behaviour. They provide reinforcement for clearly specified desired behaviours. Sometimes contracts also include a penalty clause which specifies some form of punishment, such as a fine or a chore, for some undesired behaviour or for failure to comply with the contract.

Punishment is not generally recommended for a variety of reasons:

— it may have serious side effects, such as anxiety, depression, aggression, imitating the behaviour of the person who delivers the punishment, avoidance of the person who delivers the punishment.

— it does not help the person being punished to learn any new, useful behaviour to take the place of the unwanted behaviour.

— people seem to habituate to punishment so that in order to be effective the punishment would have to increase in intensity over time.

This said, there are times when punishment may have to be considered: when it is necessary to stop some unwanted behaviour rapidly, because it is dangerous; or when other methods (such as replacing the behaviour with an alternative, positive behaviour) would probably take too long. One type of punishment that is unlikely to produce harmful side effects is 'negative' punishment such as fines or loss of points when used within a programme that is mainly one of positive reinforcement.

Operant extinction. If the worker can identify what is currently reinforcing a particular problem behaviour, and stop the reinforcement, immediately and completely, then the behaviour will reduce and eventually cease.

Time out is a variant of extinction which has been shown to be particularly effective in dealing with child behaviour problems (in conjunction with positive reinforcement for desirable behaviours). *Time Out* involves removing the child from sources of positive reinforcement. The child is warned, then removed to a dull place, and made to stay there quietly for a brief period of time.

Based on respondent conditioning

Desensitisation. The person learns to associate a new, desirable response with a stimulus that has previously evoked anxiety or anger. This is achieved by introducing gradual 'dollops' of the stimulus while the person relaxes or engages in some other incompatible behaviour such as humour.

Flooding is where the above takes place all in one go. In between these two extremes are various forms of *graded exposure* - the person is exposed to the disturbing stimulus starting with as strong a dose as he or she can tolerate. In flooding and graded exposure it is necessary that the person stays in the disturbing situation for as long as it takes for the undesirable response to disappear.

Based on social learning theory

Modelling simply means demonstrating how to do something. (Note the features mentioned above that make for more effective modelling.) Modelling is a key feature of social skills training. For example, a group member who is confident about using the telephone to enquire about a job demonstrates this in a role play. Key features of the skill are identified, and then the member who has difficulty with this takes his or her turn to practise the skill in role play. He or she receives feedback and reinforcement and further modelling and further practice until the skill is mastered.

Modelling is very valuable in almost any programme, for example, showing a mother how to give instructions to her child, how to play with a small child or even how to ignore.

Now some common approaches which are well established packages of procedures:

Social skills training. As indicated above, the main features of social skills training are modelling and shaping. The person is given an explanation and demonstration of appropriate behaviour, then tries it out and receives feedback and reinforcement and then continues to practise. Also, to a varying extent, attention may be paid to cognitive elements - learning the social rules, examining and modifying unconstructive self-talk, etc.

Communication training is a variant of social skills training designed to deal with problems in the family. Some programmes deal with any of a large number of potential communication faults, such as interrupting, lack of acknowledgement of the other person's feelings or talking too much; others teach broadly defined areas such as expressing positive and negative feelings or making requests.

Problem-solving training is teaching a series of steps towards solving a problem or making a decision - useful for many clients and usually a key feature in family work. It involves modelling and practice with specific feedback and reinforcement and a variant of shaping - the clients learn to perform each stage of the process and then put the stages together in a set order (agree to work on a defined problem, list possible solutions, eliminate obviously bad ones, select one, agree details of implementation).

Self control training packages also involve a wide range of components. For example, in anger control, the person learns to analyse the problem situation into its separate stages, to try to interrupt the sequence of events leading to the anger outburst and to develop alternative responses, paying particular attention to the physiological aspects of anger arousal and to the self-talk that accompanies the run-up to an angry outburst. Self-control training can also play a major part in work with anxiety and with some 'compulsive' or impulsive behaviours such as sexual offending, drinking, smoking and substance abuse. These procedures are used in work with people who have developed such problems and also in preventive work.

Social learning theory, as indicated earlier, marks the interface between the 'older' learning theories and cognitive theories. Chapter 10 gives further details of what has come to be known as the cognitive-behavioural approach.

I have given a rapid run-through of some key behavioural procedures. It is important to remember that it is quite rare to use only one procedure - usually the student will have to devise a package and test it out carefully - perhaps adding or subtracting procedures as the measures produce data about effectiveness or other new information becomes available. Perhaps a case example will illustrate this point. (Details of the assessment on which the intervention plan was based are omitted for the sake of brevity). Mr. and Mrs. J had frequent rows; their teenage daughter was constantly demanding money, often came home late and was abusive; Mr. J lost his temper with both wife and daughter and sometimes hit his daughter. This case involved a whole series of interventions, beginning with a couple of difficult family interviews in which the student strove in vain to set up a contract dealing with the parent-daughter problems. These efforts were thwarted by serious communication problems and by Mr. J's outbursts of temper. Therefore, the student took a few steps back and set up (1) individual sessions with Mr. J in order to help him with anger control (2) family communication training sessions in which modelling and practice were used in order to teach family members to listen empathically to each other and not interrupt and to express concerns clearly and calmly (3) problem-solving training so that the family could learn to achieve consensus or compromise solutions first to simple, comparatively non-controversial questions such as what sort of puppy to buy and later to such questions as pocket money amount and rules about coming home late. Only then could the family contract be worked out and put into operation. Later still, the problem of the rows between Mr. and Mrs.

J was re-assessed with a view to possible intervention. It was decided that the frequency of these rows was now so low that this would not be necessary. Four packages of procedures were used in this case (anger-control, problem-solving, communication training, family contracting). In all of these, and throughout, the worker was constantly modelling, offering specific reinforcement for specific behaviours, seeking to remove reinforcement from unwanted behaviours and explaining the procedures to the family.

The evidence for the effectiveness of behavioural and cognitive behavioural procedures is abundant and increasing (See, for example, reviews by Giles 1983; Rachman and Wilson 1980; Thomlison 1984). There is no area where researchers have compared the behavioural approach with any other and found the other approach to be superior. However, there are some areas where encouraging evidence is particularly strong. These include: children's problems such as conduct disorders at home and at school, bedtime problems, toileting, phobias, and prevention of smoking, alcohol abuse, and unwanted pregnancy; with adults, anxiety problems, sexual problems, family problems; and with people with mental handicaps, teaching new skills and coping with behaviour problems. Cognitive-behavioural approaches are making headway, particularly in the field of depression. Other areas where there is encouraging preliminary evidence include: alcohol abuse, self-control problems, sex offending, child abuse and failure to thrive. Social skills training shows considerable promise in many fields of endeavour, although evidence for long-term effectiveness is still lacking. However, if one rates the evidence in terms of research methodology, representativeness, length of follow-up, and so forth, anyone studying this literature is bound to conclude that no other approach has anything like the same track record of effectiveness.

Where the required social work contribution is to do with assessment alone, such as a court report, making a behavioural analysis of current and recent behaviour and the discipline of being specific, concrete and non-speculative will lead to a clear account that will be helpful when it comes to deciding on future action.

Like any other psychology-based approach, the behavioural approach is severely limited in the face of major social problems such as unemployment, homelessness or poverty and in dealing with severe forms of mental illness such as schizophrenia, where medical involvement is essential. (Though even in these situations, 'thinking behaviourally' can help to clarify problems and suggest solutions, if only partial ones.) Sometimes it seems better to combine the behavioural approach with cognitive therapy techniques (see Chapter 10) although with problems other than depression and some forms of anxiety the evidence for doing so and the circumstances where this is appropriate are still being researched.

This paper is intended only to indicate a minimum amount of information that needs to be provided for those who are new to the behavioural approach so that they will be able to understand what behavioural social workers are talking about; and it should remind fieldwork teachers of the key principles and procedures. But in no way can this superficial account substitute for training and detailed knowledge. An introductory reading list is appended. I recommend that beginners should be encouraged to take the opportunity to attend training workshops and I would emphasise the importance of very detailed discussion and planning before and after each session with clients. It is probably best for beginners to start off working with a client group that is already familiar. This said, the behavioural approach does have a built-in safeguard: the baseline and continued careful monitoring should ensure that all concerned (fieldwork teacher, student and client) can keep a check on progress. The same attention to ethical issues as in any other form of intervention is necessary and we need to bear in mind that this approach can be quite powerful and its use in settings where clients are very much under the worker's control, as in some residential establishments, must always be subject to scrutiny. A little knowledge can be a dangerous thing in this field, particularly a limited grasp of some of the techniques without close adherence to a professional code of ethics.

Note

References have not been given for every statement for which there is research evidence available. Only a few key references to important topics and references relating to matters of possible controversy have been cited.

Recommended Reading

Bandura, A. (1977), *Social Learning Theory*, Englewood-Cliffs, New Jersey: Prentice Hall.

Herbert, M. (1988), *Working with Children and their Families*, London: BPS in association with Routledge.

Hudson, B.L. and Macdonald, G.M. (1986), *Behavioural Social Work: an Introduction*, London: Macmillan.

McAuley, R. and McAuley, P. (1978), *Child Behaviour Problems*, London: Macmillan.

Sheldon, B. (1982), *Behaviour Modification*, London: Tavistock.

References

Abramson, L. Y., Garber, J. and Seligman, M. E. P. (1980), Learned Helplessness in Humans: An Attributional Analysis, in Garber, J. and Seligman, M. E. P. (eds) *Human Helplessness: Theory and Applications*, New York: Academic Press.

Bandura, A. (1965), Influence of a model's reinforcement contingencies on the acquisition of imitative responses, *Journal of Personality and Social Psychology*, 1, 589-595.

Beck, A. (1976), *Cognitive Therapy and the Emotional Disorders*, New York: International University Press.

Giles, T. R. (1983), Probable superiority of behavioural interventions: I. traditional comparative outcome, *Journal of Behaviour Therapy and Experimental Psychiatry*, 14,1, 29-32.

Rachman, S. J. and Wilson, G. T. (1980), *The Effects of Psychological Therapy*, Oxford: Pergamon.

Seligman, M. E. P. (1975), *Helplessness*, San Francisco: Freeman.

Thomlison, R. J. (1984), Something works: evidence from practice effectiveness studies, *Social Work*, Jan-Feb, 51-6.

Watson, J. and Rayner, R. (1920), Conditioned emotional reactions, *Journal of Experimental Psychology*, 3, 1-14.

Chapter 8

Crisis Intervention in Social Work

Kieran O'Hagan

Introduction

The need for effective crisis intervention by social workers has never been greater. To the well known crises which often erupt in cases of child abuse, the elderly and elderly confused, the terminally ill and bereaved, the mentally ill, battered women, adolescents in conflict with parents, etc., may now be added the rapidly increasing crises generated by the exposure of child sexual abuse, the spread of AIDS, and the increasing frequency of national disasters. How well do social workers cope with these crises? How effective and tested is their training? What theoretical and conceptual frameworks underpin their practice?

This chapter will begin by looking at our crisis heritage, ie the intellectual, cultural, and professional origins of crisis intervention. It will then identify the principal features of crisis situations most common to social workers, and also of those for which they have a statutory responsibility to try to resolve. The unique challenges of intervention in crises like these clearly dictate crucial and necessary components in training. These are:

1. A sound ethical base

2. A theoretical framework which can accommodate and imaginatively impose order and sense upon the chaos and dangers of crises

3. Self knowledge in crisis situations

4. Principles, techniques, and skills.

These are also the most significant characteristics of a professional and effective crisis intervention service. The principal objective of this chapter is to define and explore each of them.

The definition of crisis

Professionals always seek to define the challenges which face them, but they are unlikely to make any more progress in defining 'crisis' than their earliest predecessors. The fact is that crisis is indefinable. One person's 'crisis' may be another person's ecstasy. Langsley (1968) and many other pioneers attempted to find that elusive definition: 'crisis is . . . ' but sensibly gave up. He admitted what a futile and frustrating task it had been, and wisely concluded (to the benefit of us all): 'crisis theory has defined the crisis as the hazardous event (stress) and the subsequent reaction to that event' (p.156). What Langsley is saying, in effect, is that crisis is defined as the impact of an event rather than the event itself. As yet, there is no definitive listing and prioritising of the numerous impacts of what social workers would call crisis situations, but the following can generally be regarded as the most common and predictable feelings and perceptions of crisis victims: fear, panic, violence or the threat of violence, helplessness, a sense of loss or losing control, a sense of impending doom. Common features of the crisis environment are: groups of people (ie family, neighbours and/or relatives, friends); conflict between individuals at the centre of the crisis, or between the individual and the professional who has become embroiled in it; lots of mobility and noise (people coming and going, helping and hindering), a general chaos (lack of effective leadership, order and direction).

The origins of crisis intervention

American psychiatrists were the principal contributors to the emergence of crisis intervention as a new, identifiable professional discipline. The crisis pioneers, such as Caplan (1964), Langsley et al. (1968a), and Pittman (1966), became aware of the benefits of brief, intensive, and action orientated therapy in dealing with crises, as opposed to the then well established long term psychoanalytical and psychotherapeutic treatment programmes. Their literature, theories, and models of crisis intervention heavily influenced social work training in Britain throughout the sixties and seventies and (still do in some quarters). Some aspects of these pioneers' achievements will be long lasting: for example, the rigour and discipline of Lindermann's (1944) observations of the relatives of disaster victims and the pioneers' emphasis upon theoretical underpinning and systematic thought and strategy in approaching crises. Many of the principles and techniques devised by the pioneers remain crucial tools in understanding crisis processes and in extricating crisis participants from the dangerous and damaging scenarios which they have created for themselves.

There are however, some aspects of this crisis heritage which have limited its relevance to social work practice. The subject matter at the centre of the pioneers' study was the mental illness of individual psychiatric patients - more often than not American, middle class, articulate, professional and managerial people. The location of study and intervention was often the psychiatric ward or clinic. Such a clientele and locations are far removed from the vast majority of social work clients in Britain living in conditions of poverty, deprivation and family fragmentation, and from generic social workers working in understaffed inner city area offices, responsible for far too many cases. In these living conditions and environments, the dominant feature of the crises which social workers encounter is *conflict*. It is a feature which, in the flower-power peace-loving sixties, was likely to be denied. An even more important characteristic of the 'classical' crisis heritage, particularly from the point of view of social work students, was its failure to recognise the importance of self awareness in crisis situations. The clients were the only focus of attention; they were the only people with a problem; the worker (ie the psychiatrist) never had a problem, and was always portrayed in the literature as omnipotent and never-failing. Today, welfare professionals are likely to have a little more humility than American psychiatrists of the sixties, and social work trainers are becoming more aware of the pivotal position of self awareness in crisis situations, and of the specific need for social workers to recognise and acknowledge their own vulnerabilities. Finally, the crisis pioneers could never have predicted the importance of ethnic and gender issues in professional welfare work. Social work students and their trainers today are unlikely to be similarly unaware.

Foundations for crisis work

It is therefore time to lay a new foundation for training social workers to do crisis work. There is ample experience in British social work practice (much of it painful and tragic) which determines the principle ingredients of that foundation. There is the absolute necessity for 1) a sound ethical base; 2) a flexible theoretical underpinning; 3) frameworks and methods which aid effective and rigorous self exploration, and, 4) not least, a repertoire of skills and techniques.

1. The ethical base of crisis intervention

The Cleveland report has demonstrated once again a peculiarly narrow and blinkered perception of ethical considerations in crisis work. Child sexual abuse is in many ways the most traumatic, complex and challenging crisis encountered, thereby demanding a well formulated ethical code; yet when social workers, their managers and trainers, and paediatricians and police officers, were asked to justify ethically the actions in Cleveland, the reply invariably was something to the effect that 'the child's welfare is paramount'.

Similar naive platitudes - conveniently concealing a multitude of dubious practices - can be heard throughout the short history of social work. In the sixties, ethical considerations meant little more than ensuring 'the client's right to self determination'; then 'respect for clients', and, 'recognition and acceptance of their innate dignity and worth'; today, great ethical emphasis is placed upon 'the need for partnership between social worker and client'.

Social workers, spokespersons and writers undoubtedly mean well when they make statements like these, but such statements have no place as an ethical base for crisis work. Ethical principles need to involve more depth and complexity and to be more specific and realistic. For example, crises seldom if ever revolve around one individual; nor is there ever likely to be only one individual whose rights, dignity, or worth are under attack. A more serious naivety in social work's traditional ethical thinking projects the notion of every client as oppressed and deprived, and of the social worker's paramount need to champion and protect them against the harsh, non-sympathetic world. Even after the callous and brutal murders of seven social workers by those same clients during the last decade, it is alarming to know that some social work students still emerge from training courses totally oblivious to the pathology and danger of clients, and determined to uphold the rights of clients at all costs.

Ethical principles in social work generally and in crisis work in particular evolve from three main necessities: knowledge and experience, the use of power and control, and resources.

KNOWLEDGE AND EXPERIENCE

There cannot be a more unethical act than to give a newly qualified, inexperienced social worker the responsibility of solving a major crisis. Similarly, social workers themselves can be unethical by not making strenuous efforts to acquire the necessary skills, knowledge and experience which will enable them to cope with crises.

Social workers in the front line of crisis work must be experienced, knowledgeable practitioners. They must be experienced and knowledgeable in the type of crisis they are attempting to resolve, particularly if aggression and violence are features of that crisis, and if there is a threat to the life and liberty of individuals at the centre of it (including the worker, of course). Acquiring that knowledge and experience usually begins with professional training: trainers can quickly enable students to identify, categorize, and prioritise crises, and to recognise the most significant and challenging features of different categories of crises. They should be enlightened about the social and political contexts of crises, and how gender, culture and ethnicity may influence and dominate crisis processes. They must learn about and accept without equivocation their future statutory and moral obligation to try to resolve certain categories of crises.

After training, this crisis learning process becomes the responsibility of the worker and her or his manager and department. Differing locations, area offices, communities, families and clients may experience crises and their impact differently. Wherever the qualified worker finds herself, her manager should ensure that she becomes familiar with the category of crisis most common and most challenging. Will it be the crisis of the elderly confused (probably the fastest increasing type of crisis encountered by social workers) or is it the crisis of child sexual abuse, or could it be the crises generated by AIDS? The manager and the department have the responsibility of knowing what particular features of each of these categories of crises pose the greatest challenge, in particular, to their newly appointed staff and what precisely is required to ensure that the worker continues to acquire knowledge and experience without exposure to unacceptable risk.

Knowledge and experience of what one is doing, of the client(s) and the crisis(es) one is dealing with, and a commitment to the statutory and moral obligation to help resolve the crisis, is the first and most important principle in the ethical base of crisis work. It is a principle that should be underlined in the designated tasks of trainer, student/worker, and manager alike.

THE USE OF POWER, AUTHORITY AND CONTROL

Acquiring knowledge and experience will quickly enlighten the worker about the ugly, dangerous and conflictual nature of many crisis situations. The worker cannot manage or minimize conflict and danger merely by listening to clients; crises most often demand immediate action (Puryear 1979), particularly those crises in which families, relatives and other agencies are demanding the instant removal of clients, are screaming out that the client is driving them crazy, and that if she isn't removed, something terrible will happen.

In this minefield of conflicting demands and rights, the social worker's ethical duty is to attempt to impose some order upon the chaos, to take control of the crisis situation, and eventually to enlighten the participants that resolving the crisis does not mean upholding the 'rights' of any one individual, but, on the contrary, means that each and every participant is likely to have sacrificed some of their own rights. This is no small task, even for two workers, or a crisis team. The workers cannot begin to tackle such a task unless they are willing to exercise the power, authority and control which the law and their training has bestowed upon them. It is not so long ago that 'power', 'authority' and 'control' were anathema to many students (a regrettable inheritance from many trainers). Happily, there is a greater realism in training today, with students and trainers alike more conscious of the paralysis (most unethical) which can result from a reluctance to exercise power, authority and control in ugly dangerous and violent crisis situations. Clients at the centre of the crisis and the numerous crisis participants, who have begged or demanded that social workers intervene, are not likely either to understand or appreciate that reluctance. O'Hagan (1986) and Davies (1981) both offer a comprehensive analysis of the power factor in social work, arguing convincingly for the legitimate, professional and ethical use of power.

RESOURCES

Effective crisis intervention requires resources additional to that of knowledgeable, experienced and competent front line professionals. It needs a management who is committed to achieving a high quality crisis intervention service, and who knows that, rather than being a costly unnecessary luxury, this can save departments a fortune in terms of expenditure (eg, preventing clients from being taken into care), and tragedy (nearly all the child abuse enquiry reports since 1974 graphically and painfully describe the inadequacies of social workers dealing with crises).

Not all interventions seek to prevent clients from going into care. Sometimes 'care' is the best option, and there is a heavy ethical responsibility on management to provide adequate care facilities. The Cleveland report exposed this major ethical failure on the part of management. A principal officer responsible said:

> 'The situation was untenable; we had reached the level of looking for beds, rather than placing children appropriately' (Butler-Sloss 1968, p.62).

Resources are very much a matter of ethics, and it is crucially important for social workers to determine the quality and type of resources which are necessary for an effective and professional crisis intervention service. Social workers must also be willing to request adequate resources persistently, on the basis of the poor quality of service that must inevitably result from a lack of them.

2. *The theoretical underpinning of crisis work*

The principal feelings and perceptions of crisis victims and crisis participants have already been described. They experience fear, panic, and loss of control. The principal features of crisis situations have also been described, ie lots of people, noise, movement, chaos, and lack of direction and leadership. This is enough to caution the hardiest worker, and more than enough to frighten the life out of the novice. Clearly, the professional cannot approach crisis work thinking only of such unpleasant aspects as these. Even before reaching the crisis scene, the worker will need to have formed some firm opinions from the referral as to what kind of crisis this is. She will need to have some idea of the conflictual nature of the crisis, and who are the most significant participants on either side. Above all, she should have a theoretical framework with which she is familiar, and which can enable her to impose order (at least intellectually and imaginatively) upon the probable chaos, panic and fear which awaits them.

But which theory? The range of crisis situations which social workers encounter is so great now that no single theory will suffice. However, the most common and difficult crises for the vast majority of social workers working in social services departments are the same as always, ie plea for removal crises (O'Hagan 1984, 1986), when neighbours, families, friends (enemies) and professionals from other agencies (eg police, health visitor, GP, teacher) clamour and demand that social services remove a particular client for fear of something terrible happening. The client may be an unmanageable delinquent, or an elderly confused or mentally ill person. These are very much conflictual crises, in which opposing sides can easily be identified and conceptualized. Fundamentally, they represent conflicts between status quo and change. The client at the centre (whom nearly everyone wants removed) represents threatening change. The persons demanding removal represent the endangered status quo. Systems theory, which primarily explores the tensions between growth and change in living organisms, seems ideally suited for providing social workers with a theoretical base for this particular but very common crisis situation.

SYSTEMS THEORY

Systems theory provides concepts and frameworks which enable social workers to understand, predict, and prepare for significant processes and stages in crisis eruption. For example:

> all systems but the largest are themselves subsystems of other systems, and all systems but the smallest are environments for other systems (Forder 1976, p.26).

This central tenet of systems theory aptly illustrates fundamental characteristics of the plea-for-removal and numerous other types of crisis situations. The client referred, upon whom all attention (and wrath) is focused, is merely a component part, (as are numerous other individuals), of a larger social system, usually the family. The family is merely a component part of the larger system embracing friends, relatives, neighbours, and professionals. This, in turn, is part of the even larger living system which we refer to as the community. All of these systems and their components are likely to be interrelated and interdependent to varying degrees, and this interrelationship and interdependence is likely to have contributed significantly to events leading to the crisis. It is unhelpful, therefore, in crisis situations, to dwell solely upon any one individual, to the exclusion of others in a wider system who are probably more significant in the origins of the crisis than at first meets the eye (O'Hagan 1986).

Another example of systems theory's contribution is its provision of concepts easily applied to the typically conflictual crisis situations: 'morphostasis' (associated with the status quo, ie structure, pattern, regularity, and constraint), and 'morphogenesis' (associated with change, differentiation, innovation, and creativity) (Walrond-Skinner 1976, p.14). The worker's main task in assessment is to identify the processes and persons on either side of the 'status quo v change' conflict. Gender, cultural, and racial issues may figure prominently amongst those processes. The greatest temptation facing the worker at this point is to become identified as belonging to or as being sympathetic to either side. This is of crucial importance in crises revolving around those who have been labelled or diagnosed as mentally ill.

Other categories of crises may necessitate entirely different theoretical frameworks: the crises associated with AIDS, for example, for both victims and their loved ones; or the crises resulting from sudden bereavement, as in the ghastly catalogue of disasters which Britain has suffered in recent years. But the general principles regarding the function of theory are as applicable to these crises as they are to the more common social services crises. They are all painful, chaotic, potentially destructive experiences, all demanding an intellectual ability to theorize on how the crisis has come about, on the processes and people who sustain it and exacerbate it, and on the likely strategies for first imposing order upon it, then attempting to resolve it. It is unwise for social workers to approach crises without a firm grasp of theory. The degree of confidence one has in approaching a crisis will often depend upon a preceding imaginative analysis and resolution. Theory is the effective means by which that can be achieved.

3. Self awareness in crisis situations

The unpleasantness and danger of many crisis situations create temptations for the workers called upon to solve them. The greatest temptation arises when one wants to get away from a crisis in which it is obvious that one is doing no good at all, or possibly making the crisis worse, and then to seek out reasons within the crisis itself, amongst the crisis participants, to explain away one's own helplessness and failure in solving it. Another common temptation is to act in a way that one knows has no professional or moral validity, yet be unable to resist the enormous forces within the crisis situation that are compelling one to act in that way. There are for example, literally thousands of crises concluded by the removal of an individual client. The social worker who has implemented that decision may be full of unease for days and weeks afterwards, knowing that the removal was not in the client's best interests, nor (in the long term), in the interests of those clamouring for the removal. Despite the numerous disasters which have occurred in recent years, there is good reason to believe that many social workers and managers are falling in to the temptation of immediately demonstrating involvement and caring by being on the scene in minutes without too much idea of how best to help (Stewart 1989). It is particularly easy to fall for this temptation because the crisis victim is incapable of offering resistance, and the political necessity to demonstrate some action, any action at all, is overwhelming.

Self awareness is the most important component in crisis training. It has three main tasks:

1. It seeks to enable social workers to explore rigorously their own vulnerabilities in crisis situations.

2. It seeks to identify the precise cause of that vulnerability.

3. It seeks to enlighten the worker as to how particular vulnerabilities can seriously limit the quality of their intervention and lead to them making unprofessional and damaging decisions.

Here is one example of the crisis conditions which can lead to such a situation:

The GP, neighbours, relatives and local bobby are clamouring for the removal of Jack, aged 80, living alone, senile, and not caring for himself as much as they would like. He leaves the electric fire on; he wanders in the middle of the night; he knocks the neighbours up; he's driving them crazy.

They are all waiting for the social worker who arrives. They collectively criticize social services; they demand removal of Jack; they talk of the time he nearly burnt the whole neighbourhood down; they talk about the certainty of something terrible happening if he is not removed.

Any worker, no matter how experienced, is going to feel some vulnerability in this extremely unpleasant situation. Many workers, indeed, may succumb to the pressure so blatantly applied, and then rationalize their action in terms of 'the welfare of the client . . . it's in his own interests to be removed', or, 'the very real risk of him doing himself and others harm if he isn't removed'. Self awareness training, however, does not only aim to expose the obvious in this case, namely, that the worker succumbed to the pressure applied, but it also seeks to enable the worker to identify the strongest, most irresistible elements in that pressure, and to explain why they are so, for that individual worker. For example, there is an enormous difference between a mere recognition that one succumbed to a collective pressure and then made the wrong decision, and a detailed analysis of the intervention which identifies: (1) the GP; (2) the size of the hostile group; (3) the fear of that 'something terrible' happening, as the principal causes of that pressure and wrong decision making. Self awareness must further explore why these factors posed such difficulty. There is little prospect of surmounting a difficult obstacle if one is not aware of precisely what it is in one's own experiences, temperament, outlook, background, etc., that makes one vulnerable to that obstacle. Many social workers, for example, find it difficult to be assertive with GPs, either out of a sense of inferiority caused by the enormous discrepancy in status and power between the two professions, or, like most people, because they have been reared in a family and culture that has bestowed a God-like omnipotence upon GPs. If such a worker does not acknowledge feelings and perceptions like these before embarking upon an intervention in which the GP is playing a significant (and not necessarily helpful) role, it is more likely that the worker will be pressurized into making the wrong decision.

There are conceptual frameworks available to aid social workers in the task of self awareness (O'Hagan 1986). Students or workers should first be given every opportunity to use these self exploration frameworks alone: some may find it difficult to acknowledge their own vulnerability in a group setting or in supervisory sessions.

The frameworks are constructed on the base of particular aspects of crisis situations. For example, social workers can look at:

1. The environmental context of a crisis

2. Different categories of crises

3. Different types of clients at the centre of each crisis.

Each of these should be dissected with reference to real or imaginary cases, so that the worker can identify specific details which pose difficult challenges. The environmental context often has numerous challenges: slum dwellings; dark tenement blocks; filthy, smelly rooms; overcrowding; large dogs; bustling activity and noise . . . etc. - any or all of these can inhibit, frighten, even paralyse some workers. Having identified precisely which do that, the worker must seek the reason why? Some reasons may be obvious; appalling conditions for example, which are not only painful to look at but which physically discomfort, may be vastly different to what one is familiar with. However, the reason may not always be obvious: a large group of angry people in a small room may feel chaotic, threatening, or claustrophobic; but, in analysing why, the worker may discover that they have always had difficulty in group situations of any kind, and that they lack the social skills and confidence to function adequately in groups.

Similar considerations apply to the type of crisis and the type of client and other participants at the centre of it. Most social workers are apprehensive about mental health crises, particularly in the dark early hours of the morning (Clark 1971; O'Hagan 1987). Many female social workers may have great difficulty in dealing with crises of child sexual abuse where the suspected male perpetrator is present and remains a dominant force. Social workers with personal experience of being battered or having watched their own mother being battered may have enormous difficulty dealing with a 'wife battering' crisis. The Bengali parents who attack their rebellious daughter for whom a marriage is already arranged, may present the most unpleasant and insurmountable challenge to some social workers who are incapable of understanding or empathising with the tradition, culture, and religion that such parents are merely attempting to uphold.

(I have used these self-exploration frameworks with many different groups of social workers and students. The crisis which I have consistently found to be the most challenging and the most revealing of social workers' vulnerabilities is that generated by cot deaths. I have witnessed social workers visibly distressed when merely discussing imaginary case histories of cot death crises presented to them.)

These are some of the crises and clients and participants. But it is of little use merely knowing that a particular crisis or client or participant(s) is unpleasant and challenging; self awareness needs more precision than that. Why is a worker apprehensive about a mental health crisis? Does she have a phobic fear of madness? Does she fear violence? Does she feel that the possible hospitalization of a mentally ill person is ethically repugnant? Why might a worker be reluctant to embroil herself in a crisis of conflict between two cultures? Does she have an overwhelming sympathy for the daughter and perceive the culture of her parents as ridiculous and cruel? Is she reluctant to come face to face with parents whom she does not or cannot respect? Why are cot death crises so challenging? Is it because the worker is overwhelmed by the enormity of the loss, and feels that any reaching out, any offer of help and support, is futile, even insulting? Or is it the unbearable thoughts about the apparent cruelty of this event, and the professional ignorance as to its real cause and consequences?

The third and final task in self awareness is to attempt to predict how a particular vulnerability may pressurize one into making a wrong, and damaging decision. On the basis of the numerous vulnerabilities already referred to, it is not difficult to imagine how social workers could be pressurized into making wrong decisions. The most obvious wrong decision is to avoid all those unpleasant features which trigger off the sense of vulnerability; avoid, for example, the unpleasant environmental context by attempting to get the crisis participants to the office, hoping to solve it there; or avoid the threatening large family or group of crisis participants by contriving to see them one at a time; or avoid the incomprehensible seemingly cruel Bengali parents by . . . simply avoiding them. These understandable defensive manoeuvres - morally dubious and professionally unacceptable in themselves - are guaranteed to lead to even worse, more damaging conclusions to the crisis.

4. Practical principles, skills and technique

Many of the principles which guide present day crisis interventionists have their origins in classical crisis literature and research. They are as tenable today as when first propounded. Additional principles have emerged from a variety of more recent experiences by welfare professionals in various agencies. Here is a selection which this author believes to be particularly pertinent to social work in British Social Services departments:

1. Crisis is a time of opportunity as well as stress and danger. The opportunities arise because defenses usually collapse during the crisis, and the worker can very quickly get to the cause of the crisis. Crisis participants are more likely to be receptive to help if they have cried out for help - even if the worker is aiming towards a goal which is the opposite to the one they have originally demanded eg, removal of client.

2. Initial intervention often worsens a crisis, particularly child care and mental health crises. The clients (parents or patient) often perceive the worker as a threat, and treat the worker accordingly. Workers must be prepared for this and be capable of a very speedy enlightening of clients to the contrary. They should, both in word and action, broaden the focus of concern: the clamouring relatives and neighbours who are pointing to and accusing the wayward stepchild, or the elderly confused, or the one they have already diagnosed as mentally ill, can and should be engaged on something entirely different: mere introductions, comments on introductions, comments about home and contents, recalling previous involvements (particularly if they've had nothing to do with the cause of the present involvement). As well as temporarily removing the focus from the one upon whom everyone else wants the focus to remain, these efforts will reduce tension, and undermine any determination by the 'identified client' to attack a worker whom they perceive as an enemy (O'Hagan 1980).

3. Discussing a crisis with one of the participants in one's own office is infinitely more appealing than immersing oneself in the family and

crisis in some Godamn awful slum. But it is also likely to be infinitely less effective.

4. Do not attempt to 'rescue' clients in crisis by removing them from the crisis state and placing them in an environment that is totally different in every respect. The client's mental, emotional and physical state may not be able to adapt to such a drastic change. (Removing filthy, unmanageable, rootless kids from a dangerous abusing or neglectful crisis situation, and placing them in nice quiet middle class suburbia, is the most typical example.)

5. The right kind of minimal intervention during a crisis can achieve a maximum and optimum effect.

6. Workers who intervene in crises should commit themselves to being available to the same crisis clients during the following days.

Techniques and skills

Social work students are likely to be very impatient at this stage, having waited (and possibly waded through all the previous pages), to reach what they instinctively regard as the most exciting, important aspect of training for crisis intervention work. Of course techniques and skills are exciting, but they are most certainly not that important. And it is a thorough training and acceptance of the previous components, ie ethics, theory and self-awareness, which will often determine the appropriateness and effectiveness of particular skills and techniques.

In the preceding section of this chapter, dealing with self-awareness, there was much emphasis upon the need for the workers to realise their own particular vulnerability. In determining appropriate and effective skills and techniques, however, there needs to be just as much emphasis upon the numerous strengths possessed by workers, upon their degree of confidence and experience, and upon what one might term the worker's 'personality and style'. Let us illustrate the point by considering this very common type of crisis:

Mary and John are the very young, inadequate parents of Tricia, two months old. They both come from terribly deprived, neglectful and abusing family backgrounds. They present problems of lack of hygiene, poverty, law-breaking and inability to care for Tricia without the constant monitoring and attention of health and social services agencies. A frightened neighbour rings, saying that they are having a flaming row with Tricia in the midst of them. You quickly arrive on the scene and confirm that this is the case. John has the baby - obviously taken or wrenched from the arms of Mary. Mary is running after John around the room, screaming to get the baby again. Every time she reaches out, John swipes at her with one hand whilst holding the baby with the other. Naturally, you are extremely worried about the baby's safety.

Now, which techniques and skills would be most appropriate in this situation? The simple answer is, those techniques and skills which are perfectly compatible with the worker's personality, style and experience.

At first sight, this scene may appear to warrant the 'strong arm of officialdom' technique, ie the worker to barge in between them, firmly gripping the arm of John, stretching oneself to look down upon him, and demanding he had over the child immediately, or face terrible consequences. To accentuate authority the worker might also demand that Mary sits on her backside and says nothing. Whilst bellowing out this command, the worker purposely avoids even glancing at Mary.

This might indeed be effective, if one is six feet tall, has a deep voice, a charismatic, authoritative, personality, many years' experience in the police force, and lots and lots of confidence. It is hardly likely to be effective if one is 4' 11" tall, soft spoken, and visibly frightened by the scene in front of one. However, very different techniques and skills are available, and should be equally effective at the time. They may also create the opportunity later for worker and parents to discuss the causes of these recurring crises.

This child is not in any danger from either parent if either parent is looking after the child on their own. But she is in danger from the behaviour of both parents together. The most important feature in the scene is that this danger to the child is functional, ie, each of the parents have a vested interest in maintaining it, as it is their most effective way to gain the sole attention - albeit the attention of hatred and aggression - of each other. The cycle of violence and hatred is such that whatever technique one attempts to use in response to this situation, it must have a very powerful initial impact. Ignoring these screaming parents, and walking over to the windows and quietly opening them, is certain to break their concentration - if not the cycle of violence itself and will gain a few precious seconds in which to say: 'I'm just opening these so that you can throw that parcel out when you're finished with it . . . you're obviously have a wonderful time playing with it!' A less shocking technique would be again to ignore the danger to the child, place oneself between the parents and ask either of them whether they are the person whose name is written on the referral (which you just shoved under that parent's nose). Here the strategy of the technique is the opposite: to compete against their theatre of violence with your own theatre of naivity (how could anybody be so stupid as to ignore us fighting over our child by asking who I am?). The result, however, is likely to be the same as when the more shocking tactic is used - a few precious seconds in which the worker's incredible naivity or blindness momentarily breaks the vicious cycle of violence and danger. Once broken, even for a few seconds, it will be extremely difficult for the parents to regenerate the cycle; if they do, it will sound and look contrived. Finally, as has already been said, the danger to the child stems chiefly from the presence of both parents. In this kind of scenario, there will be numerous such utterances as 'I'm taking *my* baby now and I'm not coming back'. The worker would do well to facilitate this in any way possible: opening the door for that parent; restraining the parent left behind; assuring the latter that the one who has left will be back for sure. Once either parent leaves the room, whether they have the child or not, the danger to the child is drastically reduced.

This is an extremely challenging yet very common crisis situation for social workers. They should be encouraged to say - if that is how they feel - that none of these techniques and approaches seems safe to them, or that they would not feel confident in using any one of them. The only condition allowing them to feel confident and capable in such a crisis may be the presence of another worker. There is nothing wrong with that; indeed, I, as an experienced practitioner, have on one occasion had to rely on the presence of another worker and two police officers standing outside the door awaiting a call (the fighting parents were very drunk). But the important common factor is that those intervening have prepared a strategy and technique beforehand.

Let us now consider some other common crisis obstacles and suggest techniques and skills for coping.

The Obstacle	*Possible Solution*
Large numbers of people, many of whom are making the crisis worse. You need to get them away from the crisis so that you can talk to the main protagonists. They are basically well-meaning, caring neighbours and friends.	Thank these folk for 'trying to help'. Say how fortunate it is that the client(s) has such loyal friends. Say how sorry you are in having to ask them to leave . . . but that you are duty bound to talk to the client(s) alone. Apologise to the client(s) for having to ask such caring friends to leave.
The threat of violence from someone who is much taller, stronger, and fitter than you.	Comment on the fact that they are fitter, stronger, etc. and that you realise they feel like killing you, and how easy it would be for them to kill a mere 'pittance!' like you. (There is nothing as effective in reducing the

risk of violence than removing the 'surprise' and unpredictability factors, upon which the perpetrator depends.)

The 14-year-old is unmanageable, defiant, aggressive, and won't speak to you about anything. His parents are threatening to kill him if he is not removed immediately. They have already attacked him, which is why you have been called out.

Having tried and failed to get the lad to speak to you, you can now pretend to ignore him. Turn your back on him. Tell the parents you now know what the problem is: Their 'lad' is not 14, 'he's only 10'. Emphasise your experience in these matters. Tell parents you regret having to give them this news. But you've carefully watched the 'child' and his behaviour has all the characteristics of a 10 year old. (This technique is highly effective in breaking the cycle of violence between them. It invariably leads to the lad - grossly insulted by your suggestion - trying to prove he's 14 and it usually compels the now worried parents to defend him.)

Anger, hostility, and resentment towards social services (without the threat of violence).

Allow clients to express these feelings. Do not resist, or try to defend. Wait until such feelings have burnt themselves out. They inevitably do, leaving clients full of guilt because you have taken it all. They are likely to be receptive then to a more civilized exchange.

Crises that seem so negative and destructive that they are beyond resolving, and it is also apparent that some crisis participants have a vested interest in maintaining the crisis and all its unpleasant features.

1. Acknowledge that it is indeed a terrible crisis, unresolvable, the worst crisis you have ever encountered. Say it would be a waste of your and their time trying to resolve it.

2. Laugh immediately and apologise. Explain by saying you've never encountered a more ridiculous situation in your professional life!

(The key feature here, of course, is the participants' 'vested interest in maintaining the crisis'. The ordinary civil niceties of intervention, in which social workers excel, are not going to work here. Hence the shock tactics of 1 and 2 above. First, the apparent surrender: yes, indeed, I can see there isn't a hope in Hell's chance of me solving this crisis . . . etc . . . But this is the last thing those type of crisis participants want to hear. Their vested interest is not just in maintaining the crisis, but also in sustaining their blatant gratification in watching some hapless professionals making fools of themselves trying to solve what has been made unsolvable. There is no more effective way of both deflating the crisis and of drastically reducing the power of those kind of compulsively obstructive participants. The second technique above is merely a more direct and much quicker means of achieving the same end. It requires much confidence and experience, and the worker's certainty that such technique is perfectly compatible with their own style. The successful application of either technique will establish the worker in a position of influence, enabling them to dictate the future course of the intervention.)

The surgeon informs the parents that their child is terminally ill. You are then left with the parents, stricken with confusion, anger and grief.	Stay close to them, comfort them in whatever way is necessary; a quiet room, comfortable chairs; dissuade them from shrinking from this terrible news, or acquiring false hopes. Above all, let them see you are not embarrassed by their anger and grief.

These represent only the tiniest fraction of approaches and techniques to differing crisis situations. They are described here not to attempt to convince the reader that they are always effective, but, to re-emphasise that their effectiveness will largely depend upon the crisis context, their compatibility with the worker's style and personality, and the degree of confidence the worker feels in adopting them. 'Know thyself' is the principal determining factor in choosing both the right approach, and the most effective skills and technique.

Summary and conclusion

An increase in the number of crises that social workers are called upon to resolve, is inevitable. For example, the increase in the number of elderly people will ensure a corresponding increase in crises revolving around the confused elderly; more divorces will increase the crises revolving around reconstituted families, particularly crises of child abuse and unmanageable, rebellious, adolescent step children; we are already seeing enormous increases in crises revolving around the thousands of mentally ill people unceremoniously dumped into a so-called 'community care'; child sexual abuse is rampant; AIDs is spreading relentlessly, and, despite mind boggling technical sophistication, the general population remains as vulnerable to natural and man-made disasters as it has always been.

Before suggesting an appropriate response to these developments, this chapter has looked at the origins of classical crisis intervention and literature. There are major limitations in the relevance of the crisis pioneers' work to the majority of crisis tasks faced by staff in British social services departments. Not the least of those limitations is the lack of any consideration of how factors of culture, race, and gender influence crisis processes. A new foundation of crisis training for social workers is necessary. The main components in that foundation are, a sound ethical base, a theoretical underpinning, self awareness, and, a repertoire of skills and techniques. It has been suggested that self awareness in crisis situations is the most important component in crisis training; it is fundamentally an awareness of one's own vulnerability in the crisis situation, and how that vulnerability can lead to one feeling compelled to act immorally or unprofessionally. Frameworks and step by step procedures have been provided to enable the worker to explore rigorously and honestly their own vulnerabilities. Important principles of crisis intervention have been listed, and some techniques have been demonstrated. But social workers must be aware of attempting to use techniques which are entirely incompatible with their style of work and their personality, or which require a level of experience and confidence they have not yet acquired.

Crisis intervention is minimal intervention which seeks to achieve the maximum and optimum effect. Its focus of aim may be ruthlessly confined, yet its goals are nothing short of revolutionary. These are: 'to replace blind ugly passion with enlightenment and tolerance, chaos and panic with order and safety, helplessness and despair with a sense of hope' (O'Hagan 1986, p. 142). These are ambitious goals, but they are also attainable; more easily so if a secure and reliable foundation has been laid in crisis training.

References

Butler-Sloss, E. (1988), *Report of the Inquiry into Child Abuse in Cleveland*, London: HMSO.

Caplan, G. (1964), *Principles of Preventative Psychiatry*, New York: Basic Books.

Clark, J. (1971), 'An analysis of crisis management by mental welfare officers', *The British Journal of Social Workers*, 1(1), 27-38.

Davies, M. (1977), *The Essential Social Worker (A guide to positive practice)*, London: Heinemann.

Forder, A. (1976), 'Social work and systems theory', *British Journal of Social Work*, 6(1), 23-43.

Langsley, D. G., Pittman, F. S., Machotka, P. and Flomenhaft, K. (1968) 'Family crisis therapy - results and implications', *Family Process 7*, 753-9.

Langsley, D. G., Kaplan, D., Pittman, F. S., Machotka, P., Flomenhaft, K. and De Young, C. (1968a), *The Treatment of Families in Crisis*, New York: Grune and Stratton.

Lindemann, E. (1944) 'Symptomatology and management of acute grief', *American Journal of Psychiatry*, 101. Reprinted in Parad, H. J. (ed.) *Crisis Intervention*, 7-21.

O'Hagan, K. P. (1980), 'Is social work necessary?', *Community Care*, 297, (Jan).

O'Hagan, K. P. (1984), 'Family crisis intervention in social services' *Journal of Family Therapy*, 6, 149-81.

O'Hagan, K. P. (1986), *Crisis Intervention in Social Services*, London: Macmillan.

O'Hagan, K. P. (1987), 'Mental Health crises at night', *Community Care*, 4th December.

O'Hagan, K. P. (1989), *Working with Child Sexual Abuse: A Post Cleveland Guide to Effective Principles and Practices*, Milton Keynes: Open University Press.

Pittman, F. S. (1966), 'Techniques of family crisis therapy' in Masserman, J. (ed.) *Current psychiatric therapies*, New York: Grune and Stratton

Puryear, D. (1979), *Helping People in Crisis*, California: Jossey Bass.

Stewart, M. (1989), 'Crisis counselling' *Community Care*, 2nd, 9th and 16th February (3 articles).

Walrond-Skinner, S. (1976), *Family Therapy: The Treatment of Natural Systems*, London: Routledge and Kegan Paul.

Chapter 9

Task-Centred Practice

Peter Marsh

Introduction

This chapter examines the model of task-centred social work practice from its origins in research, through its development in many settings, to its uses and applicability in current practice. There is both a brief summary of the model's main stages and a more detailed examination of each of those stages. The task-centred model has made a particular contribution to the development of effective problem-solving and participatory practice. The history of that contribution now stretches back over some thirty years of research and development.

Early stages

Many elements of social work come from outside the discipline itself; social workers need to understand social policy, to work within the law, to have knowledge of human growth and development. However, it might be assumed that the methods of social work would be developed within the discipline. In fact imports from other disciplines have dominated most social work practice models, and task-centred social work stands as one of the most developed examples of a practice model which has been initiated, refined and tested by social work practitioners and researchers.

The origins can be traced to a number of sources, but one of the earliest demonstrates the point very well. In 1963 Bill Reid submitted his doctoral dissertation - a 'study concerned with the treatment operations of caseworkers: what caseworkers do in their efforts to help clients' (Reid 1963, p.1). This study contains the hallmarks of the thirty year development of the task-centred model of practice: a focus on practice research, based on the actions and needs of social workers and their clients.

The 1963 Reid study used an analog experiment to examine the influence of training and experience, and to see how responses varied when workers were faced with different degrees of client problem. What effect does the practitioner's work have on the client's problems? What is it that helps client problem-solving? These questions have been at the core of the many studies that have contributed to the building of the model. The 1963 Reid study, for example, asked 65 experienced workers and 56 students to complete an exercise which acted as an analogue of their real-life response to a client in an interview. The research examined the ways in which their experience affected their responses. This initial exploratory study was followed by the more famous experiment contrasting short-term and longer-term approaches (Reid and Shyne 1969) and by many more studies after that (some are listed in the Brief Guide to the Literature at the end of this chapter). The model has been built up by social workers and social work researchers using exploratory and developmental studies, focusing on the impact of particular practice elements on the client's problem-solving abilities. Each element of the model that is outlined here has some degree of empirical backing for its effectiveness in problem-solving.

Two building blocks

Helen Harris Perlman, one of the early doyennes of social casework and the author of a classic text (Perlman 1956) wrote the Foreword to the 1969 Reid and Shyne study and succinctly summarised the change in the approach to social work development shown in this study. She highlighted the fact that the research looked at the consequence for the client of certain actions, and did not focus on the intentions of the caseworker (Reid and Shyne 1969, p.8). There is a Snoopy cartoon of a football game, where Snoopy, in the last frame, wails 'How can we lose when we have such good intentions?' Social workers often feel exactly like that. The confusion of the intentions of the worker with the outcome for the client has bedeviled social work throughout its development; social work practice is usually well-intentioned, but that does not always mean that the outcome is satisfactory and developmental research, based upon consequence and not upon intention, is one vital ingredient of beneficial social work.

Task-centred work has another equally important basic element, based both on effectiveness research and on a value statement. Underlying the approach is an emphasis on partnership with the client, which is to be sought as far as possible in all aspects of practice (Marsh 1990a): partnership in the sense of a respect for the client's view, a great deal of effort being put into good communication, a preference for joint actions on problems, and a recognition of the abilities of the client where appropriate. A commitment to this form of partnership is necessary for all task-centred practitioners.

The model

What does a task-centred practitioner do? In brief summary: he or she proceeds by emphasising the role of the client in negotiating appropriate programmes of help, with work based on an agreement between the worker and the client, covering the problems to be addressed, and outlining the goals to be achieved. When necesssary these problems and goals will include those specified by legislative duties or by a court. The work then proceeds in a series of incremental steps towards the goals and is subject to regular review. Client and worker engage in a number of tasks to reach the agreed goals, and these tasks may themselves involve collaboration with other people. The worker may need to help the client carry out certain tasks by, for example, advice, or encouragement, or skill training procedures. Tasks are therefore seen as effective because they are part of an overall action; any one task is unlikely to lead directly to a goal. Time limits for the duration of the work will be negotiated at the outset: if there is a reason for long-term involvement then work can proceed by a series of shorter-term agreements or the task-centred programme can be changed to a regular pattern of service, and the monitoring of that service. The client will be centrally involved in all stages and aspects of the work and will be encouraged to be an active and participatory partner in the agreement, in the tasks and in the reviews.

The work therefore moves from problems to goals by the use of tasks carried out in a time-limited period and using participatory methods as far as possible. A simple outline, but a complex practice, as we shall see as we look at some of the main elements.

Problems

The work begins with an examination of problems through an initial general scan of all of the areas that may need help. As clients are likely to come to Social Services via other services, and as a significant number of them will be reluctant clients, this scan is a particularly useful technique as clients may often limit the problems that they present because of their view of the agency or worker function (see Sainsbury, Nixon and Phillips 1982). Task-centred work begins with an examination of the width of the problems and not the depth.

After this the problems can be explored in more detail, and the prominent problems should be carefully discussed to establish the current patterns and severity. Without this detail the work may be misdirected and it will be harder to see progress (or the lack of it). The priority of different problems is then established, on the basis of two factors. The first consideration is the priority that the client, after full discussion and advice, wants to give to different problems. The other consideration is when there are problems that statutory processes require the client to address, such as the level of care given to children. In general, work should only proceed on the basis of the client wanting it to, or on the basis of a clear mandate in legislation (usually via a court). Client acceptance of that legislative mandate may, of course, be strictly limited and strategies may need to be devised to deal with this (see, for example, Rooney 1988a). The two mandates for work, of client wishes or of statutory process link the apparently different worlds of therapy and social control. Task-centred work is firmly rooted in both worlds; the model applies fully to both therapy and social control.

Goals

Work may not proceed beyond the stage of problem exploration, but if it does then the goals of the work need to be established. Problems are *what is wrong* and the goals are *what is needed*, and there is not necessarily a simple and direct connection between *what is wrong* and *what is needed*. For some problems, perhaps most problems, the goal will be a reduction rather than a complete removal of a problem (for example teenagers and parents may recognise that complete family harmony is unlikely, and many elderly people may be consciously using services to stop things getting worse rather than to make things much better). For other problems the client may suggest a goal which appears to be only indirectly linked to the problem. The client's view of what is needed, in the light of the informed discussion with the worker is the paramount consideration (unless statutory reasons mean that some goals must be imposed).

Goals need to be achievable - it is unjust to work on any other basis. Of course some clients may make their goals too modest and full encouragement for more ambitious goals should be given - this is part of the model's emphasis on building on strengths. But equally it is the case that workers have been guilty in the past of over-ambitious claims for social work action, and clients do not benefit from such ambition.

Goals need to be observable - all parties need to know when they reach them. If clients and workers are going to work hard to achieve goals they need to be able to judge progress towards those goals. Equally the sense of accomplishment which should be present when the work is successful will be maximised by a clear and unambiguous achievement of a goal; sorting out what will be defined as success needs to be done at the outset and not at a later stage. Perhaps the best way to make sure that the goal is observable is to ask yourself, and the client, 'would a third party be able to judge if we had reached this goal?'.

Time limit

Reid and Shyne's 1969 study indicated that planned short-term work produced results at least as good as open-ended treatment of longer duration, and suggested that the results of this short-term work were reasonably durable. We all know of the remarkable improvement in effort when we are about to reach a deadline, and presumably this effect plays some role in the relative effectiveness of short-term work. Early work may often be better motivated: as the memory of a problem fades, so the motivation to work on it can also fade. Short-term work is not just a smaller amount of longer term work: it is a different process. The planned date of ending (or of moving to a new agreement, or to a monitoring stage when contact needs to be long term) is agreed at the start. The time limit should be as short as is reasonable for the problem (with around three months as the maximum).

Tasks

Tasks are carried out after the problems, goals, and time-limit have been agreed and they are central to the problem-solving efforts in task-centred work. Tasks are not just the *jobs to be done* that usually occur at the end of most interviews between clients and workers. Tasks are discrete parts of the overall action: a series of incremental steps towards goals (see Reid 1978, ch. 5). They are effective as part of that overall action; any one task is unlikely to lead directly to a goal. They are a planned sequence; a set of steps on the ladder from *what is wrong* to *what is needed*.

Tasks are carried out by workers and by clients and the process of problem-solving is a joint one between the two partners. They establish the best way to proceed, they divide up the time period into appropriate stages and they divide up the work between them. Another factor which distinguishes tasks from the *jobs to be done at the end of the interview* is the active role that clients play in the task work. Tasks are designed in part to provide ways for skills to be learnt, and for dependency to be avoided. Clients should always be centrally involved in the development of tasks, and there should normally be a number of tasks that they carry out.

Records as an aid to participation

A participative approach is vital in task-centred work and this can be greatly enhanced by the use of written material - to remind, to inform, to clarify and to provide an account. Unfortunately, records have a poor reputation in social work with the two main areas of recording, the agency records (addresses, finance, movement of children in care and so on) and the practice records (notes about sessions, plans of action and so on) being equally ill-regarded by most practitioners. Agency records are not altered by task-centred practice, but the practice records are crucial and they need to receive a much better press from task-centred practitioners. Task-centred records are essential in order to keep the client informed of progress, to clarify the plans, and to act as aide-memoire for clients and workers in carrying out tasks (Doel and Marsh, in press, Ch. 4). They are an indispensable tool: a view which represents a considerable challenge to existing views.

What the model is not

Before considering aspects of task-centred work in greater detail, we should note that task-centred practice is as prone as any other aspect of social work to simplification and parody. A sloppy use of the term 'task-centred' is often evident in discussions about methods. It seems to be confused with a simplistic and surface approach to clients problems - 'I'm only doing task-centred work at the moment; my in-depth work is with these other cases'. Nothing could be further from the truth. Task-centred work is beguiling in its clear structure and apparently straight-forwardness, but its application is complex and it is designed to tackle the most difficult problems that face social work clients. It is 'in-depth' when that depth is needed; it is not just appropriate for simple problems.

Task-centred work is also confused with a welfare rights approach to problems, and with the provision of services. Practitioners discuss the fact that this or that case is suitable for a task-centred approach because it involves benefit problems and because it involves an application for some form of service. There is no difficulty in incorporating welfare rights work and service provision in the model but to limit it to these processes is quite unnecessary. The task-centred approach integrates these aspects of work into the overall work with the client; it is not solely a service or welfare rights model.

The heart of the model

A good analysis of problems, clarity about the basis for work (client or court mandate) and clarity of goals are vital initial steps in task-centred practice. The heart of the model lies in the task work that follows this. Tasks were described earlier as the steps on the ladder from problems to goals. They are the building blocks of change in the problem-solving process. They are designed to be cumulative, acting in sequence to move the work from the problem, *what is wrong*, to the goal, *what is needed*.

The sequence of tasks

The process of problem-solving is therefore seen as:

PROBLEM
    to Tasks
        to Tasks
            to Tasks
                to Tasks
                    to Goal

Tasks may be agreed for the worker, for the client or, with suitable involvement, for others. They may be reciprocal ('If you do this, I'll do that'); they may be repetitive (a number of visits by the Home Help to carry out the same general tasks to move towards the goal); they may be joint ('we agree to do the following'). Developing them is a challenging process for both worker and client.

The first stage in task development is to consider the general pattern of tasks that is likely to lead to the goal; is there an obvious order to tasks - are there simple and more complex ones, is there a suitable balance of worker and client tasks? These issues will inform the development of the tasks because of the need to see tasks as part of a sequence and not think of them as one activity that leads direct from problem to goal (although simple problems may lend themselves to this at times).

Using clients' experience of successful problem-solving, and their caveats about past failures will be an important part of task development. As in other aspects of the model the practitioner is a 'consultant to the client' (Doel and Marsh, in press) providing support, advice, clarification and expertise in the area where needed. Maximising the client's own abilities is one aim of all task-centred work.

Task planning and action

In 1975 Bill Reid published the report of an experimental study designed to show whether or not a particular approach to task development aided task completion. The success of the Task Implementation Sequence in this study led to its adoption within the model. It consists of five main steps to be carried out after the general outline of the task has been developed. The first stage is 'enhancing commitment' where the practitioner asks the client to review the potential benefits of carrying out the task and reinforces and encourages realistic assessments of these benefits. The second stage is 'planning task implementation', where the detail of the work to be done is covered. This should be done with great care, making sure that the plans are as clear as possible.

These two stages are followed by 'analysing obstacles', where all reasonable pitfalls are thought of and ways to handle them are explored. Then the practitioner may move on to 'modelling, rehearsal and guided practice' to help prepare for the task work. Actions could be modelled by the worker (or by others), actions can be rehearsed in the session, or actions can be guided in vivo (for example the client could make a telephone call with the worker and the client having produced a check-list of what needs to be covered and with the worker listening to the call and able to give advice as needed).

Finally the worker needs to 'summarise' the task development by restating the task (which should be in clear language) and the plan for implementation.

The full process of task development is therefore:

1. Develop an overall task strategy (in outline) that leads from problem to goal - this will be a prominent factor in early sessions and in the back of the mind in later ones.

2. For each session (including the one that first agrees goals and time limits) decide on tasks for that session.

3. Follow the Task Implementation Sequence of 'enhancing commitment', 'planning task implementation', 'analysing obstacles', 'modelling, rehearsal and guided practice', ending with 'summary of the task'.

Task development needs to be undertaken for each task. For some tasks it will be brief and straightforward, for others it may be a lengthy part of the session. Writing is again a vital tool in this work. Writing down the tasks will clarify understanding, and is a very useful 'aide-memoire' for worker and client in the period between sessions when tasks are to be carried out. Leaving a copy of the tasks with the client is the ideal way of carrying out this task work (a developmental research project, Social Work in Partnership, has developed self-carbonating sheets for 'agreed goals' and 'tasks' - a useful practical aid to the work - see Marsh 1990b).

Task work is designed to achieve change and also to be part of the 'learning by doing' approach of task-centred practice. In undertaking tasks clients and workers can see how obstacles to problem-solving can be overcome and they can learn new strategies for overcoming them. Task development, after the initial session, will always begin with a review of the tasks undertaken since the last session. This review is vital to indicate progress, enhance learning and to provide analysis of obstacles to problem-solving. It offers an opportunity to see how things are going in a real and evident way as the work progresses. It also offers the client a chance to hold the worker to account through the review of worker tasks in each session.

If tasks are not completed, the reasons for this will need to be considered. The task may be the wrong one for the purpose or there may be obstacles that were not foreseen; these two different issues would require different approaches. If the task was wrong then a new task needs to be created; if there were obstacles, then it may be that guided practice or some other form of aid to task work needs to be undertaken rather than the creation of a new task. If tasks are regularly not done despite this analysis and aid, then it may be that the problem, or the goals, are not a priority for the client. Persistently undone tasks may indicate the need for detailed review of problem and goals; this review will be greatly aided by the evidence of a number of weeks of discussion and support for tasks that are still incomplete.

The tasks outside the sessions should therefore be thought of as an integral part of the approach, and the overall pattern of the model now looks like this (the sessions are in bold):

PROBLEM + Task Development
    to Tasks
            to **Task Review**
            + Task Development
            to Tasks
                        to **Task Review**
                        + Task Development
                        to Tasks
                                    to **Goal**

Reviews and endings

Many parts of the model do, in essence, seek to make social work practice more evident, more explicit and more understandable. Tasks are helpful in this process - they allow the worker's intended actions to be seen, they provide a clear picture of the process of problem-solving and they allow progress (or the lack of it) to be judged by client and worker alike. Review of tasks is part of this process and the concept of review is built into the task-centred model in a number of ways.

Apart from the task review a date for a final review of all the work is established at the start by the creation of a time limit for the work. In addition, each of the task sessions should begin with a brief review of problems to see if changes have taken place (for example relationships breaking up or disabilities getting worse could significantly affect the client's view of problems stated at the start of the work). Changes in the problem may also have occurred due to the work on the tasks, and even though this is not sufficient to meet the agreed goal it may have altered perceptions or improved matters sufficiently so that further work on that problem is not needed. These task sessions of the work should therefore always follow the order: Problem Review, Task Review, Task Development.

Work in the task-centred model will be undertaken within a time-limited period, usually not exceeding three months. Clearly there are occasions when the time limit needs to be extended, but this should only happen in the specific circumstances of problem-solving being delayed by factors outside of the worker's and client's control (such as the policies or time scales of another agency). In general, if work is to continue beyond the time limit then a new set of agreed goals should be negotiated. This means that work will continue in chunks of three months (or to look at it another way a substantial review of work, its purpose and content, will take place at this interval in long-term work).

There may be a number of circumstances where contact has to be maintained over long periods (a Supervision Order, a frail elderly person with a wide range of services, a child in the care of the Social Services, etc). This does not necessarily mean that a sequence of agreed goals needs to be drawn up at regular intervals as it may well be the case that active intervention in the task-centred model is followed by periods of monitoring which do not involve active work from the practitioner. An elderly person, for example, could well engage in a period of active work and then a network of services could be established with an agreed process of review. A Supervision Order, for example, could have active work on the court mandated and client-agreed goals in the early period, and then a period of monitoring.

Specialised work and the model

The task-centred model is an evolving one, based on practice research and policy development within social work and the Personal Social Services. There are a number of aspects of the current development of the model which cannot be covered in this introductory chapter, for example the detail of its application in specific settings, work on the use of the model in family problem-solving and its links with family therapy, and recent work on the model and partnership approaches to child care and care of elderly people. The Brief Guide to the Literature at the end of the chapter provides a starting point for enquiries into some of these developments.

Critique

The model has probably received the greatest degree of research attention of any model of practice developed within social work and the results of this research are positive, particularly when taken in comparison with other approaches (Reid and Hanrahan 1981). The model is popular with clients (Gibbons et al 1979), has been used with all client groups and in all of the settings that social workers work in (Epstein 1988a; Reid 1985). It is congruent with anti-discriminatory practice and in its respect for the client's views it sharpens the focus of ethnic-sensitive practice (Devore and Schlesinger 1981). It is proving its worth in the development of community care approaches and in the partnership-based practice that is developing in social work (Marsh 1990a). But there are limits to the model. Some of the limits could almost certainly be overcome; some of them indicate that different approaches are needed.

Training

The evidence so far is that training workers to use the model is far from straightforward. In the USA (Reid and Beard 1980; Rooney 1988b) and in the UK (Goldberg et al 1985) there have been major difficulties in training qualified workers in the use of the model. Taking similar cases and problems, some of the trainees appear able to use task-centred work with most of their clients and some appear hardly able to use it at all. Experience indicates similar problems with students on qualifying courses.

There are probably a number of factors to be considered here. First, despite its apparent simplicity, the model is in fact a complex one, demanding notably thoughtful practice and high levels of skill. It may simply be that some workers cannot manage this, and it may also be that some individuals are more prepared than others to invest the required time and effort. Much of the development work in task-centred practice has used volunteer workers with most workers being evidently committed to developmental work (for example they have been enrolled in continuing Education or Research Programmes), and these attitudes and abilities may need to be present for good development of task-centred practice. Secondly, the training may be poor, but current evidence on training is too slim to make sound judgments possible. Too many projects fail to give any detail of the training, and there is very little direct research on training. The successful American programmes provide some 40 hours of input, as well as live and indirect supervision of practice (Epstein 1988a) and this level of training is probably needed for genuine practice change.

At present we would do well to note that this model is hard work, that it requires able practitioners and that training cannot be skimped. Much more work needs to be done on the development of training for the model.

Range of work

Two areas of work are unlikely to respond to task centred practice. The first surrounds those families and individuals who appear subject to constant crises and whose problems appear to change with startling rapidity. The second involves cases where there is a statutory reason for involvement but no recognition by the client of this statutory mandate (and no area that the client wants to work on voluntarily).

The *constant crisis* family is a source of great strain for many workers in the Personal Social Services - as fast as the income support appeal is sorted out there is a teenager on the streets due to family rows, and as fast as this is dealt with there is a housing crisis etc. These cases can occupy a great deal of time and give rise to a great deal of concern (not least because other agencies are often demanding that 'something should be done'). The task-centred model is not well suited to the extreme version of this sort of case; by the time one set of goals are agreed there is a completely new set of problems to resolve and a new set of goals to negotiate. A task-centred worker may find that a number of cases that appear to fall in this category at present could be dealt with on a less crisis-oriented basis, but obtaining co-operation and agreement in some crisis-dominated circumstances is always going to be difficult. There do not appear to be any other models capable of achieving change that handle this work well. Perhaps a 'holding' model of practice needs to be articulated and developed. The scale of this part of the workload needs some careful analysis and policies need to be developed to handle it - task-centred practice's contribution is to make the practice problem more evident and clear; it will not resolve it.

The case that requires statutory intervention (supervision orders, children in the care of the social services, etc) can, as we have seen, be dealt with perfectly well within task-centred practice. But such cases do require at least some agreement (or at least reasonable acquiescence) from the client to the mandate given by the court. Situations occur where clients refuse to accept this mandate, allowing social workers or probation officers access but not agreeing that anything needs to be done. Task-centred work cannot proceed in such circumstances (although in the unlikely event of a separate voluntarily agreed problem it could proceed on this). Work in such circumstances involves monitoring and social policing, and this will need to be acknowledged. Continuing attempts to engage such clients will need to be made but it can be extremely difficult work. We do not know how many of these cases exist but they will no doubt continue to form a small group that will fall outside the remit of the model.

Other issues

There is no reason why task-centred work should not be the basis for agreed goals which themselves lead to work within other models of practice. For example, task-centred work is not designed to deal with the personal exploration involved in counselling, but a goal, reached in a task-centred manner, of 'feeling better about the death of my wife, and being able to discuss it with my friends' could be met by a number of sessions of counselling. Similar considerations apply to links with behavioural approaches, where programmes could be set up to reach goals agreed in the task-centred beginning of the work.

Use

Task-centred work has much to commend it and perhaps three main points should be focused on when considering use of the model.

- It provides a conceptual clarity for the basis of social work that is sorely needed by practitioners, managers and clients (and probably others, such as the press, the public and politicians). It highlights the fact that social work practice covers *both* help and social control, so long as great care is taken to recognise the elements of each. Working with this model, clients should be able to understand a great deal more about the service they are getting and be in a better position to influence that service and, as appropriate, to call it to account.
- It emphasises the need to develop practice on the basis of sound evidence: to fashion development in an incremental manner which is open to scrutiny by workers, researchers and others. Changes in practice do not seem to occur predominantly on this basis at present and the service is the worse for this.
- It is outcome oriented - the good intentions of the worker are not enough. Despite all the laudable efforts of staff in the Personal Social Services the outcome of a variety of well-intentioned programmes and practices has not been satisfactory on too many occasions. The development of community care and of more effective and partnership-based child care services is urgently needed. An emphasis on the effect of the work on the client is an important part of the coming of age of social work practice.

These three areas are sound reasons for considering the task-centred approach very seriously. Despite the training caveats, aspects of task-centred work that particularly feature these areas could probably be developed without major investment - for example, making sure that clearly agreed goals are recorded and that a review of these goals is made. Or workers could develop tasks for parts of their existing work, using the task development process within their current approach to practice.

If staff receive a proper training, then the model can be recommended for wide use within the personal social services in most situations where an active professional intervention is required. The limitations and strengths of the overall model and its overall status within social work practice will continue to be explored, but we already know that a significantly better service could be given to clients by much greater use of task-centred approaches.

References

Devore, W. and Schlesinger, E. G. (1981), *Ethnic-sensitive Social Work Practice*, St. Louis: C. V. Mosby.

Doel, M. and Marsh, P. (in press), *Task-centred Social Work*, Aldershot: Wildwood House.

Epstein, L. (1988a), *Personal Communication to the Author*.

Gibbons, J. S., Bow, I., Butler, J. and Powell, J. (1979), 'Clients' reactions to task-centred casework: a follow-up study', *British Journal of Social Work*, 0, 2, 203-215.

Goldberg, E. M., Gibbons, J. & Sinclair, I. (1985), *Problems, Tasks and Outcomes*, London: George Allen & Unwin.

Marsh, P. (1990a), *Outline of Social Work in Partnership Research*, Sheffield: Social Work in Partnership Programme, University of Sheffield.

Marsh, P. (1990b), *Records in Social Work in Partnership Research*, Unpublished Research Paper, Sheffield: Social Work in Partnership Programme, University of Sheffield.

Perlman, H. H. (1956), *Social Casework: A Problem-Solving Process*, Chicago: Chicago University Press.

Reid, W. J. (1963), *An Experimental Study of Methods Used in Casework Treatment*, New York: Columbia University Ph.D. Dissertation.

Reid, W. J. (1975), A Test of a Task-centred Approach, *Social Work*, 20 (January), 3-9.

Reid, W. J. (1978), *The Task-Centred System*, New York: Columbia University Press.

Reid, W. J. (1985), *Family Problem Solving*, New York: Columbia University Press.

Reid, W. J. and Beard, C. (1980), 'An evaluation of in-service training in a public welfare setting', *Administration in Social Work*, 4, 1, Spring, 71-85.

Reid, W. J. and Hanrahan, P. (1981), 'The effectiveness of social work: recent evidence', in Goldberg, E. M. and Connelly, N. (eds) *Evaluation Research in Social Care*, London: Policy Studies Institute.

Reid, W. J. and Shyne, A. W. (1969), *Brief and Extended Casework*, New York: Columbia University Press.

Rooney, R. H. (1988a), 'Socialization strategies for involuntary clients', *Social Casework*, 69, March, 131-140.

Rooney, R. H. (1988b), 'Measuring task-centred training effects on practice: results of an audiotape study in a public agency', *Journal of Continuing Social Work Education*, 4, 4, 2-7.

Sainsbury, E. E., Nixon, S. and Phillips, D., (1982), *Social Work in Focus*, London: Routledge and Kegan Paul.

Brief guide to the literature

The following selected references provide a starting point for further exploration of task-centred practice.

General Introduction:

Doel, M. and Marsh, P. (in press), *Task-centred Social Work*, Aldershot: Gower.

Epstein, L. (1988), *Helping People: The Task-Centred Approach*, Second Edition, Columbus, Ohio: C. E. Merrill.

Reid, W. J. (1978), *The Task-Centred System*, New York: Columbia University Press.

Articles covering the model very briefly:

Atherton, C. (1982), 'The task force', *Social Work Today*, 14, 2, 8-10.

McCaughen, N. and Vickery, A. (1982), 'Staging the play', *Social Work Today*, 14, 2, 11-13.

Work with Families and in Child Care:

Fortune, A. E. (ed.) (1985), *Task-centred Practice with Families and Groups*, New York: Springer Publishing.

Reid, W. J. (1985), *Family Problem Solving*, New York: Columbia University Press.

Reid, W. J. (1987), 'The family problem-solving sequence', *Family Therapy*, 14, 2, 135-146.

Rooney,R. H. (1988), 'Socialization strategies for involuntary clients', *Social Casework*, 69, March, 131-140.

Work with Elderly people:

Cormican, E. (1977), 'Task-centred model for work with the aged', *Social Casework*, 58, October, 490-494.

Dierking, B., Brown, M. and Fortune, A. E. (1980), 'Task-centred treatment in a residential facility for the elderly: a clinical trial', *Journal of Gerontological Social Work*, 2, Spring, 225-240.

Probation:

Goldberg, E. M. and Stanley, S. J. (1979), 'A task-centred approach to probation'. From J. F. S. King (ed.) *Pressures and Change in the Probation Service*, papers presented to the 11th Cropwood Round Table Conference, December 1978. Cropwood Conference Series No. 11, University of Cambridge.

Marshall, P. (1987), 'Task-centred practice in a probation setting', in Harris, R. (ed.) *Practising Social Work*, University of Leicester, School of Social Work.

Research:

Goldberg, E. M., Gibbons, J. and Sinclair, I. (1984), *Problems, Tasks and Outcomes: The Evaluation of Task-Centred Casework in Three Settings*, National Institute Social Services Library, No. 47, London: Allen and Unwin.

Rooney, R. H. (1988), 'Measuring task-centred training effects on practice: results of an audiotape study in a public agency', *Journal of Continuing Social Work Education*, 4, 4, 2-7.

Chapter 10

A Brief, Highly Structured and Effective Approach to Social Work Practice: A Cognitive-Behavioural Perspective

Windy Dryden and Mike Scott

Introduction

The primary emphasis in social work in the last decade has been on the 'amelioration' of client's problems, acting as an advocate, mustering resources and providing support. The upshot of this approach is that case files grow ever thicker as underlying problems go untackled. Two major factors serve to underpin the 'amelioration' orientation; first, most social workers lack confidence in their ability to practice any therapeutic modality and second, they believe that therapy is necessarily too time consuming. Cognitive-behaviour therapies share a set of attributes that can help social workers rediscover a therapeutic orientation to the benefit of not only clients but also of their own ailing morale.

Cognitive-behaviour therapies

Cognitive-behaviour therapies are:

- brief
- widely applicable
- highly structured
- relatively easily learnt
- relatively effective

Traditional behavioural formulations of human behaviour assume that, apart from genetic influences, human behaviour is controlled exclusively by environmental events that are ultimately beyond personal control. In its strict form such formulations assume that subjective processes such as thought or images can never exert a causal effect on behaviour, although the existence of subjective experiences would not be contested. The thoughts, images and attitudes involved in subjective experiences have been termed cognitions. However, in cognitive-behaviour therapy, cognitions are held to play a pivotal role. In particular, faulty thought patterns are held to play an aetiological role in a variety of emotional disorders. Bandura's (1976) social learning theory analysis has integrated the behavioural and cognitive perspectives. His concept of reciprocal determinism views psychological function as an interaction among three interlocking sets of factors: behaviour, cognitive factors and environmental influences. Reciprocal determinism is one of a number of paradigms that inform the practice of cognitive-behaviour therapies (see Carmin and Dowd 1988 for a more detailed discussion).

Cognitive-behaviour therapy targets both cognition and behaviour as primary change areas. Thus, for example, cathartic models of therapy, whose primary focus is the expression of excessive emotions (Janov 1970), would not qualify as a cognitive-behaviour therapy. Nor would rewarding good classroom behaviour with extra play time be regarded as a cognitive-behavioural intervention. Rather, it is an expression of the traditional behaviourist stimulus-response model of human behaviour.

Most forms of cognitive-behaviour therapy can be conducted on a group or individual basis. For example, cognitive therapy for depression as described by Beck et al (1979) consists of 15-20 individual sessions over a 12 week period, whilst Scott (1989) provides weekly sessions of individual or group therapy over a 12-week period. Cognitive-behaviour therapy is not confined to depression but has been applied to problems as diverse as anxiety (Beck & Emery 1985), anger control, social skills, marital problems and substance abuse (Scott 1989; Trower, Casey and Dryden 1988). Detailed, session by session manuals are available to therapists in the treatment of the different disorders (Beck et al 1979; Beck & Emery 1985; Scott 1989), but cognitive-behaviour therapy is no cookbook approach. While it is accepted that the traditional counsellor conditions of empathy, warmth and genuineness are prerequisites for client change, cognitive-behaviour therapists would maintain that these are necessary conditions for change, but not sufficient.

The first author has found that social work students on a three month placement can become confident cognitive-behaviour therapy practitioners by the end of the placement. Typically these students have had a caseload of six to ten clients with a range of problems, eg anxiety, depression, child behaviour problems, and shyness. They have been provided with reading and audio material at the start of the placement and the opportunity to sit in on therapy sessions. Regular case discussions have also been an important part of their placement.

Cognitive-behaviour therapies are located in an empirical tradition in which they key question is 'what treatment works, with what type of problem, with what type of client, under which circumstances?' (Paul 1967). the emphasis is then on outcome rather than process, and on the measurability of results. Within this perspective the final arbiter of the worth of a therapy lies in a controlled trial. It is also important to replicate findings in different social contexts to ensure that they are generalisable.

Cognitive therapy was the first psychotherapy (Rush et al 1977) to perform at least as well as antidepressants in the treatment of depression. Since the initial study there have been a host of further cognitive-behaviour therapy studies (reviewed by Williams 1984) replicating the original findings and attesting to the generalisability of the results (Ross and Scott 1985). The utility of a therapy should be judged not only by whether it produces better results than a standard treatment for clients who complete both modalities but also by whether it has a lower drop out rate. The cognitive-behaviour therapies have typically had a drop out rate of 5% whereas the comparable antidepressant medication group had drop out rates of 36% (Rush et al 1977; McClean and Hakstian 1979).

The most important feature of cognitive-behaviour therapies is that they teach coping skills, thus empowering the client, preventing relapse and avoiding dependence on the therapist.

The relapse rate in the 12 months following cognitive therapy for depression is only half that of patients given antidepressants (Kovacs et al 1981). Within a cognitive-behavioural perspective the therapist essentially assumes the role of psychological coach, imparting skills.

The cognitive-behaviour therapies can be categorised under four main headings though there is some overlap between them.

1. Coping skills

Stress Inoculation Training (SIT) (Meichenbaum 1985) is the most well known therapy in this category. SIT is aimed at the reduction and prevention of stress. Stress is viewed as an interaction between the individual and the environment. Both may need to be targetted for change. At an individual level, clients may be taught what to say to themselves and how to respond in situations that they find difficult.

2. Problem solving

Problem Solving Therapy (Nezu et al 1989) has been the most widely applied therapy in this category. Essentially it involves the precise definition of a problem, the generation of as many alternatives as possible, choosing the best solution, implementing the solution and reviewing progress. The process is repeated until the problem is solved. This approach can be applied to both impersonal and interpersonal problems.

3. Cognitive restructuring

The two main therapies under this category are rational-emotive therapy (RET, Ellis 1962) and cognitive therapy (CT, Beck et al 1979).

RET contends that irrationality is a major cause of emotional disorder. Ellis (1962) has suggested that much of the neurotic person's thinking is dominated by 'musts', 'shoulds', 'oughts' and 'have-tos'. These are typically expressed in thoughts such as:

- I must do well or very well!
- I am a BAD or WORTHLESS PERSON when I act weakly or stupidly.
- I MUST be approved or accepted by people I find important.
- I am a BAD, UNLOVABLE PERSON if I get rejected.
- People MUST treat me fairly and give me what I NEED.
- People who act immorally are undeserving, ROTTEN PEOPLE.
- People MUST live up to my expectations or it is TERRIBLE!
- My life MUST have few major hassles or troubles.
- I CAN'T STAND really bad things or very difficult people!
- I NEED to be loved by someone who matters to me a lot!

The goal of RET is the modification of such irrational beliefs. Cognitive therapy attends more immediately to distorted aspects of reality, whereas rational-emotive therapy gives more attention more quickly to irrational beliefs. In cognitive therapy the distressed person is seen as taking inaccurate pictures of reality. The faulty pictures are seen as arising in a number of ways:

a) arbitrary inference - drawing a specific conclusion in the absence of substantiating evidence or even in the face of contradictory evidence.

b) selective abstraction - conceptualising an experience on the basis of a detail taken out of context, ignoring other more salient information.

c) overgeneralisation - drawing a general rule from one or a few isolated incidents and applying the concept broadly to related or unrelated situations.

d) magnification and minimization - assigning a distorted value to an event, seeing it as far more significant or less significant than it actually is.

e) personalisation - attributing external events to oneself in the absence of any such connection.

f) absolutistic, dichotomous thinking - categorising experiences in one of two extremes; for example completely good or totally bad.

4. Structural cognitive therapy

The first three categories have been criticised by some theorists in the field as adopting a surface-structure model in which the focus of therapy is directed towards the modification of maladaptive self statements and behaviour, supplanting them with more adaptive ones. However, rational-emotive therapists and cognitive therapists refute this criticism, maintaining that underlying assumptions and irrational beliefs are a key focus and necessary to understanding a client's self-talk or automatic thoughts. In the structural approach the goal is to identify invariant deep structures that are held to provide the individual's entire knowledge organisation with coherence and stability. A structural cognitive therapy approach to agrophobia would, for example, begin with the behavioural strategies of helping the client to try going gradually greater distances alone, but therapy would not be terminated when the client had learnt to travel alone. Therapy would also explore deeper issues such as 'who am I getting out and about for anyway?' and developmentally linked events, such as frequently having been put on various kinds of transport as a child to be looked after by a variety of adult carers because 'mum wasn't well'.

The ABC model

All cognitive-behavioural approaches embrace a mediational model in that the traditional behavioural stimulus-response (S-R) model of human behaviour is extended to stimulus (A) - interpretation and evaluation of event (B) - emotional response (C).

This ABC model suggests that people are less disturbed by events in themselves and more by the way in which they view events. This helps to explain why it is that two people experiencing the same event (A) have a quite different emotional reaction (C) - because their B's are different.

The fundamental postulate of cognitive-behaviour therapies is that the B's of emotionally distressed people are likely to be inaccurate and/or irrational. The core therapeutic task is therefore the identification and modification of dysfunctional B's. (It should be noted, however, that the ABC model as presented above is something of an oversimplification in that it is not actually a unidirectional model, not only do B's influence C's, but to be in a negative emotional state will also enhance the recall of negative events so that C influences B).

Approaches to cognitive-behaviour therapy differ somewhat as to the nature of the B's. Structural psychotherapy looks more at historical material and the evolution of self-image to uncover B's, whilst rational-emotive therapy and cognitive therapy takes a less historical approach to making explicit the criteria by which clients evaluate themselves.

Common elements in the cognitive-behaviour therapies

1. Therapy begins with an elaborated well planned rationale.

This rationale provides initial structure that helps the patient to acquire the belief that he or she can control his or her own behaviour.

In practice this means explaining the ABC model described above. If one can explain the model using experiences that the client has provided as examples, so much the better. Analogies are also often useful, for example 'the mind is like a camera, it depends on the settings, and the lenses you choose as to what sort of photograph of events you take. It is possible to teach people to choose the settings and lenses so that you get a more realistic picture of situations that you are typically disturbed about'.

The rationale for the behavioural dimension of therapy is usually explained in terms of activity as a prerequisite for a sense of mastery or pleasure. It is therefore necessary to overcome the inertia that emotional distress can produce.

The cognitive and behavioural dimensions overlap considerably; for example a client may refuse to go to the theatre, something he used to once enjoy, ie he resists the behavioural task on the cognitive grounds that 'I know I am not going to enjoy it, so why bother'. The roadblock would be tackled cognitively by suggesting that the thought that he would not enjoy the play was only a hypothesis; he does not have crystal ball, and as such he needs to conduct an experiment to assess the veracity of his prediction. At the start of therapy it is also important to outline the time scale of therapy, the likelihood of success and the importance of homework assignments.

2. Therapy should provide training in skills that the client can utilise to feel more effective in handling his or her daily life.

Clients are asked to record events between sessions that they experience as upsetting. These may be external events (or interpretations of events) such as being criticised by a spouse, or internal events, for example, a sudden change of mood looking out of the window watching the traffic go by. Having identified the triggering events and the emotional responses to these events, clients are asked to record what they might have said to themselves to get so upset, ie find the B's of the ABC model. Clients may have greater or less access to the B depending on whether it is at primarily a conscious or non-conscious level. Part of the therapeutic skill lies in making the B's explicit and then helping the client to challenge whether or not they are valid and useful and by what authority they are held. For example, a client who experiences a downturn in mood watching the traffic go by may have been saying to himself 'life is just passing me by, I'm always getting myself into a bad mood, I'll always be this way, I am a failure'. A more rational response might have been 'I am only 40, life begins at 40, some things I have done well, some badly, join the human race'.

3. Therapy emphasises the independent use of the skills by the client outside of the therapy context.

If, in the therapy session, the therapist had, for example, drawn a client's attention to a constant theme of 'failure' in his B's, then there would be an expectation that outside therapy the client would immediately check out the failure theme when he experienced emotional distress. First the client might be instructed to pause when he noticed the first signs of emotional distress.

Then he would have to inspect his likely self-talk triggers such as 'failure'. Having identified which theme or themes were operative, he would then apply the alternative rational response which had been selected and prac-tised in therapy in order to behave in a way that could enhance his sense of mastery or pleasure.

4. Therapy should encourage the client to attribute improvement in mood more to his own increased skillfulness than to the therapist's endeavours.

To the extent that a client sees his improvement in mood as a product of his own change in thinking habits and behaviour the therapist will be able to terminate therapy. Clients can be prepared to make such attributions by the therapist's constant emphasis on the importance of homework assignments. Essentially, the client is being taught a skill for his independent use, and the more he or she practises it the more skillful he or she will become.

A case example

Jane and her husband, Peter, had a five month old baby who died suddenly in a 'cot death'. She was their first child. Shortly afterwards they began attending a parent support group for parents who had undergone the same tragedy. The group was held in a local children's hospital facilitated by a hospital social worker. Two years previously Jane's mother died. Jane had been very close to her, 'more like a friend', was very upset by her mother's death and became severely depressed three months afterwards.

She vividly remembered that her husband (then boyfriend) took her on holiday, to cheer her up, but she just couldn't be bothered with anything and 'wasted' the holiday. As the preparations for their wedding became more intense, the depression seemed to lift. There were, however, lots of conflicts between Peter and Jane, as she became irate when things did not go her way. In retrospect Jane thought she had been spoilt by her mother, who had always solved problems for her. Not long after they were married Jane became pregnant and she and Peter were delighted at the prospect of having a baby. The birth was trouble free, but soon after Jane developed post-natal depression. She felt guilty that she didn't want to be near her son, but with the help of her husband, performed the physical necessities for the baby. By the time the baby was three months old, Jane felt much more warmly to him, and she and her husband began to enjoy him. One morning she found him dead in his cot, totally without any warning; he had not been ill and the post mortem revealed nothing.

Jane and Peter derived comfort from the parents' support group run by a social worker but after three months' attendance Jane was not simply very sad, but very angry at herself, irritable with her husband over the smallest inconvenience, unable to concentrate on anything and very pessimistic about the future.

It was arranged that Jane should see another social worker for sessions of individual and group cognitive therapy for depression, which involved individual sessions each lasting three quarters of an hour, once a week for three weeks. Simultaneously, Jane began attending group cognitive therapy, of 12 sessions, each of one and a half hours, at weekly intervals. There were six group members and the leader and co-leader.

The main criteria for therapy was that patients had been depressed for at least a month, and scored 20 or more on the Beck Depression Inventory (BDI, Beck et al 1961). The BDI is a 21 item self report instrument to measure the severity of depression.

In the individual sessions, Jane experienced considerable guilt over the way in which she treated the baby in his first three months of life. She felt that she was being punished by his death. She also felt considerable guilt about her hot temper with her husband, which on two occasions led to them physically fighting on the street and neighbours becoming involved. The early individual sessions were used to establish rapport and note important areas that had to be covered in therapy, whilst preserving Jane's confidentiality as far as other group members were concerned. The early group sessions were used to promote a general discussion of 'how you look at things effects how you feel'; this orientation was facilitated by distributing copies of Beck's and Greenberg's booklet (1974) 'Coping with Depression'. This article explains Beck's theory of depression and its symptoms, and the steps involved in recovery using cognitive therapy. In addition, the early sessions stressed the importance of being active and rediscovering past interests. The rationale presented was that it was only possible to get a sense of achievement and pleasure if activities were attempted (depressives characteristically justify their inertia on the grounds that they know they will not enjoy things, so there is no point in attempting them).

This roadblock to activity was countered by suggesting that the belief that group members would derive no enjoyment from an activity was, at best, a hypothesis which needed testing to determine whether the therapist's or the patient's worst predictions were correct.

The emphasis in the early sessions of cognitive therapy is on overt behaviour, particularly when depression is severe, but much of the time in the sessions is in practice spent by the therapist helping patients to remove the cognitive roadblocks to activity. As part of her homework assignment Jane decided to ring an old friend, and to go and visit an aunt. She was apprehensive about renewing contact with both people, because she thought she had let both of them down in the past. In fact, she was pleasantly surprised by how well she was received by both of them and enjoyed the contact.

In session three of the group sessions members were instructed to keep a diary of upsetting events: what had happened, how they felt and what thoughts went through their minds to make them so upset (these thoughts are termed automatic thoughts). It was explained that an important feature of therapy was to produce a rational response to automatic thoughts. Such rational responses may not produce much immediate improvement in emotional state, but they would, with rehearsal, be filed away at a non-conscious level and percolate through to a feeling level in time. It was possible to anticipate the sort of automatic thoughts that would cause problems for Jane because she had already completed the Dysfunctional Attitude Scale (DAS, Weissman and Beck and reproduced in Scott 1989) at the start of therapy.

The DAS contains 40 attitudes that are purported to predict vulnerability to depression. In Jane's case the dysfunctional assumptions included:

'If I do not do well all the time people will not respect me'.

'I cannot be happy unless most people I know admire me'.

'I am nothing if a person I love doesn't love me'.

'It is awful to be disapproved of by people important to you'.

'What other people think about me is all important'.

'Being isolated from others is bound to lead to unhappiness'.

'If people really knew what I was like they wouldn't like me'.

Patients' thought records are regarded as private between the patient and therapist. In the group the therapist will, however, ask the patient's permission to discuss a particular upsetting incident if it would be of general interest to the group or had not been satisfactorily resolved.

Jane had recorded that she often felt fed up just before going to bed because she recalled that she hadn't done her best by the baby and she was asked by the group leader if we could focus on that in the group. Jane agreed. The therapist suggested to Jane that this feeling depended on which video she wanted to play of her time with the baby. She could play video one of just the first three months and feel bad, or she could play video two of the last two months and feel good. This underlined for Jane that there were definite choices in how she viewed her interaction with the baby. The therapist suggested that perhaps the more accurate video would be a video three, an amalgam of one and two. Other parents in the group were then asked whether their experience of parenting was of a mixture of good and bad patches, or of uniformly good or uniformly bad patches.

Again, this served to highlight for Jane that she had used arbitrary criteria in defining herself as having been a 'bad' mother and that a consensus view of her mothering was very different from her own harsh standards. The therapist asked Jane humourously whether given the standard she set herself was she actually a God or a human being? Subsequently Jane would check her perfectionism with a question - What species am I?

Jane's material provides the opportunity to illustrate the various ways in which people process information to their own detriment.

The following faulty ways of processing information taken from Burns (1980) were presented:

1. All or nothing thinking

You see everything in black and white like the student with Grade A's who gets one B and then thinks he is a total failure. It 'will set you up for discrediting yourself endlessly. Whatever you do will never measure up.'

2. Over-generalisation

You expect uniform bad luck because of one bad experience. A shy young man asked a girl for a date. When she declined, he said to himself 'I'm never going to get a date. I'll be lonely and miserable all my life'.

3. Mental Filter

You seize a negative fragment of a situation and dwell on it. It is like wearing a special lens that filters out everything positive. According to Burns 'You soon conclude that everything is negative'.

4. Automatic discounting

One instance of this is the way we often brush aside a compliment: 'He's just being nice'. Burns argues that this is a destructive distortion. Usually a depressive hypothesis is dominating your thinking, some version of 'I'm second rate'.

5. Jumping to conclusions

Two examples are 'mind reading' and the 'fortune-teller error'. In the first, you assume that others look down on you without checking the validity of your assumption. In the second, you look into the future and see only disaster.

6. Magnification and minimization

Burns calls this the 'binocular trick' because you either blow things up or shrink them out of proportion. You look at your imperfections through binoculars and magnify them, but when you think about your strengths you look through the other end of the binoculars and shrink everything.

7. Emotional reasoning

'I feel guilty; therefore I must have done something bad' is a prime example. Your emotion seems to be evidence for the thought. It rarely occurs to a depressed person to challenge this pattern of distorted reasoning.

8. Should statements

'I should do this' or 'I must do that' are examples of the kind of thinking that makes you feel guilty rather than motivates you to do something.

9. Labelling and mislabelling

If the shares you invested in go down, Burns warns you might think 'I'm a failure' instead of 'I made a mistake'. Such self-labelling is irrational. Your self cannot be equated with any one thing you do.

10. Personalisation

You think: 'Whatever happens, whatever others do, it's my fault'. Burns says: 'You suffer from a paralysing sense of bogus guilt'. What another person does is ultimately his or her responsibility - not yours.

From a series of Jane's thought records it became apparent that she characteristically processed information, using 'mental filter' and 'personalisation', (processes three and ten on Burns' list). For example, one of her thought records referred to a New Year's Eve Party, which she said was ruined because a neighbour made a pass at her and she felt she must have done something to invite his attention. Upon further examination it turned out that she had quite enjoyed the party up to the point when the neighbour made the pass, that there was no evidence she had encouraged him and, in automatically blaming herself, she had neglected to consider he had already had quite a bit to drink.

A week or so after the New Year's party, Jane had become upset in a pub with some friends. As it drew near to closing time, she was 'persuaded' to invite them all back to her home for supper. She dreaded the prospect and felt trapped. As she and her husband and friends journeyed home, she began to feel angry with herself for not making an assertive response and her automatic thoughts were 'I have got nothing prepared, it will be a mess. If ever we go back to Mary's house everything is spot on. What are they going to think of me?' By the time the 'party' arrived at the house she was anxious and agitated and hardly joined in the subsequent conversation. This scenario made explicit two of Jane's dysfunctional silent assumptions: 'If I let people get close and really know me they won't like me' and 'I must do everything perfectly'. In therapy the therapist asked Jane whether or not there was any evidence that the 'party' disliked her or her supper. Jane conceded that there was no such evidence, she just felt that they 'must' be looking down on her.

The therapist used this material in the group to illustrate the problems that 'jumping to conclusions' and 'emotional reasoning' (processes five and seven on Burns' list) can cause.

Within four weeks of therapy Jane was scoring in the normal range on the Beck Depression Inventory. In cognitive therapy the largest changes in depression usually occur in the first six weeks and early depression scores are predictive of long term outcome (Scott 1988). Consequently, if there is not say a change from severe depression (26+ on the Beck Depression Inventory) (BDI) to at least moderate depression (20 to 26 on the BDI) one might encourage the client to consider an alternative or supplement to therapy. In Jane's case, had she not shown a clinically significant change by four to six weeks into therapy she may have been encouraged to consider taken antidepressants or for her and Peter to consider coming to cognitive behavioural marital therapy. The techniques of the latter are described in Scott (1989).

It is customary in cognitive therapy for therapists to schedule periodic booster sessions in the year following treatment.

In Jane's case she was fine at both the one month and three month follow up but at the six month follow up she was highly anxious, although not depressed - she had just found out she was pregnant. Both she and her husband were delighted that she was pregnant, but extremely fearful lest this child also became a 'cot death' casualty. Jane knew another mother in the parents support group who had had two 'cot deaths' and this fuelled her anxiety. In therapy Jane was asked whether she knew any mothers who had gone on to have toddlers after a cot death and she reported that there were a few who still had contact with the parents' group. Jane was again using a mental filter, to focus on the one tragic case of the mother who had suffered two 'cot deaths' but in addition she was predicting 'I just could not stand it if I had another cot death'. The therapeutic strategy was then two-fold:

1. to help Jane make the distinction between possibilities and probabilities and

2. to challenge a catastrophic evaluation of a second cot death.

With regard to strategy one, it was agreed that one was indeed more likely to have a further 'cot death' if there had already been one. But nevertheless, the chances were still no greater than the chance of being burgled in the next twelve months. Jane reported that she spent virtually no time worrying about being burgled.

(*Note:* If rational-emotive therapy (RET) were used instead of cognitive therapy in this case, the first strategy would be termed the inelegant solution and the second strategy the elegant solution. Within RET the elegant solutions are regarded as the major target, because they are purported to provide greater inoculation against life's viscititudes, whereas within cognitive therapy the bias is probably more to the inelegant solution.)

In addition, the hospital specialist had assured her that the new baby could be fitted with a monitor to register early signs of distress and enable them to take preventative action. Accordingly, Jane was instructed to use a set of coping self-statements each time she found herself worrying about the new baby: she was to say to herself 'it is no more likely that the new baby will die than that I will be burgled, I don't worry about burglary because it is so unlikely, so why should I worry about a new baby dying? A second baby dying is anyway much less likely because there are now monitors I could use'. If Jane found that the worry was nevertheless repeating itself she was to say 'I know what the answer to my worry is. I'll agonise about it in my worry half-hour, from 7.30 to 8 p.m. tonight. Half-an-hour worry a day is more than enough for anyone'. (The use of coping self-statements in this way is an example of Meichenbaum's (1985) Stress Inoculation Training and is particularly useful where difficulties relate to specific situations, such as intense anger arousal when a parent's sleep is disturbed by a child crying for attention). The therapist went on with Jane to consider her belief that she just could not cope if there were a further cot death. It was pointed out that the data suggested that she had already coped with a cot death and that, therefore, any betting person would put money on her coping with a sub-sequent cot death. Jane continued to have strong feelings that she would not be able to cope with another death but did nevertheless concede that there was a possibility she could cope, given her increased personal and social resources. After the birth of her second child Jane did suffer some maternal blues which she overcame within a few weeks. She very much enjoyed her child but became very anxious again as the child approached the five month mark, which was when her first baby had died. Fortunately all went well.

Cognitive-behaviour therapy and the client's social context

The cognitive-behaviour therapies offer a comprehensive approach to clients' problems. Stress Inoculation Training (SIT, Meichenbaum 1985) has been applied to problems with anger, anxiety, circumscribed fears, general stress reactions, preparation of patients for medical interventions, cancer patients, patients with chronic tension headaches, and as a preventive measure with a wide range of professional groups. Rational-emotive therapy has primarily focussed on the general neurotic patient, whereas cognitive therapy has been more specifically applied to depressed or anxious clients. Problem solving therapy has been almost as widely applied as SIT in addition to a detailed application in the treatment of depression. There is clearly some overlap between the target populations of the different cognitive behaviour therapies; how then does one choose which treatment is best for Mr X? This is not an easy question to answer, as the comparative studies between the various cognitive-behaviour therapies simply have not yet been conducted. At the moment therapists can only be guided by the practical constraints under which they are working and the clinical impressions of existing practitioners. From a practical point of view a therapy such as structural cognitive therapy is likely to be so time-consuming that, until its efficacy is fully demonstrated, a social worker is unlikely to consider it seriously as a therapeutic option.

The choice between say, cognitive therapy and problem solving therapy for treating depression is not an easy one to make, as there is empirical evidence to support both, and they involve similar time considerations. The deciding factor may well be whether the client is primarily reporting a long list of problems in living rather than low self-esteem, in which case problem solving therapy may be preferable. More generally the choice of therapy should only be made after a thorough psychosocial assessment. If we continue to use depression as an example, it would be important to know whether Mr X's depression was largely a product of high levels of dysfunctional attitudes, decreased activity and opportunities for enjoyment or the absence of a warm relationship in which he felt special. If the depressed Mr X had low levels of dysfunctional attitude (a low DAS score), then from a cognitive therapy point of view there is less material to work with, and a problem solving programme incorporating support elicitation skills training, for example, might be more appropriate. Similarly, if Mr X's depression seems to be largely a product of his distressed marriage, then provided his spouse is willing, cognitive-behavioural marital therapy might be preferred. Essentially, in conducting the psychosocial assessment one is returning to Bandura's (1978) model of reciprocal determinism and gauging the relative contribution of cognitions, behaviours and the environment (particularly the interpersonal environment) in promoting emotional distress. The particular form of cognitive-behaviour therapy utilised can thus be tailored to the needs of the individual client.

References

Bandura, A. (1978), The self-system in reciprocal determinism, *American Psychologist* 33, 344-58.

Beck, A. T., Ward, C. H., Mendolson, M., Mock, J., and Erbaugh, J. (1961), An inventory for measuring depression, *Archives of General Psychiatry* 4, 561-71.

Beck, A. T., Rush, A. J., Shaw, B. F. and Emery, G. (1979), *Cognitive Therapy of Depression*, New York: Wiley.

Beck, A. T. and Emery, G. (1985), *Anxiety disorders and phobias: a cognitive perspective*, New York: Basic Books.

Burns, D. (1980), *Feeling Good: the new mood therapy*, New York: William Morrow & Co.

Carmin, C. N. and Dowd, E. T. (1988), Paradigms in cognitive-psychotherapy, in Dryden, W. and Trower, P. (eds) *Developments in Cognitive Psychotherapy*, London: Sage.

D'Zurilla, T. J. and Goldfried, M. R. (1971), Problem solving and behavior modification, *Journal of Abnormal Psychology* 78, 197-226.

Ellis, A. (1962), *Reason and emotion in psychotherapy*, New York: Lyle Stuart.

Guidano, V. F. and Liotti, G. (1983), *Cognitive processes and emotional disorders. A structural approach to psychotherapy*, New York: Guilford.

Janov, A. (1970), *The primal scream*, New York: Dell.

Kovacs, M., Rush, A. J., Beck, A. T. (1981) Depressed outpatients treated with cognitive therapy or pharmacotherapy: a one year follow up, *Archives of General Psychiatry*, 38, 33-39.

Liotti, G. (1986), Structural cognitive therapy in Dryden, W. and Golden, W. (eds) *Cognitive-Behavioural Approaches to Psychotherapy*, London: Harper and Row.

Meichenbaum, D. (1985), *Stress inoculation training*, New York: Pergamon Press.

McClean, P. D. and Hakistan, A. R. (1979), Clinical depression: comparative efficacy of outpatient treatments, *Journal of Consulting and Clinical Psychotherapy* 47, 818-36.

Nezu, A. M., Nezu, C. M. and Perri, M. G. (1989), *Problem Solving Therapy for Depression*, New York: John Wiley.

Paul, G. L. (1967), Strategy of outcome research in psychotherapy, *Journal of Consulting Psychology* 31, 109-18.

Rehm, L. (1977), A self-control model of depression, *Behavior Therapy* 8, 787-804.

Ross, M. and Scott, M. (1985), An evaluation of the effectiveness of individual and group cognitive therapy in the treatment of depressed patients in an inner city health centre, *Journal of the Royal College of General Practitioners*, 35, 239-42.

Rush, A. J., Beck, A. T., Kovacs, M. and Hollon, S. (1977), Comparative efficacy of cognitive therapy and pharmacotherapy in the treatment of depressed outpatients, *Cognitive Therapy and Research* 1, 17-37.

Scott, M. (1988), An evaluation of individual and group cognitive therapy for depression and an examination of the process of change. Unpublished Ph.D thesis, University of Manchester.

Scott, M. (1989), *A cognitive-behavioural approach to clients' problems*, London: Tavistock/Routledge.

Trower, P., Casey, A. and Dryden, W. (1988), *Cognitive-behavioural counselling in action*, London: Sage Publications.

Williams, J. M. G. (1984), *The psychological treatment of depression*, London: Croom Helm.

Chapter 11

Psychodynamic Counselling

Michael Jacobs

The psychodynamic approach to counselling has long had an important place in social work, even if in some schools of social work it has at times come under criticism from those who only have time for a behavioural approach. By the eighties in Britain counselling (as distinct from psychotherapy on the one hand or advice-giving on the other) had achieved a high profile amongst most caring professions, including social workers. Approaches to counselling are strongly influenced by various parent bodies of psychotherapy, the two most dominant schools in Britain being the psychodynamic and the person-centred. Since psychodynamic ideas have also permeated Western culture, this approach to counselling frequently proves most appropriate and satisfying in the end, even though in the early stages of training the person-centred, non-directive approach is often attractive, with its apparently simple emphasis on conditions for change rather than on techniques and method, and with its confident humanistic faith in the efficacy of love and concern. In fact, the basic skills and conditions - that is, ways of listening, alternative types of response, and ways of relating to clients - are common to many counselling styles, and will not therefore be especially considered here. Practice teachers need to ensure that students have a firm grasp of the basic skills: that they listen carefully to their clients; that they consider their own responses, both implicit and explicit (especially to material which makes client and/or counsellor feel anxious); and that they show respect for and acceptance of the other person. Both person-centred and psychodynamic, as well as other approaches hold all these to be essential to the therapeutic process.

The psychodynamic approach is occasionally caricatured as having a rigidly systematic theory into which people are slotted; in fact, while psychodynamic counselling acknowledges the immense value of the accumulated knowledge about personality development and structure, built up as a result of working in depth with clients, this knowledge base is so immense that it is only by careful listening to each new client that some 'match' of understanding is possible. To begin with, however, students are likely to have a limited, and even unthought-out and unexperienced knowledge of theory, and they need to be aware on the one side of the danger of trying to make clients fit into what they know, and on the other side of the opportunity for change that is possible simply through listening to and learning from the client. The psychodynamic approach is ultimately so rich in possibilities for understanding that the counsellor requires as much 'information' as possible. Where the student shows the capacity to listen, to experience what it is like to be with the client, to remember, and then to record the sessions in detail, the result will be more 'raw material' with which to work, both in the sessions and in supervision.

The psychodynamic approach might be characterised as more than 'being with' the client; important as is the central relationship between client and counsellor, it is what this relationship means, and what it is saying about the client, that leads eventually to what is known as 'insight' - a type of knowledge of 'seeing' which comes from the combined use of heart and head. 'Insight', both in counselling and in supervision, makes an essential contribution to the process of change, whereby the central experiencing and observing 'ego' (the sense of 'me') is strengthened; or, in less technical terms, it is partly through insight that a client is enabled to assume a type of 'control' over inner feelings and reactions, a control that comes from understanding their force and their significance.

Because Freudian theories have been assimilated so thoroughly (and often uncritically) into Western culture (popular as well as intellectual) it is tempting to think that psychodynamic counselling is the same as psychoanalysis. While it owes much to Freud, students will need to understand that psychodynamic thinking has developed since Freud's day, even if they do not yet fully grasp the subtleties and distinctions. Most will have heard of Jung, and in the course of their studies will probably have gained some acquaintance with Erikson, Melanie Klein, Fairbairn and Winnicott, all of whom have taken Freudian ideas in different directions. While they will not be able to make a detailed study of these developments, it is important that students recognise the considerable changes and developments have taken place in the one hundred years since Freud's first published work. This will help prevent them from confining the psychodynamic approach to a few rather standard theories and techniques (and then, perhaps, rightly dismissing them as too limited to one culture at one point of history). More positively practice teachers may open up for their students the relevance of these theories, by pointing to examples of key phrases and concepts in their experience of clients.

Ridding the psychodynamic approach to counselling of stereotypical Freudian thinking will sometimes be necessary. Sex is not the sole cause of neurosis (but neither was it for Freud). Penis envy is not by any means obvious in all women, and is probably if anything rather stronger in men; women's envy of men's potency may have a more realistic basis in the way things are in our society. A single traumatic event in childhood is rarely sufficient in itself to explain a client's pathology; it is more often the subsequent responses to a single trauma, or more generally patterns of behaviour in the family of origin which make the major contribution to present misery. Instinct theory (with its implied pressure to find release for sexual or aggressive feelings) has by and large given way to the centrality of mother-father-child relationships in helping to explain how people have become the persons they now are. Catharsis, whether it is the uncovering of a long repressed memory and/or the release of pent-up feelings, is seldom now seen as sufficient in itself to effect permanent change. Transference does not simply mean that clients fall in love with their counsellor, but has widened to include the carrying-over of all manner of strong feelings into relationships, with counsellors, and with other significant persons; and not only in clients, but in anyone, including counsellors. It will therefore be valuable in supervision to explore with students their fantasies about the Freudian approach. Not only may this help some of the myths to be exposed and their misconceptions to be challenged; it will provide openings for attention to be drawn to later developments, and to other authorities within the psychodynamic field, as well as to some of the mistaken assumptions about what Freud or other writers actually wrote.

Yet at the same time, some of these earlier, simpler ideas, inadequate though they may be, provide somewhat easier ways of beginning to use the psychodynamic viewpoint to look at people and their personal difficulties. As long as their limitations are made clear, some concepts, such as id, ego and super-ego may initially present a clearer way of understanding the divisions within the 'self', and of the conflicts between different aspects of the same person: for instance, my powerful needs (id) come up against a sometimes equally powerful conscience (super-ego) and get pushed down; yet part of me still wants to find expression, and the resulting conflict within me (the self) helps me to understand why I (my ego) should be feeling anxious, frustrated, guilty, or confused. Using these terms may have much the same appeal as 'parent-adult-child' does in Transactional Analysis. But the appeal of such terms (which even now provide a useful description of intra-psychic dynamics) needs later to give way to the recognition that the Self is often split into many more than three parts, and that we carry around within us aspects not only of our early self, but also of others who have been important to us. In later psychodynamic theory expressions such as internal objects, internalisation and introjection help to conceptualise the exceedingly complex picture of what appears to be going on within a client's inner world.

Students may come close here to seeing what the term 'psychodynamic' is about, since it represents a way of seeing people as made up not only of many experiences, each of which has had some impact upon the person; but also of many aspects of self, some of them informed, if not actually formed, by these life experiences. They can begin to recognise that there is not only a dynamic relationship between people, whereby each contributes to the way the other relates to them ('it takes two to tango'), but that there is also a dynamic network of relationships within each individual, seen in the way the different parts of the self relate to each other. Furthermore, they need also to begin looking for ways in which this inner dynamic influences, and is influenced by the dynamics of external relationships. The internal dynamics will be seen at work in a variety of ways, but not least in the therapeutic relationship between client and counsellor. Given time, this external thera-peutic relationship may in its turn help to correct some of the most damaging aspects of the client's internal world.

The interrelationship between the internal world (that which goes on within the client) and the external world (that which goes on between the client and others) is seen in yet another interrelationship, known as 'the triangle of insight': here the triangle consists of three points, all connected within the one figure: past relationships, present relationships, and the counselling relationship. Connections may be made, as they are detected, between the way in which a client describes present relationships, and those which took place earlier in the client's life, which in the client's inner world go on influencing the present. Patterns tend to repeat themselves, in what may be seen as learned responses, but also in what a psychodynamic approach sees as an attempt to rework the past, in the hope that this time it may be different. Students will already be familiar with such phenomena as the cycle of deprivation; but there is more to the repetition of the past than this: each new relationship is often seen as a new beginning - this time, it is often felt, it will not go wrong. Yet it frequently does, because past assump-tions and attitudes once more interfere: sometimes it is the wrong person who is chosen, someone who sooner or later turns out to be a carbon copy of those who have failed the client before: sometimes it is the client who behaves in ways which are inappropriate, and tests the new relationship beyond its limits. Family histories are often full of such repetitions.

This bleak scenario stands more chance of being reversed given a re-sponse which refuses to be drawn into past damaging patterns. This can take place, given the right person, at any time - although there is no reason to assume that only counselling can provide a therapeutic relationship. Perhaps it is the capacity of a counsellor to step back from what is happening, to be more 'objective' than those directly or continuously caught up in the life of the client, which makes it more possible for the counsellor (and in turn the client) to survive many of the effects of the repetition of the past in the present.

Yet, paradoxically, the counsellor needs to be involved sufficiently deeply in the relationship with the client to allow the repetitions to take place at all. One of the most important parts of supervision of psychodynamic counselling will be the encouragement of the student to become fully involved in what the client makes the student feel and experience: only in this way will the student be able to reach some understanding (from experience, and not from theory alone) of the type of relationships the client currently has, and probably always has had. For example, one student was describing how a client walked out on her session, the client accusing the student of not caring. 'I felt a bit angry at that, I'm afraid,' she said. The supervisor assured her she need not feel guilty about feeling angry, and invited her to say more. This enabled the student to describe just how angry the client had made her. In turn this lead the student to remember how the client had been angry with her mother for not ringing her when she was depressed; and from that point onwards the student had a clearer understanding of why the client's mother might have reacted this way: the client had the capacity to make people feel very angry, and then would accuse them of rejecting her. The client's inability to accept her 'greed' for more and more led her to create situations where she could not even accept what she was offered. All this came from the student's ability to describe how the client made her feel, including a feeling of being simultaneously 'drained' and 'poisoned' by the client's venom. In turn this gave an opportunity to explain how Klein's theory of the 'bad', persecuting breast fitted this client's view of relations with others.

Students possess this capacity for involvement in what they and the client feel, since they often have a keenness and a freshness of approach which is eager to get immersed in the counselling relationship. Yet at the same time the supervisor will often need to pull the student gently back from too ready a response, or from over-identification with the client, in order to help the student to achieve the necessary perspective upon what is happening within the therapeutic relationship; upon how this might (often in subtle ways) be a repetition of damaging patterns from the past; and upon the particular features which the student may need to watch out for as the counselling proceeds. Only in this way will the student find the capacity to resist being unconsciously drawn into the client's all too familiar ways of relating. What is essential in psychodynamic work is that the counsellor provides the milieu in which past relationships can be repeated and can be re-lived, but with a new and more hopeful result. Yet the client may not always choose to stay with this milieu - the opportunity to change can present, at least initially, as much threat to some clients as it does hope. The angry client who walked out and rejected her counsellor, had she stayed, might have experienced intense feelings of rejection herself, from being with a counsellor who refused to comfort her physically because she was getting so upset. The client wanted everything 'made better', without having to endure any pain.

As already indicated, the counselling relationship represents the third point of the triangle of insight, connected with the other two points, past and present relationships outside counselling. These other relationships are re-flected within counselling, and at the same time changes that occur in patterns of relating within counselling are slowly translated into new ways of relating to others - currently, and within the internal world - the place where the past remains accessible and open to some degree of change. Given a client who is prepared to stay with what is often a disconcerting experience - for instance, with a counsellor who does not reject her when she gets angry with the counsellor, and who is still there the following week, even when she has walked out - change begins to take place.

None of this is straightforward, and students will learn that it can be a rough ride, and that clients can resist the best of help which is offered to them. Students will need considerable support themselves in coping with these rejections, especially since they are themselves trying out new ways of relating to clients, which might otherwise be seen as less immediately effective than, for instance, being directive and telling the client what to do.

The attempt to work in this way is further complicated by unconscious factors in client and counsellor - that a client should resist help which threatens to bring about real change can only be understood as an uncon-scious dynamic, because the client's conscious wish is to become better. To begin with, students will naturally veer towards the obvious explanation or the conscious meaning of a client's words and behaviour; they often find it difficult to accept unconscious meanings without thinking that in some way they are maligning their clients: for example, lateness, which an experienced counsellor will recognise as saying something (often negative) about the counselling process, is more easily excused by the student, as something that could not be helped. Understanding some expressions of feeling as masking other emotions cannot readily be accepted by the student until (quite rightly) he or she has more tangible evidence to confirm what to an experienced counsellor or supervisor is no more than an intuitive hunch.

The concept of the unconscious, essential though it is to psychodynamic theory and practice, is liable to mystification, although it can be relatively simply described as that which we ourselves do not often see, but which is more obvious to others. Counsellors sometimes make remarks which to them seem very obvious, but which to their clients are 'eye-openers'. The more experienced a counsellor becomes, the more readily can he or she perceive aspects of their clients which are far from obvious to the clients. Students therefore need to be encouraged to make use of their observations, feelings and hunches about their clients, so that, appropriately expressed, they can help their clients become more aware of the hidden aspects of their thoughts and feelings. Such observations are often simple, so simple that the student sometimes feels it would be too obvious to express them. But it is frequently a simple observation, much more than the deep and clever interpretation the student would like to make, which proves effective in making the unconscious conscious. If a student reports a response to a client (either a thought, or expressed directly) which sounds technically impressive but nevertheless makes little actual sense, it often helps to 'cut through' the jargon with a simple question: 'What would you *really* like to have said?' or 'What were you actually *feeling* at that point?'. As one experienced counsellor put it, 'I was trying to work out what sort of interpretation I would need to make to get him to take his dark glasses off. Then I thought, and said to him, "I'm feeling terribly uncomfortable with you wearing those things; I suspect you are feeling uncomfortable behind them." He took them off and we began to meet for the first time.'

So, too, practice teachers in supervision can in turn help their students to recognise that students also have blind spots (unconscious blocks) in their work with their clients, and that some of their ways of relating to their clients contain unconscious factors which need to become more accessible to consciousness. The more open a counsellor becomes to her or his 'unconscious', the more the counsellor will be open to what is hidden away in and by the client. The student whose client walked out colluded with the client by arranging an appointment for her with another counsellor in the agency, because the student did not recognise at the time how her own anger with her client meant she would rather not see her again. In reacting this way she showed how much the client also feared the strength of her own angry responses to apparent rejection.

Psychodynamic counselling places considerable stress upon working with the defences of the client, and their particular expression in the counselling process in what is known as resistance. Some patterns of relating are defensive, attempts (often successful) to keep feared feelings at bay. Those who cut themselves off from intimacy frequently fear either rejection or loss of identity should they try to make a close relationship. While the seeking of help is often a sign that defences have broken down, it is a commonly expressed wish that the defences should be set up again, and status quo be restored. 'I want to be my old self again'. Nevertheless, as far as the counsellor sees it, that something has gone wrong at all may indicate that some change in the client is necessary. Simply to return to the status quo is to continue to court difficulty.

The skills of confronting or challenging clients are partly dependent upon a willingness to speak openly, but also to phrase remarks gently enough for the client to hear rather than to turn a deaf ear. But psychodynamic counselling suggests a way of reaching to unconscious thoughts and feelings which takes defences into account, and works with them rather than attempts to meet them head on. It is important for the practice teacher to convey to students a sense of understanding the reason for defences: for example, when a client cannot speak of some event, feeling, or thought, the counsellor does not cajole or pressurise the client to 'spit it out'. Frustrating though it may be for the counsellor who is impatient to help, the counsellor recognises that a client who cannot speak about certain matters may be afraid that putting hidden thoughts and feelings into words will prove overwhelmingly painful, or in saying what he or she really feels, fears a response from the counsellor that is full of judgement and criticism.

Some students may prove too blunt in confronting, but most are sensitive enough to avoid causing discomfort and, if anything, err on the side of colluding with the defences which they see their clients exhibiting. They prefer not to confront lateness, or absence, or the denial of feelings which appear obvious to the counsellor. It is here that the practice teacher can effectively demonstrate the psychodynamic approach to defensiveness, which is to try to identify not only what feelings or thoughts might be hidden; but also the ways the client succeeds in avoiding acknowledging these to self or others; and what it is that makes it necessary for the client to do this. Supervision provides sufficient space for attention to be paid to these three aspects - the form of defence, the reason for the defence, and what is defended against. This can help students, rather than respond immediately to the client, to formulate alternative ways of enabling clients to take the responsibility of lowering their own defences, and so choose to express what they previously felt was inexpressible. Given the need for extreme sensitivity towards clients who have suffered abuse or sexual violence, the recognition of the importance of defences underlines the value of allowing clients to exercise control over what they reveal. Needless to say, while some defences are consciously employed, others are unconscious, and by no means deliberate. Learning that 'will-power' is not enough, that desensitization or bluntness is not the answer to defensiveness, and that the 'mind' is a delicate and intricate part of the person are all essential lessons in psychodynamic counselling. Resistances, including often the 'symptoms' which first introduce a person to a counsellor, have reasons.

Resistance is sometimes shown through the use and abuse of boundaries. Missing sessions, coming late or leaving significant material to the last minute, often indicate anxieties about counselling, or even anger with the counsellor. Boundaries are of crucial importance to the counselling process, and reactions by the client to time, to breaks in the continuity of sessions, as well as to the ending of counselling are full of significance: it is often in such circumstances that past reactions to losses of various kinds become more obvious. Both the application of boundaries, and also the way in which they heighten and intensify the whole counselling process, are two vital areas for students to understand, and indeed to incorporate into their practice. Practice teachers will themselves model the importance of regular and reliable times in the way they adhere to supervision arrangements, and themselves work with breaks in and endings of their own contracts with their students. Sticking to time, not giving more time than agreed without very good reason, staying within the professional boundaries that provide the essential security for very intimate things to be talked about - all these are essential areas of psychodynamic practice.

The reliability of the counsellor contributes to the building up of trust, the dependability of the counsellor to the necessary dependence of the client. Breaks and interruptions to counselling, whether unintentional or foreseen provide openings for counsellors to explore with their clients their reactions to change and loss, influenced as these are by earlier experiences of loss and disappointment. The failure of the counsellor to provide time and space when it is sometimes most wanted need rarely be an ultimate failure in the counsellor. An important part of the counselling process is learning to cope with the inability and even inadequacy of the counsellor to meet the client's needs, and yet an equally important lesson for the client is that the counsellor survives the effects of the client's subsequent feelings of anger and disappointment. Since students will themselves often feel inadequate as counsellors in meeting the urgent needs of some of their clients, it is all the more important that practice teachers assist them in recognising the therapeutic value of 'failure': often it is when the counsellor fails, and then helps the client to come to terms with that failure, that the client succeeds in taking significant steps.

The centrality of the counselling relationship has been a key feature of this summary of psychodynamic counselling. This centrality is seen in the phrase which Freud used to describe the relationship, a 'living laboratory', where, albeit in miniature, the client's past and present life is reflected. Much that has been referred to, such as the triangle of insight, and the use of the counsellor's experience of the client, shows examples of transference and counter-transference at work; students will benefit from going deeper into the recognition of their own experience with the client, to ask what that experience is telling them about the client, and relationships which the client may have had as a child or adolescent to parents and to significant others.

At the same time the student needs some help in distinguishing how far her or his own feelings about a client are to do with the client, and how far they are the result of the student's own past experience; this understanding of counter-transference helps reduce the possibility of confusing personal and client experience. The student whose client walked out also felt angry with the client because her behaviour reminded her of the student's ex-husband. This confusion of persons, which she recognised and which made her cautious about expressing any anger back to the client, partly contributed to her difficulty in seeing how genuinely angry the client had made her.

It is frequently in this central counselling relationship that theories of personal development will begin to be understood by the student, as the recognition of the phenomenon of the past in the present throws light on what the past has been like, or might have been like. The counsellor begins to realise that the very dependent client shows every sign of being like a hungry baby, desperate for the comfort of mother's arms and breast; or that the angry disappointed client is like the let-down child who cannot bring himself to show his need for comfort, even though he is longing to be held; or that the client who asks about others in the counsellor's life is like the child who feels some jealousy towards siblings; or the acting out client is like the adolescent who deliberately flouts the rules. Indeed, as the child or the adolescent in the adult begins to show itself, and to be re-lived within the relatively safer context of the counselling relationship, in all its pain and sadness and anger and need for love and need to give love, book knowledge about child development begins to make sense. The counsellor, instead of responding simply as an impatient adult to an apparently wayward adult, invites the client to use their adult self (their observing ego) to look at the experience of being the hurt and unhappy child, so clearly emerging in the relationship with the counsellor.

Past and present are so intimately bound up in each other that work with clients cannot help but illustrate the most relevant and enduring aspects of psychodynamic theories of psycho-social development - based as they themselves are upon the observation and analysis of client material. And such theories will also from time to time throw light upon puzzling aspects of client thought, feeling and behaviour. Students may find value in adopting, as a type of map for use in understanding where the client 'is' in developmental terms, the stages of development suggested by Freud or Erikson. Practice teachers will need to be alive to the predominance of male development in such models, and to the need to pay more attention to gender issues and differences generally than do these male writers. Limited though the terms oral, anal and genital may now be, in appearing to emphasise development as related primarily to libidinal pleasure attached to specific parts of the body, the stages of childhood to which such terms refer are important in the understanding of older clients. Erikson certainly extends the developmental map beyond erotogenic zones, and beyond childhood and adolescence.

Rather than clear-cut developmental stages, apparently negotiated (or not) once and for all, it is helpful to see development towards maturity as consisting of three (or four) major sets of themes, which are continuously worked and reworked throughout life, particularly at times of loss and change. These themes are related to childhood, but clearly have great significance for later adult life as well, just as the child lives on in the adult. Although our knowledge of childhood is always open to greater clarification and deeper understanding, these major themes in development often help the counsellor to identify possible emphases when listening, responding, focussing interpretations and links, and when considering how best to understand the present and future relationship with the client.

These pivotal themes are:

Trust and dependency

Particularly related to the first stage of childhood, when the baby is so dependent upon mother, these issues are characterised by problems in trusting, or depending upon the counsellor, either by distancing or by over-dependent and clinging behaviour; such difficulties tend to indicate experiences of deprivation or loss in infancy, although where the history reveals a relatively good initial two years such clients will often benefit from work with an experienced counsellor; understanding of this period of development is particularly important for working with borderline or psychotic personalities. Problems related to this stage tend to hinge around a basic sense of 'being' or 'not-being'. Clients with obvious and long term difficulties related to these themes are not suitable for those beginning counselling.

Authority and autonomy

These are more closely related to the second stage of childhood, where increasing independence and mobility brings with it questions of conformity to parental rules, standards and expectations, and where the slowly growing autonomy of the child might come up against authoritarian attitudes in parents, or in other powerful figures. In the counselling setting such clients may show undue reliance upon the counsellor's authority, want to be told what to do and how to behave, and show concern with how far they meet expectations set by themselves and others; alternatively they may be antagonistic towards authority, especially when those who exercise it show any sign of being controlling of them. Problems related to this stage tend to hinge around 'doing' rather than 'being'; or upon being recognised for what one does, or does not do, rather than who one is. While people showing obvious obsessional patterns of thinking and behaviour are not good clients for those starting counselling, helping clients towards greater autonomy often makes for rewarding work.

Competition and co-operation

These themes, which comprise apparently somewhat varied issues, all relate in one way or other to the genital or oedipal stage of development. They include questions about gender and sexuality (even though these issues are present in earlier stages); and competition and co-operativeness between and amongst men and women; as well as problems about rivalry and jealousy, three-person triangular situations, and issues about relating socially, in groups, work teams, etc. Acceptance of oneself, and by others (including by the counsellor), as a man or woman, together with a sense of the full expression of oneself which is not limited to gender stereotypes from family or culture, will form an important part of counselling clients in whom these themes are particularly important. Problems related to this stage tend to hinge around 'relating' rather than 'being' or 'doing'. Many of the most common relationship problems tend to centre around these themes.

Change and loss

To the above three themes it might be valuable to add this fourth theme which runs throughout life, and which cannot be as closely identified with any one stage as the other themes are. Personal development means continuous change; growth always implies some sort of loss, although its intensity and effect will differ according to the type of loss and according to the personal circumstances and disposition of the person at the time. It has already been recognised above that counselling involves the possibility of considerable change (almost inevitably involving the letting go of outworn but familiar patterns of being, doing and relating); and counselling involves the certainty of loss, since it sooner or later has to come to an end. Since students are normally on placements which mean endings are sooner rather than later, the termination of the placement, and what this means for the student's clients, needs always to be borne in mind by the practice teacher, whose awareness will then inform supervision, and the students' handling of endings.

The psychodynamic approach involves an attempt to understand the client on many levels at once. Attention has already been drawn to the interrelationship between the client's private inner world and the client's involvement (or lack of it) in the world outside the self; to the parallels between past experiences and present ways of being and relating; to the way in which the counselling relationship reflects (for those who have eyes to see and ears to hear) the client's relationships elsewhere, both in the past and present, and in the inner and outer world. The practice teacher needs to be aware, when following a psychodynamic model, of one further level which is of crucial importance to supervision, to the student's work, and ultimately to the client. Indeed it is the one way in which the supervisor makes a 'direct' connection with the client. This is the way in which a particular counselling relationship is always mirrored in some respects in the supervisory relationship.

Rather as an image passes through a complex series of ground glasses within a single camera lens, so an individual's personality starts with the early relationships in infancy and childhood, passes through changes in those relationships into adolescence, is often reinforced by later relationships in adult life, and in time comes to act also upon the counselling relationship - to which, of course, the counsellor also brings her or his own past and present experience. But the lens continues, since the light carrying the image passes on into the supervisory relationship too. As the supervisor becomes aware of the changing patterns of her or his own relationship with a student, of the different manner in which a student presents various clients, or the same client at different times, so the supervisor is informed, at one remove, of what might be happening within the counselling relationship, and within the client's inner world. At all times the supervisor's own inner feelings and associations are evoked partly by the supervisor's own knowledge and previous experience, partly by the student, and partly by the client. The dynamics of human relationships are so powerful that they carry over from one relationship to another, and from one period of time to another.

However, to counterbalance this, the growing psychological distance from the original events and relationships enables first the counsellor, and then the supervisor, to step back sufficiently far to monitor their own experience of the client (and, for the supervisor, her or his experience of the student); to get in touch with their emotional reactions, and then to use the resulting thoughts and feelings in an attempt to shine light back upon the client's inner experience.

If the practice teacher can help a student to become aware of the way in which all these factors constantly interweave in the life of the client, and aware of the constant repercussions that all of these factors have not only upon the various relationships which the client has, but also upon the student, and even upon supervision itself, perhaps the most important lesson about psychodynamic counselling will have been learned: on that basis, the student will be better able to develop a deeply therapeutic style.

Further Reading

For psychodynamic technique:

Jacobs, M. (1988) *Psychodynamic Counselling in Action.* London: Sage Publications.

For the application of psychodynamic theories about personal development:

Jacobs, M. (1986) *The Presenting Past.* Milton Keynes: Open University Press.

For further understanding of the psychodynamics of supervision:

Mattinson, J. (1975) *The Reflection Process in Casework Supervision.* London: Tavistock Publications.

Searles, H. (1965) 'The Informational Value of the Supervisor's Emotional Experiences' in *Collected Papers on Schizophrenia and Related Subjects.* London: Hogarth Press.

Chapter 12

Community Social Work

Stuart Watts

Since the late 1960s, there has been a debate within social work between the proponents of a client centred approach and those who favour a community based approach for the provision of social work services.

The strength of feeling about this issue emerged publicly and officially in the Barclay Report (1982). The Barclay Committee was set up in 1980 by the National Institute of Social Work at the instigation of the then Secretary of State for Social Services, Patrick Jenkin (the report did not include Scotland). The report affirmed the value of social service departments but proposed a wider conception of their role, including both the traditional work of *counselling*, but also *social care planning* where social workers provide help indirectly. It argued that social work should be informed by an attitude of partnership with the community. In pursuing these aims the report defined and advocated community social work as follows:

> By community social work we mean formal social work which, starting from problems affecting individuals or groups and the responsibilities and resources of social work departments and voluntary organisations, seeks to tap into, support, enable and underpin the local networks of formal and informal relationships which constitute a basic definition of community (Barclay 1982).

An opposing minority view articulated by Robert Pinker (1982) argued:

> Our present model of client-centred social work is basically sound but in need of a better defined and less ambitious mandate. Social work should be explicitly selective rather than universalist in focus, reactive rather than preventive in its approach and modest in its objectives. Social work ought to be preventive with respect to the need which

comes to its attention, but it has neither the capacity, the resources nor the mandate to go looking for needs in the community at large (Barclay 1982a).

An additional minority report, presented by Brown, Hadley and White (1982), argued that the report's main recommendation failed to acknowledge:

> the extent to which community orientated social work represents a significant departure from current practice (Barclay 1982b)

The Barclay Report was published eight years ago and since then there has been no concerted move by social service departments to implement its main recommendations. What has happened is a gradual polarisation between centralised teams, specialised by client group, and decentralised, generic patch teams which incorporate, to a greater or lesser extent, a 'community social work' approach.

What is community social work?

It has always proved difficult to formulate a precise definition of community social work. By its nature it involves a process of change from an existing model of reactive social care to what is described in the Barclay Report (1982) as 'an attitude of mind in all social workers from the Director of the department or agency to front line workers which regards members of the public as *partners* in the provision of social care'.

The key components of community social work are listed by Bennett (1986) as follows:

1. Community social work embraces the functions of a whole social work agency and should not be seen as ancillary to them.

2. It is based on collaborative working within teams providing services and involves working in harmony with both formal and informal social networks.

3. It focuses on the type and nature of relationships between the individual, individuals, families, organisations and groups and the community.

4. It recognises that the bulk of care, supervision, and control in the community is undertaken by members of the community ie parents, neighbours, relatives and other informal carers. These people constitute a vital part of the pattern of care and, in social planning, account should be taken of both their contribution and need for support.

5. It is proactive and resources are readily available to those in need. One major aim is that those disadvantaged by social networks and structures are encouraged to engage in new, more advantageous activities within their community.

6. It involves planning to help maximise effectiveness. Typically, this planning will necessitate continuous review of resources and needs in an area or community and an analysis of the interaction between needs and resources. Priorities and methods of work are based on this analysis and on judgments about how these various elements should relate to each other.

Bennett (1986) continues to clarify the components of community social work by also establishing what it is not and what it is moving away from:

Community social work is not the practice of 'a community social worker'; it is not the occasional project group / volunteer scheme tacked on to a predominately case orientated practice: it is not the same as community work. It seeks to move away from a model of professional 'cure' of individuals' problems, away from a service delivered by a group of otherwise anonymous workers organised in large (to the consumer) overly bureaucratic area teams; away from a service which is separated, organisationally, professionally, and in practice, from domiciliary, day and residential services; away from a service where the professionals know and are known only to 'clients' or to other helping professionals in the area.

On taking into consideration all these factors the exponents of community social work would say that it has the following aims:

1. to provide a visible and accessible social work service

2. to encourage local participation in defining the nature and style of social work services

3. to develop a wide range of methods of intervention which are responsive to needs in the community

4. to create and formalise links with other agencies

5. to establish networks of support

6. to develop appropriate community care projects and resources in collaboration with local groups and resources.

There are currently three main models of social work provision.

1. The client centred approach: a centralised intake team with supporting specialist teams serving a large geographical area.

2. The community social work approach: a decentralised system with out-posted generic teams serving smaller specific geographical areas and with a centralised headquarters.

3. A combination of the two where out-posted teams are made up of workers with an individual specialism to a greater or lesser extent eg 75% specialist/25% generic or 75% generic/25% specialist.

Though the providers of all three types of provision would argue that they provide an efficient social work service, the underlying principles and philosophy of 'the client centred approach' and the 'community social work approach' are, in practice, quite different. The third type of provision, the mixed approach, can incorporate a balance between the two, depending on how it is implemented. What are the main differences between the two approaches?

	Client Centred approach	Community orientated approach
1. Area served and organisational unit population	Area team 20,000 - 50,000 population	Patch team 5,000 - 10,000
2. Accessibility	Centralised teams not easily accessible to public; specialist teams do not have a communal base or responsibility	Localised patch/ neighbourhood teams offer easy access for advice, support, and information
3. Reactive/proactive approach	Team reacts to demands for services	Team takes part in creating services in partnership with local community
	Many third party referrals	Many client self referrals
	Usual interventions are at crisis level	Frequently involves early warnings of people at risk
4. Volume and allocation of referrals	Comparatively low demand with a high proportion dealt with by formal allocation	Comparatively high demand with a high proportion dealt with informally

5. Dominant mode of work	Routine treatment of identified cases using departmental or other service's resources. Many statutory cases	Treatment (as traditional) plus prevention using informal networks and community resources; fewer statutory cases
	Practice heavily influenced by bureaucratic norms, departmental programmes and monopolised by demands of individuals	Practice defined by community needs, service users' demands, and based on the concept of empowerment
6. Team organisation	Centralised, bureaucratic determination of the definition, nature and style of social work services	Local participation in defining the definition, nature and style of social work services
		Co-ordinated planning at local level
	Client centred approach	*Community orientated approach*
	Centralised management of resources	Locally managed resources
	Central budgets	Local budgets
	Central planning	Local planning related to local conditions
	Social workers deal with cases, ancillaries provide support and practical service delivery	Senior social worker manages patch team, responsible for overall service delivery; many cases dealt with by non-social workers
7. Supervision	Professional/ bureaucratic	By peer group and senior. Participation and entrepreneurial style encouraged
8. Professional responsibility	Worker responsible for solution to client's	Based on a shared responsibility with

	problems	local people, other statutory and voluntary agencies
9. Service evaluation	Only target of intervention is the individual; evaluation of service provision based on resolution of individual problems	Target is the wider community; evaluation based on resolution of community problems
10. Relationships with local organisation	Bureaucratic/ hierarchical	Direct, low level and informal; frequent.
11. Links with local networks and non-user services	Tenuous	Frequent and informal

If one examines these differences more closely it becomes obvious that to implement a philosophy of community social work within a department requires, as the Barclay Report (1982) urged 'an attitude of mind in all social workers from the Director to front line workers'. Major implications for this 'attitude of mind' are now explored under five major headings: area served, accessibility, proactive approach, organisational implications and professional responsibility.

Area served

A community social work approach requires complete awareness of the geographical/demographical area that is served, and commitment to research the problems that are associated with the area, the transport links, and the role and boundaries of other agencies eg DHSS, hospitals, health centres, schools, which also offer services to the community. This information is crucial in defining the community which an office will serve and the possible location of the office. It is easier to form links with a small defined geographical population of 5000 - 10,000 than with a larger population that is distanced both in terms of access and awareness of the social work service provided.

Accessibility

Accessibility to social work services is not only about the provision of local social work offices but also about publicising their existence and the services that they offer. It is about approachable premises and friendly buildings, rather than grey, intimidating monoliths with brusque receptionists, appointments systems, drab reception areas and claustrophobic interview rooms. Offices need to be inviting and client-friendly.

Departmental policies on recording also have to be looked at. Is it appropriate that everyone who calls at a social work/services office should have referral forms on them completed and thus be 'clientised' even though they may simply be asking for advice and information? In most departments this is the policy: the statistics that such recording mechanisms produce are then used as validation for the existence of the social work department and for demands for more staff. It is interesting that agencies which do not use such sophisticated recording techniques and do not have the same need to gain personal information, eg CAB offices and advice and information centres, tend to have become a more attractive alternative venue for people to visit rather than the more formal social work/services department. In a community social work setting the office or home need not be the only contact point between consumer and social worker. The community social worker has to be available and known within the community where he or she works. Contact points with consumers can be varied and take place in neutral venues eg on the street, in community centres, shops, schools, and playgroups.

Workers from statutory agencies are not the only providers of advice and information and are often the last resort for someone experiencing a problem in his or her life. Within most communities there are various forms of supportive networks involving a range of informal advice givers including postmen, milkmen, shop keepers, bar persons, ministers, childminders, playgroup leaders, all of whom should at least know of the existence of the social work/services department and the services it offers. It is essential that a community social worker develop these contacts.

Finally, access to social workers is also important to workers in other agencies, serving the same community. It is necessary for them to know the local social work/services department and be aware of the services the department can offer. A high community profile is therefore essential.

Proactive approach

The community social work approach is designed to be proactive; it aims to give early warning of cases at risk rather than simply becoming involved when situations have reached a crisis point. For example, social workers are frequently confronted with the possibility of taking a young person into care who (it emerges from the social history) has always been seen as a behavioural problem by his parents and the educational authority, though he or she has never been referred to the social work department. Similarly, we encounter an elderly person or family, with multiple debt problems about to be evicted or have their electricity cut off, saying, 'If only I'd known you existed before I probably would not have got into this mess'. Though this justification may seem simplistic, the community social work approach may overcome some of these crises. Because the social worker is available and has developed a 'street credibility' and contacts in the community, he or she is more approachable. Consequently, the number of self referrals increases and prevention, rather than crisis management, may be possible. Workers in other agencies can suggest to those who confide in them that it may be useful for them to talk to the local social worker.

Organisational implications

The provision of social work services to a local authority area is generally determined by centralised decision-making bodies, operating departmental programmes which frequently have to satisfy political demands. Such programmes, though proactive, will be influenced by central government policies and priorities. Thus additional funding will be targeted on client groups with a high national and political priority. Since local government services are heavily dependent on central government finance, central government decisions and priorities will influence the provision of local social work services, and a local community social work team may find itself confronted with resources, determined by central government, which it does not need and which may be unnecessary to service the particular community.

In a local authority area that comprises both rural and urban areas, the centralised decision-making body is always to be found in the urban area and, consequently, often imposes urban models of social work provision on rural areas which are totally inappropriate.

The community social work approach seeks to develop more local participation in determining the nature and style of provision of social work services for the community. This could be defined by local living conditions and perceived demands made by the community on the social work team. The social work department would then co-ordinate the planning of such services at a local level. This would involve the decentralisation of budgets to a local level and, consequently, the management of these resources also at a local level.

The decentralisation and local responsibility for these budgets can also encourage innovation, often the first quality to be lost in a newly appointed worker (given the traditional bureaucratic decision-making processes within local authority social work departments). This aspect is the 'entrepreneurial' part of community social work. Where local teams are allocated money which is not restricted by 'heading' or 'client group' it can be utilised immediately rather than having to wait for a request to go through the normal hierarchical framework, only to discover that there is no relevant heading within the existing budgets, or there is no money in that particular budget for the year, with a consequent delay. There are, of course, implica-tions for management structure in such decentralisation.

Professional issues and responsibility

Historically, clients have been allocated to individual social workers who are then responsible for a solution to the clients' presenting, underlying prob-lems. For the client there is often no choice in social worker and the only opportunity for change of worker is if the client complains. There has also been a tendency for social workers to become very possessive of their clients and see social work involvement as the only solution to the client's problems. The individual client is often looked upon as the only target for social work intervention at the expense of consideration of family networks and the community. Traditional social workers are likely to see the solution to prob-lems as lying within the individual psyche and therefore tend to deal with each case separately and privately. The community social worker would instead look at all the different systems that affect the client's perceived problem and from this position plan appropriate social work intervention. Community social work recognises that the social worker cannot work in isolation from workers from related social work departments or other agen-cies and that sometimes it may be more effective to utilise one of these other workers. The emphasis is therefore on a team approach and responsibility.

For community social work to be successful a continuity of contact between team members and the local community is essential. Through this meaningful relationships are formed and trust is developed with members of the community and staff from other agencies. It is interesting that studies (Simmons 1985) of community social work and patch work show that staff turnover is lower than in traditional teams. Social workers are also more committed and optimistic about their work and consequently job satisfaction is high.

Constraints on the implementation of community social work

The concept of community social work has emerged as *the* way to provide a social work service in all the major national reports on the provision of social services. Seebohm and Kilbrandon emphasized the 'one door' generalist approach in the early 1970s and Barclay in 1982 strongly recommended a community social work approach. It is therefore surprising that only a minority of local authorities within the United Kingdom are totally com-mitted to this way of working and the majority have moved or are moving to the alternative more specialist approach.

Why should such resistance to the approach occur?

Attitude of senior management

It is particularly interesting to speculate why there appears to be such reluctance at senior management level to implement a community social work since it also appears that field work social workers generally support such a philosophy. In discussing the move towards patch systems Hadley (1983) suggests:

> It seemed that experiences of the same kind of frustration with the inadequacies of the conventional model of team organisation were leading people in a wide range of different settings to come to some kind of conclusions about the changes that were needed.

It is possible that the reluctance of the majority of senior managers to move towards the community social work approach is related to the devolution of power and budget control that is inherent in such a system and the consequent loss of centralised power and hierarchical control.

It may also reflect the fact that the role of community social work does not naturally lead to the professional status that social work continues to seek.

Attitudes of other staff

While social workers engaged in community social work appear to enjoy high levels of job satisfaction (Simmons 1985) workers in traditional teams may view this approach with some anxiety: the principle of empowering clients involves workers in relinquishing power and the protection they might feel it affords them. Community social work also involves practice becoming more public and visible (Pithouse 1981) and more accountable to the community, all of which may appear threatening to some workers.

Evaluation of community social work

Because community social work is primarily a proactive form of intervention it is very difficult to measure its effectiveness. Whereas evaluation of the traditional reactive social work approach is based on the number of individuals who approach the social work department and thus become clientised, the evaluation of a community social work approach would have to be based on the number of non-referrals to the department or a negative referral rate. It is therefore unfortunate that traditionally the allocation of social work resources is related to increases in referral rates and high case loads. If one accepts this principle, a reduction in formal referrals and case loads, which is part of the ethos of community social work, could mean a reduction in resources.

Most social work teams are under-resourced, particularly in terms of personnel. Given the amount of statutory work faced by individual social workers there is often little time left for teams to become involved in an innovative community approach to problems. This leads teams into the 'if only we could' syndrome; 'if only we could start a parent-child behavioural group, an IT group, a group for single parents, a group for unemployed people, a young offenders group, we might prevent so many statutory referrals.' Here is a recognition that the community social work approach works, but unfortunately if a team which operates such groups is under pressure, it is these forms of proactive intervention that are the first to go.

The long timescale required

A team cannot develop a community social work approach overnight. First, one has to define the community, which is often a problem in itself as obvious demographic boundaries may be irrelevant to the people who reside there. The development of participating relationships takes time to develop and careful negotiation is needed.

Conflict of interest

If service provision is based on the needs and demands expressed by the community there can be a risk of unrepresentativeness with a bias to demands articulated particularly strongly by specific groups.

Conflicts of interest can emerge between community demands and local authority wishes and requirements. A worker, whose aim is to empower a local group, may find herself in opposition to her employing body.

The role of the department, the structure of a community social work team, and the authority, autonomy and role boundary of the worker have to be carefully considered and delineated, but the potential role conflict and ambivalence can render community social work a complex endeavour.

'Community care' and its relationship to community social work

The Griffiths Report (1988) and subsequent White Paper 'Caring for People: Community Care in the Next Decade and Beyond' (1989), though concentrating on those people who are affected by problems of ageing, mental illness, mental handicap or physical or sensory disability, builds on the recommendations of the Barclay Report. It emphasises a community approach to individual problems involving a close relationship between a variety of agencies offering services and a greater involvement of consumers, carers and their families in decision making about what services are provided at what times and in what ways.

The White Paper (1989) stresses the following objectives which are in common with a community social work approach:

— To enable people to live as normal a life as possible in their own homes or in a homely environment in the local community

— To give people a greater individual say in how they live their lives and the services they need to help them do so.

— To ensure that services respond flexibly and sensitively to the needs of individuals and their carers.

— To ensure that services allow a range of options for the consumers.

— To ensure that services intervene no more than is necessary to foster independence.

— To ensure improved access to information about local and national facilities including respite care and a greater involvement of patients, clients and carers in the development of services.

Finally, under the heading of 'Working Together' the report states:

There is no room in community care for a narrow view of individuals' needs nor way of meeting them.

The Griffiths Report (1988) also highlights the following areas as a pre-requisite for the implementation of community care: collaboration, networking and control.

Collaboration

The Report puts the onus on social work departments to ensure that the voluntary and local sectors are encouraged and stimulated to create new community initiatives. They must also ensure that local and voluntary groups are fully involved in both the preparation and implementation of plans for any new initiatives taken by the social work department and in the total management of community care services, *not* just in the delivery of a few special projects.

Networking

The Report stresses the need for adequate provision for the support of local community groups and for integration of all the resources of a geographical area/community in order to support the individuals within it. Social work departments must advertise the services that they provide in order to give informal carers information about immediate support. Another task for social work departments is to identify where informal caring networks have broken down or cannot meet the needs that are placed on them and decide what public services could fill the gap.

Control

The co-ordination of services to a community should as far as possible include the support of voluntary community groups. If there is conflict about priorities and between different groups any final decision should be made as locally as possible. It is essential that any services provided should meet the needs of the community.

Essentially these principles appear to have much in common with those of a community social work approach but there are considerable problematic aspects which may conflict with a true community social work approach based on the needs of the community and on the empowerment of its members. In particular there is the question of the adequacy of resources underpinning community care and there is the question of who will carry it out.

Problematic issues in the implementation of the Griffiths Report

The Griffiths Report (1988) follows in the tradition of Section 12 of the Social Work (Scotland) Act and the Barclay Report in advocating a role for social work beyond that of client counselling and service provision. It appears to implement the Barclay Report's recommendation that social work and social services are marginal to the provision of care in the community.

The role of the social worker is not automatically that of a direct care provider and it is often not necessary for a social worker to become an integral part of the process of meeting client needs. Instead the role is that of an outsider, a broker, who links those with needs to those who have resources to meet them.

Resources

The White Paper (1989) employs the principle of 'consumer choice' and 'empowerment' but nowhere addresses the mechanics of creating this consumer choice. It rather assumes that the existence of a variety of services automatically means choice for consumers. The White Paper reflects the government's belief in the application of market economics to increasing areas of what has traditionally been public service. It also reflects the belief that community care will be more effective if market forces operate to select and reward only services desired by the consumer. The crucial emphasis, however, is on financial efficiency rather than efficiency of service provision for the user.

The principal financial change under the new proposals is that money will be transferred from DHSS to local authorities but will not be specifically earmarked or 'ring fenced' for the care it is to provide. Community care will have to compete with other service demands for it. In reality there will be little extra money to underpin community care unless local authorities sell off services to free additional funds.

Otherwise the only extra money available will be

a) the transitional protection allowances given to those already in residential care.

b) the extra money the government calculates will be necessary to cope with demographic changes.

The timing or phasing in of these changes is uncertain.

Given this poverty of financing for community care, the choice for individuals needing care is likely to be restricted by shortages of resources, or by manipulation of assessment criteria governed by availability of resources. There is a danger that users may encounter the same problems with community care budgets as experienced by users of the Social Fund ie when they approach with a demand the budget has already run out.

Choice in market economics relies on the consumer approaching the services available in the market *with money*. They can then select the services *they* decide they require. Choice for the majority of users under the community care legislation will involve the local authority receiving money and providing or buying in services assessed as appropriate for the management of each case, thereby limiting the direct choice of any consumer. At the moment it is also not known whether or not there will be any course of appeal against individual assessments made by case managers.

Carers

The White Paper has assumed that there is a hidden army of willing carers waiting to become part of the community care network. Smale, (1990) in his address to the Association of Directors of Social Work, estimates that there are some six million informal carers in Britain, 1.4 million of whom devote over 20 hours per week to their caring tasks. If one compares the £200 per week that the Government is willing to offer to finance a place in residential care with the amount of benefit received either under the Invalid Care Allowance or the Attendance Allowance (with all the restrictions placed on eligibility for these allowances) there is little incentive to care for a relative at home.

The White Paper also has implications for the majority of reciprocal, kinship and neighbourhood ties which form the current 'delivery of care' in the community. How will a carer feel when the support they give freely to an elderly or disabled person is replicated next door as a result of a cash transaction? Will more people demand such payments, thereby increasing the strain on limited financial resources?

If they do not, how ethical is it, particularly for social workers, to collude with a situation which exploits the goodwill of informal carers generally women, to provide community care on the cheap? Finally, current demographic and economic demands require women, as 'surplus labour', to return to paid work to meet a labour shortage. Given that the majority of current informal carers are women, their return to paid work may result in the demand for residential places increasing rather than decreasing under the community care legislation.

Voluntary organisations

In the White Paper it is envisaged that there will be a much closer working relationship between social work departments, voluntary organisations and community groups both in planning and in the provision of services as a shared partnership. Voluntary organisations, though until now often grant-aided by statutory authorities, have been seen by consumers of services as independent of social work departments and therefore in the position to act in an advocacy role. However, the new relationship, where the local authority may actually sub-contract services to voluntary organisation could make them more dependent on statutory financial resources and, to some extent, they could lose their autonomy and perceived position of independence. This could lead to a change in the values of the voluntary sector service delivery in terms of integrity and the cost of provision of a service could take precedence over client's needs. If voluntary organisations lose their image of responding to the needs of the public and therefore cease to be one route by which the statutory authorities can discover what a community needs, a considerable part of the philosophy of 'empowerment to the people' contained in the White Paper would be lost.

These are just some of the potential problems involved in implementing the White Paper which the government has now decided to phase in over a period of years rather than implement totally in 1991. Again, the reasons for phasing appear to be based on financial and political decisions rather than on the overt principles on which 'Care in the Community' is supposedly based.

Conclusion

The original philosophy of the Griffiths Report (1988) can be seen to have many elements in common with a community social work approach.

There are a number of common objectives

1. Accessibility of services.

2. Active participation between consumer and service deliveries.

3. Inter-agency working.

4. Developing new initiatives.

5. Establishing networks of support.

6. Decentralised control over method of intervention and budget.

7. A proactive approach.

8. Services close to the community.

9. Flexibility.

However, the current priority of financial stringency is compatible neither with the principles of Griffiths nor community social work. Responsiveness to users' needs and consumer choice will be limited by inadequate resources and users and carers will be disempowered if cheap, unresourced care in the community is the only option. Case management seems to imply power of decision making by the local authority, rather than a response to the consumer's demand.

The Community Care Bill has major implications for the training of social workers and the reorganisation of existing service provision and management structures. The necessary changes require resources. It remains to be seen whether the implementation of community care is based on principles shared with a community social work approach or the current political preoccupation with financial stringency.

References

Barclay Report (1982), *Social Workers: their Role and Tasks*, Report of a working party (Chairman Peter Barclay), London: Bedford Square Press.

Barclay Report (1982) ,*Social Workers: their Role and Tasks*, 1st Minority Report of Working Party (Pinker, R.), London: Bedford Square Press.

Barclay Report (1982b), *Social Workers: their Role and Tasks. 2nd Minority Report of Working Party* (Brown, H., Hadley, R. and White, K. J). London: Bedford Square Press.

Bennett B. (1986), *Directory of Community Social Work Initiatives Scotland: An Introduction to Community Social Work*, London: National Institute for Social Work.

Caring for People: Community Care in the Next Decade and Beyond, (1989), London: HMSO.

Griffiths Report (1988), *Community Care: Agenda for Action*. London: HMSO.

Hadley, R. (1983),'Tapping Experience'. *Community Care*, March 31.

Hearn, B. (1989), *Community Social Work Exchange: Training for Care*, Issue No. 10 Oct/Nov. London: National Institute for Social Work.

Pithouse, A. (1987), *Social Work: the Social Organisation of an Invisible Trade*, Aldershot: Gower.

Simmons (1985), 'Becoming Part of the Network', *Community Care* August 8.

Smale, G. Address to ADSW, April 1990.

Social Work (Scotland) Act (1968), London: HMSO.

Additional Reading List

Beresford, P. and Croft, S. (1985), 'Whose Welfare?' *Community Social Work, Patch and Community Care*, Brighton Polytechnic.

Cooper, M. (1983) 'Community Social Work' in Jordon, B. and Parton, N. (eds.) *The Political Dimensions of Social Work*. Oxford: Blackwell, 146-163.

Hadley, R. (1987), *Community Social Workers' Handbook*, London: Tavistock.

Hadley, R. and McGrath, M. (1980), *Going Local*, London: Bedford Square Press.

Smale, G. (1988), *Community Social Work: A Paradigm to Change*. London: NISW.

Smale, G. and Bennett, B. (eds) (1989), *Pictures of Practice, Volume 1, Community Social Work in Scotland*. London: NISW Practice and Development Exchange.

Chapter 13

Working within the Life-Space

Colin Keenan

The concept of life-space

The concept of life-space derives essentially from practice and research undertaken by Fritz Redl and David Weinmann in the USA in the late 1950s and early 1960s but does not appear to have reached this side of the Atlantic until the mid-1970s. While the language of Redl and Weinmann (1951) has never attained a strong foothold in group care practice (with such terms as 'ego hygiene', 'milieu particles' and 'manipulation of the boundaries of self', that is perhaps less than surprising), the concepts underpinning it probably remain the most effective framework for the development of a coherent theory of social work method and practice in group care settings.

It was at the time, and remains today, probably the most successful attempt to break away from the value laden and ideologically based frameworks which have operated since the time of the Poor Laws and before. This notion of life-space conceives of the residential milieu as an organic whole within which is located a constantly varying set of systems and subsystems. The literature does not yield any operational definition of life-space, but for the purposes of clarity and comparison within this article, I offer the following:

> a therapeutic and institutional environment wherein residents or atten-
> ders enact both existential and historical aspects of their lives in the
> context of relations with each other, professional and other staff, their
> systems and sub-systems.

There has always been an ambivalent relationship with family care, with the group care environment being regarded as either a replica or a replacement of family life. 'The relationship, then between the family and residential care is a relationship riddled with contradictions. This is because residential solutions not only can remove prime responsibility for caring from the private sphere of family life to the public sphere of welfare and social work, but can also be a complete substitute for family life' (Davis 1981). Although it can provide for all the normal functions of family life, (parenting, identity etc) in group care these still take place in an artificial, constructed, environment so that normal family life can never exist in such a setting.

The idea of life-space transcends narrow notions of family by addressing itself solely to the nature of the setting in which residents in care live their lives and wherein professional social work intervention takes place. The extent to which the residential environment can or cannot encompass certain of the features of family life is incidental to the overall nature of the setting itself.

A life space formulation can also transcend other 'models' deriving from custodial, militaristic, or educational assumptions as it is essentially therapeutic and goal oriented in its conception and concerned with the whole of that environment in its own right. It has been created out of group care practice experience and is only very tangentially concerned with comparisons with other social work settings.

Within the student training context, group care placements have moved on from family based assumptions, but the extent to which they have matured into providing a conceptual basis of their own, must only be regarded as partial. There remains a tendency to translate out of other models more familiar to fieldwork. These include both individual casework and different approaches to, and methods of, groupwork as well as some community work assumptions. Life-space work is neither individual casework nor group work, nor even individual casework conducted in a group context, but a therapeutic discipline of its own.

The fact that there may be a substantial overlap in the area of skills and techniques does not gainsay the implications of the fundamentally different context in which they are deployed.

The characteristics of a life space milieu comprise the following elements:

Social structure

The life space is a mini society in its own right. No matter how well it is integrated with the society in which it is located, it has a cultural life of its own. Redl (1959) once wrote that it was more of harem society than a family one, in the sense that there are generally more women than men care givers and that caring roles in respect of any one individual resident/client were carried out by a number of different professionals. Personal and familial life cycle events such as beginnings, endings, arrivals and departures all take place in this context.

It is by no means uncommon for an old people's home to experience several deaths in the space of one week or for a childrens' home to have a number of admissions and discharges in a similar period. These and myriad other major experiences become part of the routine experience for all (staff as well as residents) who are part of the life-space. The frequency rather than the magnitude of such events makes the life space experience very different from the familial one. Families experience arrivals and departures, crises and bereavement, but seldom (because of scale), on anything approaching the frequency with which these take place in a residential establishment.

Within the care giving group, there is also a pecking order which derives from both formal structural authority and informal considerations such as personal authority, popularity and experience. Routines and rituals are part and parcel of the cultural regime of any given establishment but, at the same time, the resident's experience will be of differing interpretations and applications of these according to the personality and individual value system of each particular care giver 'the sequence of events and the conditions under which people undergo certain repetitive manoeuvres . . . can have a strong impact' (Redl 1959). This implies that although one might expect a degree of standardisation of the daily routines of an establishment the impact these will have on residents will vary according to both the life history of the resident and the individuals within any staff group who operate them. Bedtime, when one member of staff is on duty, can vary significantly, in the experience it affords residents, from the same routine operated within the same normative structure by a different worker. Furthermore, that variability will, of its own right, produce additional experiential dynamics to impact upon the resident.

There is a sense in which the immediate environment in meeting dependency and caring needs has a significant effect on the sense of self or identity of those within it. The life space can, therefore, constitute an intense cauldron of experiences which impact on the selves of its residents.

An institutional context

All residential establishments are institutions and subject therefore to the processes and dynamics of institutions. The extent to which any one establishment is or is not a total institution is incidental to the fact that it remains an institution at all. The concept of 'total institution', perhaps because of the prevalence of Goffman's work (1981) in this area, is frequently mistaken for that of institutions per se. Whereas all residential establishments are institutions, by no means all of them can be seen as total institutions. The process of institutionalisation is more subtle and profound than that indicated by Goffman in *Asylums*. What he identified in respect of total institutions in the arena of 'batch handling', or 'stripping away of the outside world' is beyond dispute and residential establishments which produce these features are likely to be total in character. Other residential establishments will not produce these at all, but will still be institutions. While different institutions have their own unique cultures and sub cultures and some (eg voluntary care day centres) are likely to be less 'total' in character than others (eg secure units) such cultures and sub cultures remain institutional in nature.

Polsky (1962), writing of his research findings in an establishment for delinquent male adolescents, demonstrates the primacy of the resident subculture over others.

'Like adolescents the world over, the boys in Cottage 6 experiment with the roles and values that are integrated into a youth culture. Delinquent boys want to be free from adult controls as do all adolescents. Because of their histories and staff accommodation, they evolve a social organisation built upon force and manipulation.

A pseudo-environment is thus constructed between two social systems (staff and resident) in a common interactional field . . . the two systems are extraordinarily independent of each other, yet complementary' (p.149).

The content of the boys' delinquent, authoritarian sub-culture owes much to their previous history and experience, but the existence of independent, complementary cultures for residents and staff is central to the life of all institutions. It is in the nature of residential institutions that they produce this tension between the two principal cultures. As the size of the institution increases, the disparity between the two cultures is likely to increase while, at the same time, the number of different sub cultures and sub cultural sub systems is likely to increase. These operate on worker and resident alike. A significant danger in this, as demonstrated by the work of Menzies Lyth (1988) is that workers become so enmeshed within their own cultural systems that they become blind to the existence, or despondently accepting, of those operating within the resident group.

All cultures have their own rituals and the rituals of institutional life not only vary in nature from those of the 'outer world', but because the context is different, the meaning and significance they hold for residents and workers is likewise different from the outside. Meals and bedtimes, and the conditions of coming and going are cases in point.

There is frequently a time scale dimension to the structure of institutional life which ranges from admission and discharge to more subtle aspects of seniority and status. The group care life-space is, however casual and informal in its ethos, a formal, permeable organisation. It is therefore an inescapable fact of life in such a context that there will be a tension between the needs of the individual for personal space, choice and the expression of individuality and that of the organisation towards standardisation, impersonality and 'efficiency'.

The scale on which many residential establishments operate (many old people's homes still serve upwards of thirty residents with almost the same number of full and part time staff in different roles) extends a highly complex interplay of inter- and intra-group processes and dynamics. These necessarily impact upon the lives of residents as well as the 'intended' caring and interventive processes which go on within the life space. This is true of all the above structural and institutional considerations.

Institutionalisation is the product of life in such an environment and because of the complexity of this, traditional views about it which focus only on the simple erosion of, or lack of opportunity to develop, certain social and coping skills can be regarded as true but dangerously simplistic. Life in such an environment with all its splits and potential splits impacts on the inner world of the resident. The idea of complete consistency of response to any resident is no more possible in a residential setting than it is in most families. But, because of the scale of the operation (most establishments are bigger than most families) as well as its complexity, inconsistency and 'mixed messages' abound in even the best managed establishments. A degree of dependency is present in all resident worker relationships. The dependency needs of the resident towards the worker can be easily understood but the counterpart of those of worker on resident are less easily acknowledged. It is nonetheless of major importance to any true understanding of the dynamics of institutionalisation that these are considered. They contain elements of transference and counter transference (see Brearley and Jacobs in this volume) and more. Consciously and unconsciously, such worker to resident agendas as need for approval, ambivalence about authority, or difficulty in living with the physical intimacy implicit in the bathing and toileting of others, produce adaptive and maladaptive responses which are picked up by residents at subliminal and sometimes more conscious levels.

Frequently, workers and residents will form collusive relationships against other workers and residents. The outcome of this is a climate where both staff and residents can play one off against another. While the extent to which this occurs is variable, I have yet to see a residential establishment where it did not happen at all. I am tempted to argue that it is endemic. A resident whose request is met by a consistent series of 'no's from one shift of staff may well find a collusive 'yes' from a member of the next. This sort of split is at the heart of the process of institutionalisation. In the context of resident to worker dependency, constant exposure to splitting of this type can frequently lead to a position where the resident begins to substitute manipulation for the more painful business of sustaining close relationships. This is a sort of deprivation in that true caring and sustaining is blocked off by the manipulation of transactions, thereby depriving the resident of the caring we all need to sustain self and to face reality. The process of splitting is explained in greater depth by Gibson and Brearley in this volume.

When a resident is socially and emotionally dependent on an institutional outer world, it is very easy for him or her to incorporate such splits, but his or her capacity to sustain adult relationships characterised by give and take rather than take/take can be eroded. Lack of opportunity to make choices and live through their consequences results not only in the loss of decision-making skills but can erode confidence, assertiveness and ultimately in some cases the capacity to distinguish adequately between reality and fantasy. The nature of institutionalisation is therefore insidious and to be fully understood requires a knowledge not only of social learning theory but of psychodynamics. The sort of institutionalisation which produces an ignorance of the price of a pound of mince, or the inability to cook it, is serious enough, (although ultimately easily counteracted by simple skills training), but the kind which leads to emotional impoverishment through splitting is both far more insidious and much less amenable to simple remedial intervention because inner world process is always harder to engage with than that which is more conscious.

Practice within the life-space (see *Life Space Interview* below), must therefore accommodate the impact of all these features on the lives of residents and workers alike as well as on the helping relationship.

Targets for intervention

As good life-space practice is goal oriented, there must be reason and purpose as justification for residence. There is a richness and complexity to what must be managed in the process of helping and assisting in change and growth for clients. 'Casework' approaches borrowed from field settings, applied in the life-space situation, are not, however expertly they are undertaken, anything like enough to engage with the variety of systems at work.

Workers need to be able to influence the resident sub-culture as much as the agenda of the staff systems. Individual lives are lived out in that context and effective intervention must engage with the person-in-situation configuration. Dealing with the person in ignorance of the context and situation is pointless. While an active understanding of the structural and institutional dynamics is relevant to the social, structural and institutional aspects of that configuration, the situational dimension requires something more. A valid grounding in the sociology and social psychology of social systems and institutions may cover the structural and institutional, but the situational needs an amalgam of developmental and group dynamic approaches. In particular, the process agendas of worker to resident needs and the consequent requirement for self awareness constitute crucial areas for student supervision.

Systems within systems

Just as the resident and staff sub cultures operate within the context of the wider institution, there exist both groups and sub groups within these larger groups. In addition, both staff and residents generally have lives which predate their beginning in the institution and which also operate outwith its boundaries. These systems within systems can also have a profound effect on the functioning of residents. The extent to which they are open to intervention may be variable but this does not in any way alter the effect they can have on how a resident or group of residents may function. Generally speaking, such effects are of two sorts: *direct and indirect*.

Direct

A family crisis in one resident will have an effect on him/her which will be determined by previous life experience and its influence on coping mechanisms. This in turn may have a 'knock-on' for the other residents according to how that resident handles the crisis. It can become a direct variable on his life-space as well as the other way round, eg how he reacts can influence the life-space and how the life-space is can influence how he copes. That is a direct two way relationship. To engage with it the worker needs to understand the dynamic interplay between past and present in the resident's make up, the nature of defences, such as projection, displacement and reaction formation (see Brearley and Gibson in this volume) as well as the determinants of group functioning such as the stages of its life cycle and common dynamics such as scapegoating and mascot creation. The other crucial element is, of course, the worker/resident relationship.

Indirect

That same family crisis can set off echoes of repressed painful past experience in other residents who then act this out according to their own experience and pathologies. In this there may also be an interplay between the individual actors and the wider systems with which they interface. Workers are by no means exempt from this process and frequently act out the pathology of their residents. A resident who is actively ambivalent about male/female aspects of his or her familial experience can trigger off such splits in other residents as well as within the staff group. Therefore, to sustain professionally effective relationships within the life space, the worker requires a high level of self awareness about where within his/her own life such reactions derive, as well as a good working knowledge of how such processes can interact with each other.

The life space interview

Redl and Weinmann's formulation of the life space interview (Whittaker and Treischman 1972; Redl and Weinmann 1951) starts from the premise that life space intervention depends on 'the clinical exploitation of life events' with the broad term 'exploitation' referring to the network of goals and sub goals that therapy, which is the raison d'être of the resident's stay, seeks to achieve. It has frequently been described as a framework for 'therapy on the hoof'.

It comprises the following elements:

a. Reality rub-in

As I have argued, the life-space is a confused and confusing environment, the impact of which upon residents can be to produce a 'delusional' system of life interpretation. The abnormal in 'real' terms can seem normal in the life space. In addition, many people find themselves in institutional care in the first place as a result of confusional states, (eg elderly people), lacking the ego strength to distinguish adequately between reality and fantasy (eg emotionally disturbed children) or clients with cognitive problems (eg people with special learning needs).

In terms of goal, intervention of this sort is both short and long range in intent. In the short term the resident is presented with an accurate dose of reality, (we want to correct a particular distortion, perhaps to aid communication). In the longer term, he/she is quite likely to require 'multiple exposure' through the repeated injection of such intervention. Reality orientation can broadly speaking be considered as a form of reality rub in, but the function of reality rub in is broader and more flexible than reality orientation in that it can be included in other goals, eg behaviour modification, or counselling. Perhaps more importantly, it can be used to help people face the consequences of their actions. In such situations, it is just as capable of having applications in a group context as for a particular individual.

b. Symptom estrangement

Many clients in residential settings have arrived there as a consequence of behaviour that wider society finds unacceptable. In many cases, they themselves do not find that behaviour to be problematic but ' . . . have invested heavily in secondary gain activities to such an extent that the whole ego seems to be allied with their central pathology rather than any one part of the ego taking a stand against it. While this does not mean that the whole ego is sick with the same disease that we are trying to cure, unless its "uninfected" part can be "estranged" from the core pathology and converted into an allegiance to seeing that something is wrong, the battle cannot even get started' (Whittaker 1972, pp.242-3). Put simply, clients can become so 'stuck' in a particular role or set of maladaptive behaviours, that this can take over their personalities to the extent that their healthy, coping parts become hard to reach.

The technique consists of patiently finding and then nurturing the healthier parts of the personality to work against the maladaptive ones. The residential environment is particularly suited to helping because of the opportunity it provides for the worker for access to the client at all times of day, in different moods, and in a range of settings, situations and sub settings.

Harry (13) saw himself almost entirely as a professional thief, a role actively encouraged by his father, and had established what was for his age a very expensive life style which was funded by the proceeds of his breakings and enterings. He was also a persistent and embarrassed bed wetter. Embarrassment about the bed wetting opened up the underlying hurt and sense of rejection he felt from mother. Staff were able to help him to recognise that stealing and the 'flash' life style represented an attempt to gain friends to substitute for mother and was no more or less worthwhile than bed wetting, as both were really about the same thing. The bed wetting and its attendant embarrassment were healthy (to an extent anyway), and were focused on to 'estrange' the stealing.

Sometimes disabled or handicapped people see themselves as worthless and unable to cope in areas of their lives which are not related to the handicap at all. By challenging them and supporting them to maximise what they can do, a healthier sense of self can develop, so that they can see themselves as more than just the sum of their disabilities.

c. Value repair and restoration

Some clients have become socialised into maladaptive, helpless, disruptive or patently anti-social behaviour. The nature of residential life is such that it can (subject to constraints mentioned above), offer opportunities for modelling, managing, and education in the area of values. This may be needed in the process of 'normalisation' for example. There are, of course, obvious dangers of workers imposing their own values on dependent, malleable or needy clients. The values restored therefore need to be consistent with professional ethics rather than the idiosyncratic interpretations of right and wrong of any particular worker. CCETSW Paper 30 (1989) is helpfully explicit in the area of professional values.

d. New tool salesmanship

This quite simply refers to the social skills learning dimension to life-space work. A large part of the task is to assist residents to abandon old ineffective or inappropriate behaviours for new constructive and effective ones. This is necessary for two reasons. First, because the setting is institutional and can lead to the loss of, or failure to develop many every day social skills, there is a need to provide an antidote to that aspect of institutionalisation.

Second, it is common for people who have found their way into residential establishments to have poor levels of social skills from the outset. Given the pervasive influence of the sub culture (see above) it is crucial that care plans provide for the teaching of such skills.

As all change, even for the better, entails loss and because the adaptation to loss is a form of mourning, it is crucial that the processes of loss and change are allied to such salesmanship. Given that a known part of adaptation to loss in mourning is the idealisation of what has been lost, there is a danger of the sub culture making forbidden fruit taste very sweet indeed and sabotaging skills development. There is a correlation between 'closedness' and 'openness' in the extent to which regimes foster the existence of such sub cultures. The more closed or total in character the regime, the greater the propensity towards a strong resident counter culture. A recognition of the importance of sub cultural influences is therefore central to an understanding of what can be 'sold' as well as how and when this can be most effectively achieved.

e. Manipulation of the boundaries of self

The effects of the residential environment on the 'self' have been powerfully documented by Goffman (1981), Miller and Gwynne (1979), Townsend (1964), Berridge (1987), and King, Raynes and Tizzard (1971). they fall into two broad camps characterised by Davis (1981) as 'optimists' and 'pessimists'. Both recognise the influence of the life-space environment but the pessimists look more towards its corrosive potential on the sense of self of the resident. Anyone with a poor sense of self is vulnerable to 'invasion' by the confused and confusing abnormality of the life space existence. The interplay between the pathology of the individual and the nature of the life space is discussed above. It is crucial that the worker recognises the dynamic relationship between the sense of self and the environment it inhabits. It follows, therefore, that as much autonomy and opportunity for choice as is possible should be afforded to every resident, because it is by these means that self is nurtured and sustained. By influencing the environment, the worker is able to influence the self of the client within it.

Joe (79) was an isolated old man who, prior to admission had a fairly severe drinking problem. At the root of this was a poor level of self esteem. He had lived alone and drank alone. He was totally dependent on home help and other domiciliary services to get by in the community. He took virtually no decisions and had little opportunity for making choices in his life before admission. In care, he was helped to make choices about what he wore and when he went out and in, what he ate and with whom he associated. By being skillfully guided in these and other choices, he slowly grew in self esteem as some sense of relative values came back into his life. This in turn affected his need to drink and, as time went on, the raised self esteem allowed the drinking to return to manageable proportions.

Clearly, these life space interview headings from Redl and Weinmann (1976) constitute a useful formulation for much of the activity that is conducted within a residential environment, but it is important to remember that these are a mere beginning. All other aspects of basic social work values and skills must still pertain as much in the life-space as in any other setting. Central value issues like non-judgemental attitudes and anti-racism transcend considerations of setting. If the central task of the social worker is conceived of in terms of forming and sustaining relationships with individuals and groups towards an agreed end of change, then what is done within the life space has far more in common with practice in other settings than may at first be appreciated.

Conclusion: the student in the life-space

Students, and to some extent their tutors, display an occasional inclination to regard 'residential work' as some sort of esoteric specialism or, worse, as a lower form of the social work art. As a consequence of this, it is not unusual for both to approach a group care placement as something to be 'translated out of the fieldwork'. They bring 'fieldist' assumptions with them. In addition, the student, like any newcomer to the unit, will experience to some extent all the strangeness and deprivation of entering a new world. While responses to this, just as with new residents, will vary according to personal experience and personality, there are certain commonly repeated phenomena.

a. The 'Tell me what to do and I'll do it' syndrome

This refers to the uncertainty held by the student about the intangibility of the setting. In fieldwork certain roles and tasks are easily defined, eg interviewing for and writing a report for the court or panel. In such situations it is relatively easy for the student to understand what it is he or she has to do and why he or she should be doing it. Cases are allocated and the case itself suggests (albeit in many cases after a painful period of supervision!) what the appropriate roles and tasks commensurate with it are. In the life-space, many of the tasks are less tangible and those which are tangible (eg assisting with meals, dental appointments etc) are generally heavily rooted in primary care functions and harder for the novice to connect with his/her conception of 'real' social work. The risk here is two-fold; either the student gets involved in the primary care as a displacement at the expense of the more therapeutic aspects of the role, or fails to connect the potential of the daily minutiae with wider therapeutic goals.

b. The 'I'd rather be a fieldworker/counsellor' syndrome

Some students are disabled by the complexity of the life-space and hold onto a fieldwork/individual case work model where they conceive of their task as the provision of individual counselling to one resident at a time, sometimes even in an office setting. They often try to create a role for themselves more akin to that of an 'attached' fieldworker rather than a main grade shop floor worker. Such students lack a basic appreciation of the richness and therapeutic potential of the life-space and can sometimes be regarded as regressing to, or fixated at an earlier, safer level of functioning. A variant of this is 'if it's not individual work, then it must be groupwork' where the focus is on setting up groups for this, that and the next thing. This is a different form of the 'I'd rather be a fieldworker' syndrome, but the underlying defensive dynamics are generally the same.

c. The 'hardly anybody here's qualified' syndrome

There are some students who conceive of the social work task almost exclusively as case management and, regarding themselves from a part qualified position to have more expertise than experienced, but unqualified colleagues, see their role as directing (however nicely that is done) their colleagues as resources at their disposal in the overall management of the 'case'. In a sense, this is like an attempt at pre-qualifying level to engage with what are essentially management agendas.

This, too, is an unproductive defence. The student needs to engage with the reality that teamwork is required and that he/she needs to negotiate entry to and membership of that team. A new member, however gifted, (and one who relies on such a defence is unlikely to be particularly gifted) is unlikely to join the team in a leadership role without the peer credibility to justify it.

There are, of course, other defensive games and syndromes but the above are very common. While they need to be regarded as natural, in the sense that all defences are ways of dealing with anxiety, persistence with them to any significant extent can hardly be indicative of adequate attainment.

References

Berridge, D. (1987), *Children's Homes*, Oxford: Basil Blackwell.

CCETSW (1989) Paper 30: 'DipSW: Requirements and Regulations for the Diploma in Social Work', London: CCETSW.

Davis, A. (1981), *The Residential Solution*, London: Tavistock.

Goffman, E. (1981,) *Asylums*, Harmondsworth: Penguin.

King, R. D., Raynes, N. V. and Tizzard, J. (1971), *Patterns of Residential Care*, London: Routledge and Kegan Paul.

Klein, M. (1960), *Our Adult World and Its Roots in Infancy*, London: Tavistock pamphlet.

Menzies Lyth, I. (1988), *Containing Anxiety in Institutions*, London: Free Association Books.

Miller, E. and Gwynne, G. (1978), *A Life Apart*, London: Tavistock.

Polsky, H. W. (1962), *Cottage Six - The Social System of Delinquent Boys in Residential Treatment*, New York: Russell Sage.

Redl, F. (1959), 'Strategy and Technique of the Life Space Interview', *American Journal of Ortho-Psychiatry*.

Redl, F. and Weinmann, D. (1951), *Controls from Within*, New York: The Free Press.

Townsend, P. (1964), *The Last Refuge*, London: Routledge.

Whittaker, J. K. and Treischman, A. E. (1972), *Children Away from Home*, Chicago: Aldine Atherton.

The contributors

Jane Aldgate is a Fellow of St Hilda's College, and a lecturer in Applied Social Studies at the University of Oxford. She has undertaken several studies in the field of Child Care Practice including research on Parents of Children in Care, Foster Home Breakdown, and the Educational Progress of Children in Foster Care. She has written extensively in the field of Child Welfare and Children in Care. Her recent publications include co-authorship of the BAAF/Batsford books *Direct Work with Children* and *Adolescents in Foster Families*.

Mary Barker practised as a social worker/manager in Sheffield, Essex and Lancashire, before teaching at Liverpool and Leicester Universities. Now retired, she is involved part time at Leicester University, and with several voluntary organisations.

Judith Brearley is a Senior Lecturer in Social Work at Edinburgh University. Trained in medical social work, she gained experience of practice teaching in various medical settings. She later qualified as an Analytical Psychotherapist at the Scottish Institute of Human Relations, where she is a project leader and member of Council. She also chairs Marriage Counselling Scotland and offers consultancy to a range of organisations.

Ann Davis is the Director of Social Work Courses, University of Birmingham. She has worked as a social worker in the health and social services. Her publications include *The Residential Solution* and *Women, the Family and Social Work*, edited with Eve Brook.

Windy Dryden is Senior Lecturer in the Department of Psychology at Goldsmith's College, University of London. He is series editor of *Counselling in Action*, a series of books for counsellors and students of counselling which provides clear and explicit guidelines for practice. He is also series editor of *Psychotherapy in Britain*.

Alastair Gibson worked as an administrator in the NHS before training in social work. As a social worker, he worked at Aberdeen Royal Infirmary and a large city health centre before moving to Gateshead as a senior social worker to a paediatric unit. He returned to Aberdeen to become team leader at Woodend General Hospital and, in 1985, took up his present post as lecturer in social work at the Robert Gordon Institute of Technology in Aberdeen.

Pauline Hardiker is Senior Lecturer in the School of Social Work at the University of Leicester. She taught psychology and sociology at Stevenage College before moving to the School of Social Work, Leicester University in 1969. She has undertaken research in the fields of probation, chronic illness and child care; she has published in these fields and maintained a career-long interest in social work theory. She is currently engaged in various activities in relation to the implementation of the 1989 Children Act. She has collaborated with Mary Barker on many projects, including the volume *Theories of Practice in Social Work*.

Barbara L. Hudson is a Lecturer in Applied Social Studies and a Fellow of Green College at Oxford University. She was previously a Lecturer at the London School of Economics and before that a psychiatric social worker.

Michael Jacobs is Director of a large counselling training programme developed within the Department of Adult Education at the University of Leicester. He teaches, practices, supervises and writes. His interest is not only in counselling and therapy itself, but also in gender issues, in the nature of therapeutic relationships and in the interface between religious belief and psychotherapy. Prior to his present work he was a counsellor and therapist in Student Health, and before that a university chaplain.

Colin Keenan is Senior Lecturer in Social Work at the Robert Gordon Institute of Technology in Aberdeen. Previously he had extensive experience in group care management and practice, predominantly with children.

Joyce Lishman is Senior Lecturer in Social Work at the Robert Gordon Institute of Technology in Aberdeen. Her social work practice has been with children, adolescents and families with behavioural and emotional problems and, as Malcolm Sargent social worker, with families of children suffering from cancer or leukemia. She was editor of the *Research Highlights in Social Work* series designed to make research findings in social work more available to practitioners and managers.

Peter Marsh is a teacher, researcher and practitioner in social work at the University of Sheffield. His main interests lie in statutory child care policy and practice, the introduction and maintenance of effective models, and in developmental research methods. His work has particularly featured the inclusion of consumer views as an aid to understanding, assessing and developing services. Publications include the research study *In and Out of Care*, a forthcoming book on task-centred social work, and work on fathers, on links between children in care and parents, and on research methods, including a research column in the magazine *Community Care*. He is a research director of Social Work in Partnership, a national research and development study and is also directing a study of the management of social work student placements.

Kieran O'Hagan is a social work writer, trainer and practitioner. He has been in front line social work practice in British social services departments since 1974. He has written numerous articles and books on crisis intervention and child abuse. In 1977 he received a M.Phil in Social Work from the University of York. He was awarded Community Care's Travel Scholarship in 1979 and 1980, the latter for a highly acclaimed article on crisis intervention with the elderly. He worked in Mother Teresa's establishments in Calcutta and Los Angeles, and has recently returned from a lecture tour in Australia. In social work practice, he has pioneered a new and radical method of family crisis intervention, particularly in the field of child abuse. In recent years, he has been concentrating on training and writing about widespread damaging crisis interventions in child sexual abuse cases.

Gerard Rochford was formerly Professor of Social Work Studies at Aberdeen University and is Director of the *Research Highlights in Social Work* project which has published over twenty books relating research to social work practice and policy making. He qualified as a psychoanalytical psychotherapist at the Scottish Institute of Human Relations and is in private practice. He also conducts case discussions for Marriage Counselling, Scotland and for Camphill Community.

Mike Scott is a qualified social worker and a chartered psychologist. He works for a voluntary agency, Liverpool Personal Service society, where he is the senior counselling psychologist and he is also an honorary research associate in the Department of Psychology at the University of Manchester.

Stuart Watts is Senior Social Worker in Grampian region. He entered social work as a community service volunteer, was a volunteer coordinator in South Wales and with Task Force in Islington, and was a community worker in Peckham. Since 1972 he has practiced as a community social worker and team leader in Grampian region.

Introducing Network Analysis in Social Work
Philip Seed
ISBN 1 85302 034 6 hb ISBN 1 85302 106 7 pa
This new textbook is designed for social workers and others in social work practice as a guide to the application of a systematic method for understanding and using social networks. As the importance of informal as well as formal care is more widely recognised, social workers and others in the helping professions have come to see the services they provide more and more in the context of the people, places and activities that are significant to the client's daily life.
In part one, social network analysis is studied generally; part two deals with specific applications of network analysis. Finally, the role of day care is studied, and procedures suggested for routine reviews using social network analysis.

The Abuse of Elderly People:
A Handbook for Professionals
Jacki Pritchard
ISBN 1 85302 122 9
This book is a resource and manual for a variety of professionals who work with cases of elderly abuse. It has four main aims: to define elderly abuse; to raise the consciousness of elderly abuse; to develop skills in recognising elderly abuse; to develop ways of working with elderly abuse. Jacki Pritchard is Principal Social Worker in the Sheffield Family and Community Services Department, Nether Edge Hospital.

Gerontology: Responding to an Ageing Society
Edited by Kevin Morgan & Christopher W Smith
ISBN 1 85302 117 2
PARTIAL CONTENTS: Introduction, *Kevin Morgan*, 1. Policy Development at the Grassroots Level, *Silvana di Gregorio*. 2. Car Dependency among Older Men and Women, *Tony Warnes*. 3. What is Normal Cognitive Ageing?, *Felicia Huppert*. 4. Older Adults and Basic Skills, *Alex Withnall and Keith Percy*. 5. Assessing the Effects of Social Environment on Demented Elderly Residents of Local Authority Homes, *Anne Netter*. 6. Using Experimental Training Methods to Link Personal Ageing and Old Age in Others, *Simon Briggs*.

The Psychology of Ageing
Ian Stuart-Hamilton
ISBN 1 85302 063 X
The book covers all principal areas of the psychology of ageing: perception, intelligence, memory, language, personality and the dementias. It is written in a non-specialist language; no prior knowledge in psychology is expected or necessary. No psychological or neurophysiological terms are introduced without at least a full definition provided. People associated with the care and treatment of the elderly such as medics, nurses and others in the caring professions will find it especially useful.

Jessica Kingsley Publishers, 118 Pentonville Road, London N1 9JN

Grief in Children: A Handbook for Adults
Atle Dyregrov
ISBN 1 85302 113 X
This practical book explains children's understanding of death at different ages and gives a detailed outline of exactly how the adults around them can best help them cope with the death, whether it is of a parent or sibling, other relation or friend, or of class mate or teacher. It deals with the whole range of responses, from those on the physical and pragmatic level to psychological reactions which may be less obvious to the caring adult, and describes the methods that have been shown to work best. The author also explains when it is necessary to involve expert professional help for a child, and discusses the value of bereavement groups for children. The final chapter concentrates on the needs of the caregiver.

Social Work in the Wake of Disaster
David Tumelty
ISBN 1 85302 060 5
Case Studies for Practice 6
This volume explores the types of help which social workers offer to those affected by a disaster, and those groups of people to whom such a service is offered. The first chapter looks at the response Social Services have offered in the immediate aftermath of a major incident, the options available and some of the principal problems encountered. Chapters two and three looks at the problems involved in identifying a disaster population, gathering information and initiating longer term work. Chapter four concentrates on aspects of work with the bereaved. Chapter five looks specifically at the needs and problems of those who survive a major disaster, and chapters six and seven develop these themes by looking at the role and functions of individual counselling and group work with the bereaved and survivors. Chapter eight looks at its function, content and distribution in the wake of a disaster. The final chapter looks at the possibilities for counselling after non-spectacular accidents.

Play Therapy with Abused Children
Ann Cattanach
ISBN 1 85302 120 2
This book explores the uses of play therapy with abused children as a way of helping them to heal their distress and make sense of their experiences through expanding their own creativity in play. It introduces the concept that play is a developmental activity through which children explore their identity in relation to others. Ways of starting play therapy with abused children are described and the author explains how the child can use the process for healing. Models of intervention are described which meet the particular needs of the child and the work setting of the therapist; for example, short and medium term interventions, individual/group and sibling work.

Jessica Kingsley Publishers, 118 Pentonville Road, London N1 9JN